Alessia had always done everything that was expected of her. A dutiful daughter she had attended a good school and passed all her exams. The only blot on an otherwise unblemished report was being caught sun bathing in her bra in the sixth form garden which halted her progress to Head Girl.

She went to university and gained a good degree in law before embarking on a promising career. Now it was time for the unexpected. Newly single and no children to worry about she was free to indulge in her passion for travel by working as a holiday rep.

The Rookie Rep

Alessia George

The Rookie Rep

Vanguard Press

VANGUARD PAPERBACK

© Copyright 2013
Alessia George

The right of Alessia George to be identified as author of
this work has been asserted by her in accordance with the
Copyright, Designs and Patents Act 1988.

All Rights Reserved

No reproduction, copy or transmission of this publication
may be made without written permission.
No paragraph of this publication may be reproduced,
copied or transmitted save with the written permission of the publisher, or in
accordance with the provisions
of the Copyright Act 1956 (as amended).

Any person who commits any unauthorised act in relation to
this publication may be liable to criminal
prosecution and civil claims for damages.

A CIP catalogue record for this title is
available from the British Library.

ISBN 978 1 84386 728 9

*Vanguard Press is an imprint of
Pegasus Elliot MacKenzie Publishers Ltd.*
www.pegasuspublishers.com

First Published in 2013

**Vanguard Press
Sheraton House Castle Park
Cambridge England**

Printed & Bound in Great Britain

Disclaimer

All the incidents described in this book really happened but the characters are fictional to protect the perpetrators and the author.

Contents

Chapter 1 – July	13
Chapter 2 – August	33
Chapter 3 – September	52
Chapter 4 – October	70
Chapter 5 – November	87
Chapter 6 – December	102
Chapter 7 – January	118
Chapter 8 – February	132
Chapter 9 – March	145
Chapter 10 – April	158
Chapter 11 – May	179
Chapter 12 – June	197

Chapter 1 - July

I was so excited I could not concentrate on the task in hand. My bedroom resembled the aftermath of a jumble sale. Every light in the house was switched on and most of the cupboards and drawers were open. It was midnight already and I was leaving in two hours yet my suitcase was once again lying empty on the floor. I had lost count of the number of times I had packed and then unpacked. The travel 'experts' suggested that all the items I intended to take should be laid out on the bed and then half of them should be packed. I kept packing the wrong half.

By the time my taxi rolled into the drive I was snapping the last lock shut on my bag. During the five minute journey to the station I babbled excitedly about my forthcoming trip to Crete. I had never been there but it had been a long held ambition to visit Greece. But first I had to get to Gatwick. When the driver asked me which platform my train would leave from I realised I had no idea. It was many years since I had travelled on a train and this was my first visit to my local station.

I told the driver I would check the platform when I bought my ticket. He roared with laughter as we swung into the car park in front of the station. The glass and steel construction that housed the ticket office was shut. Outside was a row of machines that sold every variety of ticket for travel in the next twelve months. But they did not make announcements regarding the relevant platform.

Fortunately my driver was an expert on these matters and instructed me on the use of the appropriate machine. He waited and then drove me over the bridge to my platform and unloaded my bags. I was still shouting my thanks as his rear red lights receded in the darkness. He must have thought I was an idiot. Clad in my company blazer with my name badge on my lapel proclaiming to the world that I was a holiday rep and I did not even know how to buy a ticket for the train.

It was two in the morning and the platform was deserted. I sat on a bench to wait. My stomach was churning. In two hours, when I arrived at Gatwick, my adventure would begin. Once there I would be taking charge of a group of twenty tourists and I would be totally responsible for the organisation of their holiday. I was glad when the lights of my train appeared in the distance and I had to concentrate on getting myself and my luggage on board. I was surprised to find there were already several people on the train. Most of them were sleeping but I dared not relax for a second in case I missed my stop even though it would be more than an hour before we got there. At the next station a breathless young man fell into my compartment and immediately began punching numbers into his mobile phone. I was curious to know who he could be calling at such an early hour.

I listened intently. He was talking to the friend who had just dropped him off at the station. They had been out all night and now he had to concoct a story to appease his wife. He was already on a yellow card so it had to be good. I could not help listening and smiling at the thought of him arriving home to find he was locked out and his belongings were scattered on the road. I would never know, it was a snippet of someone else's life and this would be my one and only episode.

* * * * * *

"Tickets please."

I woke with a start and fumbled in my pocket. I had only slept for a few minutes but I felt refreshed and wide awake. I took out the information pack my manager, Aimee, had sent me. Aimee was responsible for all the Hosts and Hostesses at New Company Travel. I had already devoured the contents of the bulging envelope but I pulled them out and began going through them again. I perused the list of names. Soon these names would have faces and personalities. Would I remember their names? Would they like me? The thought that all these people would be depending on me to make sure they had a great holiday was nerve wracking. I read through the notes of my colleagues, Hosts and Hostesses who had already done this trip, and a source of valuable information. I had tried to memorise every detail, as my guests would expect me to have all this information at my fingertips. Could I meet their expectations? Should I be here? Why was I here?

Fate had sent me on this trip. I had been pursuing a career in the law and after teaching the subject for several years I had decided to take the final exams and become a solicitor. It was hard work doing a full time job and studying as well. I felt I deserved a year off, a chance to travel. As I did not want to travel on my own I wrote to a tour operator in the hope of being employed by them on a freelance basis. I had travelled with this company and was familiar with the role of the hosts who accompanied their groups. It seemed they spent their days going on excursions with the guests and their evenings dining and disco dancing. I felt I would be adept at both these activities so I was delighted when they called me a few days later and invited me to attend an interview. My enthusiasm more than made up for my lack of language skills and experience and I was invited to a training weekend, in Bournemouth, two days hence. My final exams were imminent and I packed some books just in case I had a few spare hours.

I barely had time to eat and sleep that weekend. When I arrived at the Highcliff Hotel Aimee, my trainer and a very experienced Hostess, was waiting in reception for me. It was an embarrassing start when I requested a room with a sea view and Aimee stepped in and cancelled this request. Our guests were allocated the best rooms and the Hostess would be allocated a room the hotel considered appropriate. Unabashed I accepted my small room with an uninterrupted view of the dustbins below and a bathroom that was bigger than the bedroom. There was just time to take my case up to this room but no time to unpack as Aimee had scheduled a meeting with the duty manager.

Within minutes I was back downstairs following in their wake as they checked function rooms against our itinerary. I scribbled notes on my own copy as we moved from room to room. I noticed that Aimee did not take any notes at all just flirted charmingly with the young manager. I was not surprised when I was given a job to do while Aimee went to her room to 'freshen up'. My role was to keep in touch with reception regarding last minute cancellations and to check the Welcome Drink was laid out properly. Just before dinner I had to confirm final numbers for the meal so any extra covers could be removed before we took our places.

Some of our guests had arrived before us and as soon as our meeting finished Aimee asked me to find them and introduce myself. I had been so focused on the travel I had forgotten this aspect of my new role as a holiday representative – the people. Naturally very shy as a child I had hated running errands to the local shop as it meant I had to speak to the shopkeeper. I had resolved this problem by bribing my younger sister with comics to do it for me. Supermarkets had been invented for people like me, the silent shopper. Reluctantly I made my way back to the bar and was surprised to find that our guests approached me. I had not realised how conspicuous the blazer and the badge made me. Then I got over-confident and approached some people who were nothing to do with my company. I was left in no doubt regarding their views on package holidays. Embarrassed I retreated into my shell.

Our first official function, when the whole group would gather together, was the Welcome Drink. Following Aimee's advice I dressed down for this occasion and pinned my Trainee badge on the pocket of my demure shirt dress. I made my way to the bar fifteen minutes before the first guest was due to arrive. My brief (and it had been brief) was to be early for every function during the weekend. I suspected being late was probably a sackable offence, along with topless sunbathing and getting drunk on duty. As we were never off-duty the latter was easily achievable.

When I got to the bar five guests were there already and hovering by a tray of drinks. I greeted them, requested their names, handed them a glass of wine and wished them a happy stay. This calm efficiency did not last long. Ten guests arrived at the same time. They pushed past me and grabbed a glass of wine ignoring me and my list of names. I could not even be sure they were in my group. Each guest was allowed one drink but it was difficult to enforce this rule – especially when some people were pleading for a second drink before everyone in the group had arrived. It was hard to refuse these pleas as I was so anxious to ensure our guests enjoyed themselves. A helpful barman recognised my dilemma and discretely replenished the tray of drinks. I smiled my thanks. Already I was discovering a camaraderie that existed amongst everyone who worked in this industry. A band of people united in the struggle to please the tourist.

When Aimee joined us she looked stunning. Tall, slim and slightly tanned she was wearing a stylish cocktail dress and heels high enough to suggest the most activity she would be undertaking that evening was the short walk from the bar to the restaurant. Clearly she did not take her own advice regarding the attire of the Hostess. Aimee was everything I was not and I gawped in admiration as she slid into her role as the charming Hostess and effortlessly ushered everyone into the restaurant.

It was a very sociable dinner – I hosted one of our two large tables and Aimee sat at the other one. My companions were very friendly and the conversation flowed as freely as the included wine. Uncertain about the closeness of Aimee's scrutiny I was careful to concentrate on the water rather than the wine. When the meal was over it was time for our disco. I loved disco dancing and I was keen to strut my stuff but I did not know if this would be allowed. Did I join in with the dancers or follow Aimee's example and maintain an elegant distance. I glanced across to her table as I jiggled to the music on the side lines. Aimee nodded her consent and I took to the floor and encouraged everyone else to join me.

When I stopped to sip some water Aimee said she was going to bed and was leaving me in charge. It was an exhilarating feeling and I took advantage of my position and slipped in a few requests for my favourite tracks. I danced until the disco finished at midnight and then joined the late night revellers in the bar for a last drink. I was not sure if I was supposed to stay up until the last guest fell off his or her bar stool. I added it to the list of questions I was compiling to ask Aimee.

Aimee was not in the mood for questions the next morning. She did not appear at breakfast and arrived in reception just in time to greet our local guide who would be leading our tour of local attractions. Aimee joined the guide at the front of the bus while I observed from the back. Swanage was our lunch stop and it brought back a lot of childhood memories for all of us as we strolled along a seafront that was peppered with fish and chip shops and ice cream outlets. Most of us succumbed to the aroma of freshly fried cod and chips and sat outside on benches at large wooden tables to eat them. After eating we were given the option of taking the steam train to visit Corfe Castle and I decided to go as well.

My decision was very popular with Aimee and our local guide. Both of them had done the trip several times already and were happy to amuse themselves in the town. I arrived at the station with fourteen guests in time to watch the steam engine chugging from the front of the train to take the lead at the back. We had a short ride across beautiful countryside before the impressive ruins of Corfe Castle came into view. We dismounted at the end of the line and then walked back to Corfe Castle to explore the ruins before returning to Swanage.

It was my first introduction to the marshalling of a group to ensure everyone arrived in the right place at the right time. As we left the station the group scattered in all directions tempted by shops, bars or a tour of the castle ruins. Innocuous phrases took on new meanings. "I am just popping into this shop" translated as I am going to spend an hour in there looking for a suitable present for Aunty Mary as I always take her something when I go away. "I need to get a drink, I'll be quick" was a code for I am going to sit down at a table and order a snack and a drink and stay there as long as I can. By the time I had flushed people out of souvenir shops and dragged them away from tables outside bars and cafés there was no time to join the sightseers in the castle before we had to board our train. I felt a sense of triumph when I fed the right number of tourists into the flock clustered around Aimee waiting to board our bus.

When I volunteered to organise the Bubbly Quiz that evening Aimee accepted graciously and I accompanied her to her suite to collect the lists of questions. I supposed that her suite came under the definition of 'a room considered suitable by the hotel management'. Once I had been acquainted with the rules of the quiz I raced back to my room to cut up strips of paper that were essential for the conduct of this game. Aimee would not be joining us as she felt I would be inhibited by her presence. She was probably right although I suspected the real reason was the chance to stretch out on her plush settee sipping a glass of the cold white wine I had seen chilling in an ice bucket in her sitting room.

The Bubbly Quiz was hilarious. As people arrived in the function room I put them at one of several small round tables. Each table formed a team and when a member of that team answered a question correctly they were given a slip of paper and once they had ten slips of paper they could swap them for a glass of champagne each. My sympathetic barman was on duty again and he raced around topping up glasses while I asked the questions, handed out the slips of paper and dealt with disputes about the correct answer. Fierce arguments raged between opposing teams in the race to consume as much sparkling wine as possible. I accepted different versions and awarded strips of paper indiscriminately. The barman kept topping up my glass as well and I giggled my way through the last few questions.

We were all very relaxed when we joined Aimee in the restaurant for dinner. I hoped Aimee would not notice my flushed cheeks and the wisps of hair escaping from my attempt at an elegant arrangement of my long blonde hair. I had been experimenting with a smart tortoise shell clip purchased earlier that day.

Aimee retired to the bar with a few guests as soon as we finished eating. I was left in charge of the disco. We had a very enthusiastic DJ who taught us the moves of the Macarena. I scribbled them down on the back of an envelope in my bag so I could teach other groups. I was really enjoying my new role and desperately hoped there would be a future for me as a Hostess.

It was difficult to remain calm the next morning as we said our goodbyes to departing guests and handed out feedback forms. I viewed these with suspicion. Never before had I been subjected to other people's opinions regarding my ability to do my job. Aimee was very encouraging regarding my performance that weekend. She also had a few cautionary tales to tell as she went through our role on the more demanding trips abroad. She drilled into me that I should never dress as though I was on holiday, I should never behave as though I was on holiday and that I should never wear jeans.

After a few days I settled back into my old routine and the buzz I had felt over the weekend fizzled out. Even in such a short time I had become used to the constant company and the busy lifestyle. I should have been concentrating on the exams ahead of me but my thoughts kept straying to the fascinating destinations in the glossy brochure I had brought home with me. The trilling of my phone roused me from my reverie. It was Aimee. My heart was thudding as I listened to her congratulate me on having successfully completed my training. She then offered me a trip to Crete immediately after my last exam. It was perfect timing and a good incentive to make sure I passed my exams at the first attempt.

* * * * * *

By the time my train slowed to a halt at Gatwick airport I had read and re-read all the information in my bundle of papers. There were rooming lists, flight manifests, requests for special diets, rooms with views, double beds, single beds, top floor and ground floor. This was one of our most popular destinations and the company had been going there for several years. There was a lot of detailed information such as where one could buy an English paper, postcards, stamps and the location and opening times of supermarkets and pharmacies. Enough to pretend I had been there before. But did I dare or did I just confess to being a rookie rep?

I had to admit my inexperience in order to complete my first task on arrival at the airport. I had to get a TOD from the Pin Stripe Representative for a member of my group but I had no idea what it was. I did a quick tour of the check-in desks which were already surrounded by crowds of holidaymakers looking for someone dressed in pin stripes. Stupidly I had expected that this person would also be looking for me. I laughed at my own naivety when I asked at the Information Desk and discovered that TOD translated as a ticket on departure and the Pin Stripe Representative was a company and not a person.

Ticket clutched in my hand I set off to find my client Mr Right. There was no one at the appointed place, the luggage shop near the check-in area. Neither I nor Mr Right could check-in until I had found him and given him his ticket. I strolled slowly up and down the fast growing queues around our check-in desks looking for a solitary male with our distinctive luggage label on his case. After each sortie I went back to the luggage shop but I could not find anyone who fitted my bill. As I hovered uncertainly in the check-in area I heard raised voices at one of the desks. Naturally curious I moved closer to see what was going on.

A harassed girl was dealing with an angry passenger. There seemed to be some problem with his ticket, the lack of it. When I moved closer I noticed that he had three of our luggage labels tied to his case. I soon understood the problem. The passenger was insisting the girl had his ticket and was pointing at his itinerary spread on the desk in front of them. The girl was pointing across the check-in area towards the luggage shop. When I intervened and asked if I could help I was greeted with a smile of relief from the girl and a scowl from the passenger. I introduced myself to Mr Right and gave him his ticket before retreating to the back of another queue. The instructions on his itinerary had been quite clear. Was this a sign of things to come?

I caught up with Mr Right and several other passengers in the Departure Lounge. They all crowded round me their eager faces alight with curiosity as they bombarded me with a variety of questions – simultaneously. I was as excited as they were but I tried not to show it by adopting the persona of the experienced traveller. It proved impossible to remain cool and aloof and I was soon caught up in their chatter as evocative names like Knossos, Spinalonga, Elounda and Santorini rolled off their tongues. I wanted to visit all of them and when I admitted to never having seen any of these places I immediately formed a bond with my companions. They did not seem to mind that I was not an expert; they just wanted to have a good holiday. As I led them to our boarding gate I resolved to do everything I could to ensure that they did.

On arrival at Iráklion airport I immediately lost one of my passengers. I was certain that Mr Right had been with us when I did my first head count. When I did a recount to make sure I had everyone he had disappeared. Had I imagined his presence on the first count? Wild-eyed I scanned the crowds surging towards the exit. Did I leave the group and go looking for him, did I wait and hope he came back or did I take them to our bus and hope he found us there? As I stood there in a quandary I felt a re-assuring hand on my arm. It was The Duchess, named for her stately appearance. "Don't worry dear," she said, smiling down on me, "I expect he has gone outside for a smoke." I seized on this explanation gratefully. She was used to travelling with a group whereas Mr Right was not. At that moment he appeared in the doorway and grinned apologetically while I beamed back at him in sheer relief. Now all I had to do was find our transfer bus. I marched confidently ahead of the group, company sign held high.

Our bus driver had abandoned his post in the Arrivals Hall. I suspected he had also gone off for a cigarette. However, his absence was not totally unexpected. A thoughtful Hostess had noted in our resort information that the drivers often did not bother to meet the group and would be in the bus in the car park. Relying on this snippet of information I led the group outside and asked them to wait while I raced up and down the lines of stationary buses. I was beginning to appreciate that the role of the rep was fraught with difficulties and wondered what I would do if there was no bus. Just as I was running out of buses I found ours. As our flight had been delayed our bus driver had snatched the opportunity to snooze in his bus and was still sleeping when we arrived. Thoughtfully he had propped our company sign up at the front of the bus and I hammered on the door to wake him up.

As soon as everyone was settled on the bus I stood in the centre of the aisle and welcomed them to Crete. I had to shout but it was better than trying to use the microphone which I had never done before and I was nervous to try in case it started squeaking at me. I informed them when and where we would meet for the Welcome Drink and then asked if they had any questions. I was peppered with them. They wanted to know everything from the weather forecast for the week (hot) to the nearest place to get a newspaper (hotel shop). By the time we turned into the drive of our hotel the flow of questions had dried up and I could turn round and look ahead through the windscreen. My attention was riveted by the panorama of small white bungalows wreathed with deep purple bougainvillea and glimpses of a blue sea sparkling below us. I hoped no one had asked me any more questions because if they had I would not have heard them as I drank in our sumptuous surroundings.

I received a warm welcome from the receptionist and we exchanged lists, completed the check-in and everyone was soon on their way to their bungalows. The Capsis Beach was a mixture of bungalows and one large block of rooms all set in beautiful grounds that sprawled across a headland. I waited in reception in case there were any problems with the rooms but nobody came back so it seemed they were all happy and I was free to find my own bungalow. It was fabulous. I had been allocated a small bungalow on the first floor in a block of four just a short walk from the main building. When I stepped out onto my secluded terrace I had amazing views of the sea in the bay below me. The interior was spacious, cool and quiet. I knew I was going to love staying there for the next three weeks.

My first attempt at organising a Welcome Drink was a flop. I had carefully checked the venue but had done so in the afternoon when it was empty. Now it was full of noisy French guests and I had to shout to make myself heard. It was impossible as the group had split up into smaller groups all chatting together and no one was taking any notice of me. If I attracted the attention of one group they would get bored with waiting while I tried to get the others to be quiet and went back to their conversation. I was getting hot and flustered and went outside to cool down. The spacious balcony was empty so I went back inside and suggested that we moved outside. It was quiet and the view was stunning. The barman was very helpful and brought the trays of ouzo and orange juice outside for us. I had not tried ouzo before and was surprised at its milky white appearance but this was because water had already been added. I liked the aniseed flavour but it was not popular with everyone and once it was grudgingly accepted that there were no other options most people chose the fresh orange juice.

After toasting a successful holiday we moved on to dinner in the restaurant and my first problem. Our brochure promised a twenty per cent discount on drinks but the maître d' was refusing to apply it to drinks ordered at the table. I suggested they went back to the bar to buy their drinks and bring them into the restaurant. I filled my plate from the tempting buffet. My first forkful of food was nearly in my mouth when The Duchess appeared and informed me that the barman was refusing to apply the discount on their drinks. I rushed off to the bar to find out what was happening. I was told that everyone should have been issued with a card in order to get their discount. I sent the group back to the restaurant and went to reception to get the cards.

Reception informed me that they had run out of cards and refused to offer an alternative solution. I needed to speak to a manager to resolve the issue but none were available as they had all gone home. I explained the problem and appealed to them for some support. I went back to the restaurant and informed both tables of the situation. My full plate of food had been cleared away so I went to the buffet to get some more food. I had just sat down again when a receptionist arrived to say that the manager of the bar was available to speak to me. When I went back to the bar and explained the problem, again, we agreed on a compromise. I was to give them a rooming list and each person had to prove their identity at the bar to claim their discount. Alternatively they could set up a line of credit in reception and the discount would be applied when they paid their bill at the end of the holiday. At last the problem had been resolved and I could settle down to eat. But there was nothing to eat as my second plate of food had been taken away as well as the entire buffet. I dined on crisps from the bar.

I was up very early the next morning. The air was fresh and invigorating at that hour so I decided to explore my surroundings. While making my way along the path towards the small pool on the headland I met a pair of pot-bellied Vietnamese pigs and some peacocks also out for an early stroll. I wondered where they had come from but there was no time to investigate as breakfast started soon and I needed to be there in case any members of my group were early risers. I wound my way along one of many paths on the cliff top shaded by trees and dotted with stone benches – ideal hideaways where I could sit and read a book.

Our tables were empty when I arrived in the restaurant. We were seated at the back of a large open terrace corralled in a corner by smaller tables for two and four. I asked the maître d' if we could have some tables closer to the sea but regretfully he explained that large groups were always seated at the back of this area. Of course I could have sat at one of the smaller tables but I had to banish this temptation. The breakfast buffet was set out round the indoor swimming pool and it looked very appetising especially the cooked English breakfast. I pounced on the fried eggs and bacon, I was ravenous. When I started to eat them I discovered they were stone cold. Returning to the buffet I noticed an egg station and was soon tucking into a fresh omelette. By the time the group started drifting in I was ready to take them on a tour of the buffet and make recommendations.

Between breakfast and our Information Meeting later that morning I renewed my quest to speak to a manger to find a permanent solution to the problem of the discount on drinks. I had to work my way through a plethora of under managers and managers up to a director. I had to wait a long time for the latter and sat patiently in the reception area. He kept me waiting so long I had to leave before he appeared in order to get to my own Information Meeting on time. I would have to go back later as the issue needed to be resolved. My guests were not impressed at the thought of having to keep their passport tucked in their swimwear in order to get a discount on their drinks.

Our Information Meeting was conducted by a representative from our local agent. I had to work through this agency rather than use the ones that lined the street outside the hotel offering the same excursions at much lower prices. How was I going to persuade them to pay the higher price? Exclusivity was my selling point. I had to convince them that our high prices were based on top class vehicles, that is, air-conditioned, and only our guests on board. After briefly describing each trip and answering a few questions the agent left. I just had to make a note of the number of bookings and collect the money. It sounded easy but there were some special offers to take into account as discounts were available depending on the number of trips each person booked. It was hard work, computing discounts, taking bookings and answering questions about trips I had never been on. But it was going to prove worthwhile as I had been promised a free place on any of the trips that my guests booked.

My head was spinning by the time I had taken all the money, stuffed it in my safety deposit box and then raced back to the main building for a meeting with another director to discuss the drinks' discount for a third time. It seemed I had to be both a diplomat and an accountant. I had prepared for this meeting and copies of our brochure page and correspondence relating to the discount nestled in my smart leather folder. The director collected me from reception and I followed him through a labyrinth of back rooms to his own palatial office. I rehearsed my arguments in my head as I swallowed frantically to moisten my dry throat. I was invited to sit down on a leather office chair opposite the desk. I took a deep breath ready to plead my clients' case. But my diplomacy skills were not required on this occasion as the problem had already been resolved by the miraculous appearance of some discount cards. These were handed to me and the director apologised because the cards had not been available when we arrived. He wished me a pleasant stay in his hotel and invited me to share with him any other problems I may have while I was there. I was now free to do some exploring.

Aghia Pelagia, the local village, was a short walk from our hotel either along the beach or down the main road. As I strolled along the public beach I met several people in my group sunning themselves by the sea. I stopped to chat with them. Olive, a retired head mistress, asked me about the possibilities of local entertainment in the evenings. She felt that the entertainment organised by the Animation Team in the hotel would be too much like the school productions she had masterminded over the last twenty-five years. I was happy to take on this mission as it gave me a purpose while I was exploring the village.

I was loitering outside one of the tavernas that lined the sea front when I was ensnared by a prowling waiter. He was charming and very persuasive. I was soon

sipping a delicious local wine and tucking into my first genuine Greek salad. Through the open window I could see the beach and beyond a shimmering sea dotted with brown rocky islands. Inside this simple taverna the atmosphere was friendly and relaxed and I was soon chatting with the owner, Kostos. I was not wearing my badge but he seemed to know who I was. When I left he waved aside my offer to pay for my food. I accepted the proffered business card for Le Gourmet. I would be happy to take my group there as the food was delicious and the setting was perfect. As I continued towards the village I wondered what I would have done if the food had been terrible – insisted he take my money even if it meant stuffing it down the front of his smart polo shirt.

By the time I reached the centre of the village it was the siesta and shops and bars were slumbering in the heat of the afternoon sun. Most of these bars would not come alive until much later that evening and when they did I was certain they would be too raucous for Olive who was looking for genuine Cretan experiences. I was not sure I would find any in this blatant tourist trap and I was nearly back at our hotel when I discovered Manolo's Bar on the main road close to our hotel entrance. There were tables and chairs set outside so customers could enjoy panoramic views of the bay across the road. It resembled an English transport caff but I decided to give it a try and sat down outside in the shade of the awning over the shop front window.

I was perusing the menu when Manolo appeared and introduced himself. I ordered ouzo and this time the spirit and the water were served separately so I could dilute it according to my own taste. My drink was accompanied by some lovely, home-cooked nibbles. I suspected Manolo had plundered his own dinner table to comply with this Cretan tradition. The high sugar content of ouzo resulting in speedy intoxication demands that it should be slowed down by the consumption of food. The prices were a fraction of those charged in the hotel bar – even with the discount. The setting was also more interesting – people strolled by and I noticed a stream of scooters whizzing past me and then returning laden with supplies from the local supermarket. Manolo joined this convoy when a customer requested a drink he did not have. Within minutes he was back with a bottle. I loved it and I was sure Olive would be delighted. I felt very light-headed as I sauntered down the drive of our hotel but this was more likely to be the ouzo than relief at having fulfilled Olive's request.

That evening, after dinner, I led my group up the drive for our first visit to the bar. Manolo was delighted to see us and rushed around organising tables and chairs outside so that we could all sit together. The group were charmed by his personal attention and fell on his little snacks as though they had not eaten for a week. After a few drinks we moved on to another bar, the Banana Bar, right on the sea front. This bar was very popular but we were able to find tables outside on the patio where we could enjoy the balmy evening, soothed by the lapping of water on the beach below us. The black water was a stark contrast against the background of the bright lights of the discos, bars and shops behind us. Some of the shops stayed open until midnight. I tried retsina for the first and last time. It was awful. There was no disguising the fact it was sap from a tree and its original purpose had been to preserve the wine rather than flavour it. I just had one drink and then walked back to the hotel. I needed an early night as we were off to Knossos at the crack of dawn the next day.

Knossos did not come up to my expectations but it was brought alive for us by our guide Andreas. He was gorgeous. I could tell by the intense silence of my female companions that they were also appreciating his physique more than the ruins that surrounded us. I loved the way his dark brown eyes crinkled at the corners when he smiled. He thoughtfully guided us from one patch of shade to the next as he used his book of illustrations to give form to the crumbling blocks of stone. I was so distracted that I forgot to collect a tip for him. I had to dig deep into my own pocket and hope that I could recoup my loss later when I owned up to my omission. But even the charms of Andreas were no defence against the searing heat and it was a relief to move on to the air-conditioned environment of the museum in Iráklion. Visiting museums was not my favourite pastime but I had no choice as I had to stay with the group. It was not the hardship I had anticipated and my attention was riveted to Andreas as he guided us through his personal selection of items weaving an interesting history of the island.

After the tour our local agent sent three taxis to collect us. He had forgotten the 'plus one' which was me. I waved my companions goodbye and set off for the bus stop. When the bus finally arrived it was already full of locals and the air conditioning consisted of open windows. An elderly gentleman stood up and invited me to take the seat next to an open window. I accepted gratefully and squeezed into the corner gulping in the fresh air. As we bumped along the local road beyond the town more and more people squashed on board at every stop. Clearly there was no limit to the number of passengers the vehicle could carry. Seats designed for two people were occupied by four. My neighbour was clutching a live hen that glared at me menacingly until we reached my stop and I could scramble off the bus. When I got back to my room I had a cool shower and then dragged my mattress on to the balcony and stretched out in the sun. The balcony was so secluded I could sunbathe nude, something I had never thought of doing before. It was so liberating. I felt totally free now that I was no longer confined by office hours and appointments.

I drifted off into a deep sleep from which, fortunately, I was aroused by the ringing of my telephone. I had placed it as close to the open door as the lead would allow – just in case. It was Olive. She wanted to know what time her trip departed the next morning, what time it got back and how much money she would need. I had crawled into my room on all fours as I dared not stand up in case someone spotted me over my parapet. Scrabbling among my pile of notes I found the relevant information and passed it on. It was a timely reminder that I would need this information when we met for our pre-dinner drinks in the hotel bar. I also realised it would be a good idea to set my alarm whenever I had a chance to relax in my room as I could have easily slept until the following morning.

Perched on the low wall outside reception at five o'clock the following morning I scanned the paths for The Duchess, her friend Lily and Olive. They were off to visit Spinalonga and I wanted to make sure that they and their transport were in the right place at the right time. They had assured me they would be fine and I need not get up especially. I had no reason to doubt the reliability of our agents either but I wanted to make sure everything ran smoothly. The three of them sat in reception while I played lookout outside. We had a few false alarms – delivery vehicles, the refuse collecting lorry and several tourist buses heading for other destinations. All excursions set off very early in the morning to avoid the heat of the day. I became anxious when the flow of tourist buses ceased.

At six I called our agent who insisted that the bus had arrived on time but my clients had not. He stopped trying to blame my clients when I said I had been with them and could confirm that it had not arrived. It was too late for the bus to come back and collect them – I suspected the bus had been running late and employed the philosophy that by missing out a stop they could make up some time. A full refund or a replacement trip and a complimentary cocktail were agreed. The Duchess and Lily were both very philosophical about it and joined me for a leisurely breakfast. Olive was not so forgiving and went off for an early swim. We incurred the wrath of the restaurant manager by shunning our empty group tables for a table by the sea. I distracted him by pointing out that some hitch-hikers had gate crashed breakfast and were stuffing their rucksacks with a week's supply of bread, fruit and boiled eggs.

When we finished I hesitantly invited The Duchess and Lily to join me for lunch at Le Gourmet. I had not really established exactly what my role was beyond organising the official itinerary. They were so enthusiastic that I extended the invitation to the rest of the group who were eager to satisfy their curiosity regarding 'my' restaurant.

They loved it. The food was simple but very tasty and the wine was light and fruity. As we ate we planned our afternoon's activities. They all wanted to swim in the sea and invited me to join them. I had not expected this as I had seen my position as purely administrative. Some regular clients in the group assured me that it was part of my role to join in all the activities. It was so many years since I last went swimming in the sea that I imagined myself sinking slowly to the bottom and having to be rescued. I could not envisage Aimee, my role model, doing more than dipping her toes in the water but nevertheless I decided to take the plunge in my sensible one-piece swimsuit. My fears were ungrounded and I had a great time splashing around in the warm water.

After dinner that evening we set off to try a bar recommended to us by the barman in our hotel bar. I had been looking for somewhere nice to take The Duchess, Lily and Olive for their complimentary cocktail. He assured me that the Pool Bar was the 'in' place to go and was buzzing with people every night. Certainly the list of drinks posted outside offered a more exotic and extensive selection than any other bar. It appeared to be ideal so I decided to chance it. The whole group had decided to come along and followed me down the steps into the murky interior. Music was blaring out and one barman lurked behind a bar illuminated by incandescent light filtered through the water of a small indoor pool. It was deserted but we decided to have one drink and see if it livened up. It did not. Clearly it had ceased to be the 'in' place overnight. The group were very understanding and put it down to experience. I was much harder on myself (and so was Olive) and as soon as I could, I excused myself as I was really tired. This job was much more demanding that I had expected but also much more rewarding. I felt a real glow of achievement when my guests thanked me for my efforts on their behalf.

I was up early the next morning, refreshed and ready for our excursion to the Samaria Gorge famous as an escape route for prisoners of war on Crete. We were not going to walk through the whole gorge but would take the ferry from the small port of Chora Sfakion to Aghia Roumeli from where we could walk into the gorge. We set off before the hotel started serving breakfast and stopped at a pretty taverna for breakfast on our way to the ferry. Our simple repast was delicious – a good cappuccino (akin to gold dust on Crete) accompanied by pancakes stuffed with goat's cheese and served with honey dribbled over them.

On the ferry I introduced myself to our local guide, a Dutch girl called Corea. Our group was part of a larger group and Corea was in charge of everybody. So much for exclusivity! But as yet no one had picked up on that point and I was hoping they would not notice. Corea was a mine of information about our role as reps. I was still bursting with questions as we approached our destination but she had to make some announcements. She went off to use the public address system on the boat to advise everyone to have something to eat and plenty to drink before setting off for our walk into the gorge. It was really hot and there would be no shade and no shops to buy water during our walk. We followed Corea to the taverna she had recommended. She arranged a free lunch for me which she assured me was normal practice on Crete – I only had to ask!

We had just gathered round a table in the small taverna when I was informed that Giles and Vera had raced off to the gorge as soon as we had disembarked the ferry. They obviously thought they knew better than an experienced guide. They had not even stopped to buy some water. I would have raced after them but Corea insisted I had something to eat and drink first. I agreed with her and eventually we all set off together and followed them into the gorge. We had not gone far when we came across Vera on the verge of collapse and Giles in a state of panic. Vera had complained of an upset stomach two days earlier and should not have attempted the walk at all. I had suggested she cancelled the trip but egged on by Giles she had refused. I suspected they had rushed off to the gorge before I had a chance to suggest, once again, that Vera did not go on the walk. We gave them some of our water and used our hats to carry water up from the river to splash over Vera who was overheated.

My companions were concerned and wanted to stay and help me but I encouraged them to continue their walk assuring them that Giles and I would be able to cope. Once they were on their way Giles and I helped Vera down to the river to clean her up. This is strictly forbidden as the water from the river supplies the village below but needs must. We got her back to the village and sat her in the shade where she sipped a glass of water and Giles and I gulped down pints of beer. I was so hot and sweaty I just walked into the sea, clothes and all, to cool down. I was dry by the time the others returned from their walk. I was sympathetic towards Vera as I was sure she had been led astray by Giles. It was difficult to understand why Giles had behaved as he had but I did not need to point this out as The Duchess was already giving Giles a hard time. They could have ruined the whole day for everyone. I was very relieved that a real crisis had been averted and decided I needed to take a First Aid course as soon as I got home. Yet another aspect of my new role had revealed itself.

Breakfast the following morning was eaten on a cruise ship at the start of our four hour crossing to the small island of Santorini. After eating we lazed on deck welcoming the regular platters of fresh fruit that the crew handed round. The first sighting of our destination was uplifting – pretty white buildings with blue roofs perched on top of the cliffs. We spilled off the boat and onto a fleet of creaking old buses which wound their way up to Fira, the capital, where we would spend the next two hours. It was a charming little town and we strolled through narrow cobbled streets darting in and out of souvenir shops. I was as anxious as everyone else to find a suitable reminder of our visit here and finally settled for a tasteful fridge magnet – there were not many of these around. As I browsed the shops I had also been looking for a suitable venue for lunch. I found a small bar with a balcony at the back overlooking the sea. It was perfect as the balcony was in the shade and a gentle breeze kept us cool as we sipped our ouzo.

Perhaps it was the ouzo or maybe it was just a moment of madness but when our local guide suggested I might like to ride down to the harbour on a donkey I agreed. Perched on its bony back I wobbled precariously as it lurched down the stepped cobble street. The beast hugged the side of the narrow track that was lined with buildings and occasionally got so close that my bare legs scraped along the walls. My yelps of pain were ignored by its owner who strolled nonchalantly behind us. Every time we swung round one of the many bends I thought I was going to be catapulted onto the deck of our boat that I could see below us in the bay. I was very relieved when I was finally standing on my own two feet and could stagger up the gangway.

After a quick head count I was back on dry land again. One of my guests was missing. Adrian the affable Australian was nowhere to be seen and the ferry was about to depart. He was not amongst the people ambling along the quay so I began to search the other ferries. They were all much smaller than ours. I had pointed this out when we had disembarked and I had also made sure they knew the name of our boat so they would not have any difficulty finding it. As everyone else was on board it seemed something may have happened to Adrian. But after a quick search I found Adrian ensconced in the ferry to Agios Nikolaos.

He was more genial than usual having clearly consumed vast quantities of alcohol. I stuck my head under the awning and called his name. No answer. He was engrossed in the story he was relating to some bewildered passengers around him. I had to scramble aboard and climb over the outstretched legs of several people until I was close enough to grab his arm and yell in his ear that he was on the wrong boat. He was adamant that he was not. He remained so even when I pointed to our ferry, the size of a small cruise ship, to try and jog his memory regarding our journey here. I was getting desperate. I could see our crew releasing the mooring ropes – time was running out. Should I stay with him and risk having to spend the night in Agios Nikolaos? I raced back to our boat and pleaded with the captain to wait a few more minutes before setting off. He agreed and just as his patience was running out Adrian lurched across the quay and boarded our boat.

On the journey back Olive repeatedly expressed her disappointment that she had not been able to swim at all that day. Swimming off the boat would only have been possible if she had been attached to a tow rope. I told her there was a pool on the forward deck without realising it was empty of water. When she came back she clearly expected me to rectify this omission. Short of organising a chain of volunteers with plastic cups between the toilets and the pool to fill it up with tap water there was nothing I could do. I kept nodding my head sympathetically until everyone was distracted by the sight of dolphins frolicking in the wake of our boat.

I enjoyed a solitary breakfast the next morning as there were no excursions. I had the whole day free before our genuine Cretan night that evening. It was billed as a unique experience. But we subsequently discovered that this 'unique' experience was to be shared with two hundred other people. On arrival in Anapoli we were given a glass of raki before starting our tour of the village. Raki is a product of the vine, a colourless spirit distilled from the residue after the grapes have been pressed. It was very strong and I soon regretted rising to the challenge of drinking it in one go. It went straight to my knees and I was lifting my feet unnecessarily high as I shadowed Olive who was lagging behind the group. When she stopped to peer through a crack in a wooden fence I nearly fell over her. She told me that she really wanted to see inside a genuine Cretan house. We hesitated long enough to arouse the curiosity of the owner who came out of his house. He opened the gate and motioned to us to go inside. We crossed a small courtyard and entered the tiny abode where we stood awkwardly in a small, cluttered room. The family was clearly very poor so after a quick glance round we put some notes on the table and made our escape. Our host motioned to us to wait but we were worried about losing the group and set off down the road. He chased after us and presented each of us with a flower plucked from his own backyard. Then he grinned and retreated.

Waving our thanks Olive and I set off at a trot to find our companions. As we rounded a corner we saw the last few people disappearing into a large shed. When we joined them they were already browsing the numerous souvenir stalls inside. I joined our local guide who admired the bloom I was still clutching in my hand. I told her where it had come from in case she thought I had been plundering a garden in the village. When I told her how insistent the man had been that we take the flowers she explained that on Crete it was not acceptable to take money for nothing. It had been a memorable experience and Olive's face was still wreathed in smiles as she staggered to the till with an armful of souvenirs. I waited for her and we were the last two to arrive at the venue for dinner.

It was a huge hall and packed with tables all surrounded by people. I was sure I would never find the rest of my group but I need not have worried as they were clustered together just inside the entrance. I thought they were being courteous and had waited for me to show them to our table. But the scowl on some of their faces made me realise that this was not the case. There was no table to take them to. I pushed my way through the crowded room to find our escort and alerted her to the situation. There were plenty of empty tables so the only problem was getting someone to set one for us. I tried to attract the attention of a nearby waitress but she was already busy serving drinks and told me I would have to wait. I knew I had to act quickly so I chose one of several empty, bare tables and told everyone to sit down.

When Olive realised what I was trying to do she rose magnificently to the occasion. She grabbed my wrist and steered me towards some large cupboards nearby and we rummaged through them extracting tablecloths and napkins. Next we started to collect cutlery and glassware. Meanwhile The Duchess set about spreading tablecloths on the bare surfaces and distributing napkins. She and her friend Lily then formed a chain and passed the cutlery and glasses from us to our table. In no time our table was ready and success had been wrested from the jaws of disaster.

Once the carafes of rough wine had been lined up down the centre of our table I could relax and watch the high-speed service of our traditional fare. Waiters and waitresses in national costume pushed large trolleys round the hall and skimmed metal dishes piled with hot food down the centre of each table. We had to be vigilant in order to halt their progress before they crashed to the floor at the other end. As we ate the ceiling was rolled back and we were sitting under the stars. The occasion may not have been unique but it was certainly memorable. It was also the last evening I would spend with this group as they were all going home the next day and would be replaced by another group.

The following morning I was on duty in reception to say goodbye to my departing guests. The first two left for the airport in taxis. The second taxi had barely disappeared from sight when a minibus arrived with the new arrivals from Manchester. I checked them in and arranged to see them later for the Welcome Drink as I had to go to the airport with the group departing for Gatwick. First I had to make sure all their bags had been collected and were ready to be loaded on to the bus when it arrived.

I sat proudly in the jump seat at the very front of the bus enjoying a clear view of my surroundings though the vast expanse of windscreen in front of me. Behind me I could hear lots of whispering and rustling. When we pulled up outside the terminal building Olive handed me a plastic carrier bag full of money – mostly coins – and thanked me, on behalf of everyone, for a great holiday. My eyes smarted with tears. I had not expected this and I mumbled my appreciation before leading them to the check-in desks. While she was checking in The Duchess realised that she had thrown all her South African money into the collection and she would need it when she got home. She asked me to return the bag of money so she could rescue it. I obliged and turned away while she hunted through the coins. Once the check-in was completed we clustered together saying fond farewells. I was sad to see them go.

There was no time to grieve as I had some new arrivals to collect. First I needed to freshen up and dived into the nearest toilets. It was a relief to drop my bag on the floor as it weighed a ton with all the coins I had been given. There was no time to sort them out and change them for notes. There was no time to do anything but head for Arrivals and find a vantage point amid the scrum of people.

I found a good place to stand holding my sign aloft where it could easily be seen. Within seconds I was surrounded by other reps, elbows dug into my side, arms obscured my view and several people trod on my toes. I backed away from the pack and retreated to another open space. I was further away from the exit and I had to stand on tiptoe to ensure my sign was visible. This jostling for position lasted for nearly an hour until all the passengers had come through. I had to chase after a few passengers who walked straight past me. While I was doing that some of the people I had asked to stay still went off to buy bottles of water so I had to parade up and down with my sign until I had fielded them all.

The first questions I was asked during the transfer were a great insight into the characters of the new group. They were not sightseers and were only interested in the activities available at our hotel. During my early morning walks around the hotel complex I had located the tennis courts and the hotel's private beach where the water sports centre was based so I was able to assure them there was plenty to do. A very different week stretched ahead of me and I was relishing the challenge. I felt much more confident now that I was familiar with my surroundings.

I had noticed that one of the women, Eliza, was very pale and stared out of the window taking no part in the general conversation but there had been no time to do more than walk down the bus and introduce myself. As I was checking everyone into the hotel Eliza suddenly collapsed into an armchair beside me and started sobbing. Immediately I went down on my knees beside her and tried to find out what the problem was. The receptionist handed out the remaining keys while I established that Eliza was grieving for an aunt who had died the night before she had travelled. I sympathised and mopped up her tears. I collected her key from reception and tried to explain where her room was but she was very confused about where she should be going so I accompanied her. The new arrivals all had rooms in the main block but I had been allowed to keep my bungalow. I was very grateful for this as not only had I become very fond of my room it would have been impossible to pack up and move while coping with arrivals and departures.

After dealing with Eliza I went straight to the bar for our Welcome Drink. Some of the group were already there and getting to know each other but one man remained aloof from the general conversation. He looked horrified when he was invited to join the early morning games of tennis. Danny did not look athletic. His short, rotund body was encased in a T-shirt and shabby jeans. He had not changed since I had seen him head for the bar and his first pint of beer shortly after we arrived. When he had taken his pint outside and taken off his T-shirt, I had followed him to check he had applied sun cream to his exposed white skin and suggested a hat would be a good idea. He told me not to fuss and assured me that his skin would turn brown naturally. I left him there and that was where he had stayed until he had pulled on his T-shirt and come back inside when I arrived in the bar. He had bought himself another pint of beer and then sat down close enough to the group to be a part of it but far enough away not to be included. I could see that his arms were already well on the way to an unhealthy shade of pink but I knew that any more interference from me would not go down well so I turned my attention to the distribution of ouzo or orange juice.

Eliza had not appeared at the Welcome Drink and after taking the group into the restaurant for dinner I went in search of her. I had highlighted times and places on her itinerary and given her a map of the hotel complex but I suspected she may not yet be ready to face the group on her own. Megan came with me as she had spoken briefly to Eliza on the transfer bus and was concerned about her. Eliza was not in her room so I urged Megan to rejoin the others in the restaurant while I continued the search. I finally found Eliza wandering around the grounds looking for the restaurant. She was totally disorientated so I went back to the restaurant with her and, as the dinner service had already finished, I organised a cold plate and some water for her. I had to leave her there on her own as I was due in reception to greet my last arrivals from Glasgow. Once the formalities had been completed I took them straight to the restaurant, introduced them to Eliza and we all ate together.

My first task the following morning was to fax my report for the first week to Aimee. It had not taken long to write it as everyone said they had enjoyed themselves and the only incident worthy of note was Vera's collapse in the Samaria Gorge. We had a duty to report any complaints made directly to us as their rep and indicate how we had attempted to deal with them. As I had not received any official complaints I had nothing to report. Maybe the feedback forms would tell a different story but I would not know immediately as they were sent directly to my company. I wondered if Lily would feedback the extreme irritation it had caused her that all the road signs were in Greek.

Our Information Meeting that morning was very brief as they were not interested in any excursions. When they escaped to the sun I was quizzed by the agent regarding this lack of enthusiasm. I responded that it was difficult to sell trips at their inflated prices. He failed to convince me regarding the argument of exclusivity as it had only applied to one trip, Knossos. I had to tread carefully as our local agents did not only organise excursions. They arranged our airport transfers, booked the hotels and helped us with major issues. I pointed out that there was still time for this group to book trips in their second week and I promised to do my best to generate some interest. As I had no money to collect after the meeting I was free to take the group on a tour of the complex. We only got as far as the hotel's beach where a fleet of canoes proved a stronger attraction and they were soon paddling round the bay.

I walked back to the main building to check on Danny who was still intent on his mission to get sunburned and had ignored my earlier observation that he was going red rather than brown. There was no sign of him but I did find Eliza who told me that Danny had been forced to retreat to his room to plaster his body with After Sun (borrowed from her). He probably had second degree burns as his shoulders had begun to blister. He was still working on the theory that he would go brown in a few days but he would need to grow a new layer of skin first. I called him in his room and he insisted he did not need to see a doctor and said he would join us for dinner later.

Danny was not at dinner so I took a tray of food to his room. It was a subterfuge to check on his condition as I was really worried about him. He was not in his room and when I returned to our table Karl told me he had seen Danny on his way out for a night on the town. Everyone else was also anxious to sample the night life so after we had eaten I took them to Nanu's, a night club, in the village. I had one dance with Karl but decided I should check my insurance before repeating the experience. I led them in one performance of the Macarena and then left them gyrating on the dance floor while I walked back along the beach paddling in the tepid water. It had been a strange day. I was still in the same resort but now I was seeing a very different aspect of it. I was already enthralled by the kaleidoscope of people and places that was the travel industry.

Chapter 2 – August

It was two in the morning when the shrilling of my bedside telephone plumbed the depths of my dreamless sleep. Eliza's shrill tones took control of my robotic state. "Go and tell reception to turn the music down in the disco". I struggled out of bed and pulled on some clothes. As I could not open my eyes wide enough to insert my contact lenses I perched some glasses on my nose before setting off.

The receptionist seemed surprised to see me but that did not match my own astonishment at being there. Or maybe it was my personal appearance that had evoked this reaction. My baggy nightshirt flopped over tailored shorts and my long spiky hair encircled a face almost entirely hidden behind the huge lenses of my old-fashioned tinted specs. I never wore them in public and had not bothered to renew them for at least twenty years. I delivered the message – please turn down the disco music. Yes, they already knew about the problem as Eliza had rung them several times and a member of staff had been sent there to ensure the music was turned down immediately. I thanked them and re-traced my steps.

By the time I got back to my bungalow my heart was still pounding following my rude awakening. I knew I would not get back to sleep and I decided to do some paperwork. As I moved papers around my desk I noticed the telephone. No wonder the receptionist had been so surprised to see me in person – I could have used the phone to deliver my message and then rolled over and gone back to sleep. It was too late now and dawn was already creeping across the bay beyond my open patio door. I went outside where the birds were stirring and trilling in the trees around me. In the distance I could hear the thudding of disco music and on the headland opposite I could see the bright lights of a small village. This must be the source of the music that had woken Eliza. If it happened again she would no doubt expect me to go and speak to the culprits.

Some of the group were planning an early game of tennis that morning and when it was light I walked down to the courts to see if they were there. They were not so after saying good morning to some monkeys in cages behind the courts I went to breakfast. My first task was to spark some interest in the optional excursions. Yesterday they had all been adamant that they did not want to do any trips but I had sensed that some people were no longer so sure. Once some changed their minds others would follow. All they needed was a little encouragement.

Revived by several cups of strong coffee I began my rounds. It took me all morning to speak to everyone in the group. Some had changed their minds but others had decided they wanted me to organise some trips that were not on the list. The ringleader regarding this request was Delilah. I was somewhat in awe of Delilah. When we had the usual 'what do you do' conversation she had announced that she was a real madam. She certainly had the makings of one as she was tall, stout, very flamboyant and clearly used to being in charge. Anxious glances had been exchanged round the table. We all feared the worse. Did we have a brothel keeper in our midst? Then Delilah gave us another clue. This was how she was greeted by the attendant when she drove into the car park at the House of Commons. She was a Member of Parliament. I was thrilled, even though I did not recognise her. This explained why she was reluctant to have her photo taken. I wondered if we should also address her as 'madam'. I evaded this quandary by only speaking when I was spoken to.

Delilah's first request was that I find a boat that would take them out to sea to watch the sun setting. Our agent did not organise any boat trips so I was free to look elsewhere. I tried all the agents in the village but drew a blank. One of them suggested I find a boat and deal directly with the skipper. I headed to the public harbour and strolled along the quay looking for a local fishing boat. When I found one I tottered up the long, narrow gangplank, found a crew member and made my request. He was surprisingly enthusiastic and agreed to take the group out to sea in return for a crate of beer.

Elated by my success, I skipped back down the gangplank. I did hear the warning shout but it was already too late. My feet had slipped from beneath me and I was plummeting into the sea below. I surfaced just in time to grab my bag as it floated past me. I rescued my new panama hat as I waded ashore. I perched on a bollard to wring out my dress and dry out the contents of my bag before walking back to my bungalow. I was still glowing with success at having achieved what our local agent had assured me was impossible.

I was about to step into the shower when my phone rang. It was Maria, the barmaid at the headland pool, urging me to get there as soon as possible. I was intrigued and raced up there to find Eliza in the middle of a heated argument with a hotel manager. She had been sunbathing there and took exception to children playing in the water. She claimed they were splashing her. She had used the telephone at the pool bar and summoned the Entertainments Manager to order the children to go away! He had driven up to the pool in one of the hotel golf buggies to speak to her. He was sympathetic but refused to accede to her request to send the children (and their parents) packing. She was furious and turned her anger on me claiming that my company only catered for adults. I agreed that we did but pointed out that we could not guarantee child-free hotels. She was not to be appeased and stormed off leaving me to make peace with the young family who were clearly bewildered by the reaction their presence had caused.

My second attempt to take a hot shower was delayed by a knock on my door. My visitor was Jason – he had been dubbed Mr Wonderful by the ladies in the group and he certainly seemed to merit the title. This good looking, athletic man seemed to be determined to ensure that everyone had a great time but he did it with such a pleasant demeanour that I regarded him as an ally. He wanted to organise some snorkelling in the large pool and asked if I could help him. I agreed and we set off to the Water Sports Centre and collected some masks and snorkels. Timidly I asked if I could join them – I had never done any snorkelling but now seemed a good time to start as Jason was a qualified instructor. I splashed around the pool learning to snorkel with a reasonable amount of success but an hour was more than enough. I was encouraging them from my sun bed when a Kri-Kri goat appeared and wandered past me. He was followed by a pony and then a mule. They were too close for my comfort so I left. I still had a faint imprint of a hoof mark on my chest from my last close encounter with a pony when I was a child.

That evening we were all meeting at Manolo's bar for pre-dinner drinks. On my way there I took a short cut through the hotel bar and discovered Danny trying to make conversation with a young Spanish couple he thought were in our group. He was very drunk and the less they understood him the louder he spoke. I rescued him from his predicament and invited him to come with me to join the others at Manolo's bar. Soon after we got there he made a clumsy attempt to chat up Tasha making the hackles rise on Jason's back. Abandoning my fresh ouzo I steered Danny out of the bar on the pretext of wanting company to walk back to the hotel. I knew Danny had not meant to offend but I had to be firm as his behaviour was threatening to spoil the holiday for other people in the group. He went off to sober up and came to dinner very late. He sat on his own, ate a large plate of dessert and then went off to his regular evening haunt, Nanu's. He fancied the barmaid there but clearly true love was not running smoothly.

Snuffling and grunting outside my door woke me very early the following morning. Guests on their way home after a late night at the disco was my first thought. In fact it was a pot-bellied Vietnamese pig and his mate. Now that I was up it seemed a shame to waste such a beautiful morning so I dressed and went out for a walk. The sun was already out and reflected in the dew on the grassy areas that were littered with ducks, swans and peacocks. They all seemed to be waddling in the same direction and I followed them – to a zoo on the perimeter. It was fascinating and included several cages housing more monkeys and a large aviary of birds. I was still exploring when a lorry arrived and dumped left-over food in a shallow pit. There was a mad rush as animals appeared from all corners of the complex, snorting, squeaking and grunting as they foraged through this bounty. I watched them for a long time before continuing my walk.

Numerous distractions hindered my progress. Puzzled by a sign that simply stated Kri-Kri goats I went down the path it indicated and found several members of this species in large enclosures. They all rushed to the fencing to nuzzle my pockets hoping they were stuffed with food. I apologised for my lack of forethought and continued along the path and into a small Roman amphitheatre. A colourful poster advertising future events and candlelit suppers indicated this was not an ancient ruin but a hotel facility. Breakfast time was approaching and I quickened my step. I skirted round a five star luxury hotel that was part of the complex and peered through the wrought iron gate at a third, empty, swimming pool. This would have delighted Eliza but sadly it was out of bounds.

After breakfast I decided to wash some smalls – my first chance since I got here and, as laundry bills were not accepted as a valid expense it was something that had to be done. I draped the freshly washed items around my balcony to dry in the sun. When I got back to my bungalow after another snorkelling session I discovered that the breeze had strengthened during my absence and several intimate items had been liberated from my balcony and were strewn all over the branches of the surrounding shrubs. I raced around collecting them but decided to abandon the pair of lacy knickers that had made their way down to the patio outside reception.

Back on my private balcony I reflected on the week so far. I seemed to be getting on really well with this group. There was just one small blot on my horizon. Karl was tall, blond and now attractively bronzed. But his muscular body was bursting out of some cut off denim shorts that he wore all the time – even at dinner. People did dress up for the evening meal especially the ladies but Karl just strolled in from the beach wearing his skimpy shorts. After dinner he changed into smart trousers and a shirt before going off to the village. I had complimented him on his smart appearance and joked that the women would appreciate it if he could dress up before he had his meal. The hotel did not allow shorts in the restaurant but for some reason they were turning a blind eye. I had to do their job for them as I had heard some comments from people in the group. My hints had fallen on deaf ears and as I had now received several direct complaints regarding his attire I had to take action.

That evening I found Karl in the bar on his own. It was the perfect opportunity and I suggested, politely, that he might like to change before joining us in the restaurant for dinner. He did not wish to change and saw no reason for doing so. When he joined us for dinner he was very unpleasant to Eliza assuming (correctly) that she was one of the complainants. Jason sprang to her defence so Karl moved to an empty table. He ignored several invitations to return to our table and then left. He was lying in wait for me when I walked out of the restaurant and re-opened our discussion shouting and using unacceptable language. I kept my cool. Fortunately the rest of the group were not far behind and Jason came to my rescue and told him to shut up. Karl vanished into the night and I did not see him again until I was walking back to the hotel on my own.

I was lost in thought and did not realise there was anyone behind me until I was suddenly thrown across the bonnet of a car. Karl was pushing his body down on top of me and murmuring in my ear that if I only I would take a course in the subject I would make a good rep. Not the best chat up line I had ever heard. My amusement turned to dismay when he tried to kiss me. I protested and tried to wriggle out from beneath him but he was too strong. Panic was setting in when suddenly everything lit up. We were bathed in the lights of a motor scooter that had pulled up beside us. Vangelis to the rescue.

I had met Vangelis in the village the previous week when he had tried to rent me a car. Since then I had often called in to his office for a cup of coffee and a chat. He was very Greek in appearance with dark, curly hair and a swarthy complexion. He was quaint and quirky and his English, which was very good, was littered with lines from sixties pop songs which were currently very popular on the island. He had declared that since meeting me "he was walking back to happiness". It was comforting to have a friend in the resort as I had discovered that being a rep could be a lonely existence. That evening he had been on his way home when he saw me walking up the road and had followed me to offer me a lift. When he saw Karl jump out on me he came roaring up on his scooter to see what was happening. His presence was enough to scare Karl off and Vangelis insisted on walking back to the hotel with me pushing his scooter along. Entry to the complex was forbidden to non-residents so I thanked my knight on two wheels and scuttled to my room – a second narrow escape that evening?

I was not sure whether or not I should warn the other ladies regarding Karl's predatory nature but I decided that in the interest of group harmony I would not mention the incident. However, it seemed I was not the only one who had been troubled by Karl's amorous advances. When Tasha joined us at breakfast the following morning she announced to everyone that Karl had called her at three that morning and invited her to join him for a drink on his balcony. She then turned to Karl, now slumped over his first coffee, and told him not to do it again. Jason leapt to his feet brandishing an imaginary sword, or so it seemed to me, and told Tasha that she must tell him if Karl gave her any more reason for concern. This exchange gave Eliza the courage to confess that she had received a similar invitation, issued in the early hours of the previous day. It seemed that I had not been at the top of Karl's list after all.

Later that morning we walked round the headland to a secluded bay we had seen from the cliffs. There was no path so we had to scramble over rocks and splash through shallow pools of water. It was worth the effort as we had the bay to ourselves and, with Jason's guidance, we were soon in the sea exploring the coral reefs below us. As we splashed ashore Tasha trod on a sea urchin. Mr Wonderful gathered her up in his arms and carried her back to the main road where he hailed a taxi and took her to the local medical centre. We stretched out in the sun to await their return blissfully unaware that the tide was coming in. When the sea encroached on our rocky platform we inched back a little more to avoid the crashing waves.

I was aroused from my daydream by warning shouts from Jason. Our hitherto calm sandy bay had become a raging torrent between us and the mainland. We scrambled to our feet and began stuffing our belongings into our bags. Jason then waded to and fro in water up to his shoulders bags balanced precariously on his head until everything was safely stowed on dry land. Although we could all swim we had to choose the right moment to plunge into the water to avoid being thrown against the rocks but with Jason masterminding our evacuation we were soon safely back on dry land. It was really scary and taught me to be more vigilant. After all I was responsible for everything – even the turning tides.

Our adventures that morning were the main topic of conversation later at dinner. We also discussed having dinner in the village one evening. I told them that all my colleagues had recommended a particular seafood restaurant. It was agreed that I should book the restaurant later that evening when we walked to the village for a drink. Vangelis joined us in the Banana Bar. He was keeping a watchful eye on me and had declared his undying love in a unique but endearing manner. He said "my heart is like a loaf of bread that can be given away a slice at a time". He was good company but no more. I was more attracted by the PC in his office – free internet access. I left them in the bar and went off to book tables at the seafood restaurant. I was made very welcome by George, the owner, who plied me with white wine and promises of the best fresh lobster in town. I agreed to take the group there the following evening.

The next afternoon both the hotel and the village had several power cuts and with no air conditioning in the rooms it was stifling. Most of us survived but Eliza did not feel well and she and Megan, her new best friend, cancelled their bookings. I called the restaurant to tell George that two people had cancelled. I was sure it would not be a problem as he had seemed very affable. He had really pushed the fresh lobster though and both ladies had selected it. My call was taken by one of the waiters who just said, "No problem".

But it was a problem by the time we arrived that evening and George insisted I would have to pay for the two cancelled dinners. He had promised me a free meal for taking the group to his restaurant and now he was expecting me to pay for two meals. I thought he was being unreasonable and said so. I had given him notice of the cancellations. As I was expecting fireworks when I paid the bill I collected the money from everyone and then told them that I would see them later. George was still insisting I paid for the cancelled meals but I did not have enough cash with me. I regretted telling the clients concerned that they would not have to pay anything at all but I felt that illness was a reasonable excuse. I said this to George and finally we agreed that I should pay for one meal (thus cancelling out my free meal). Once the cash had changed hands he yelled at me to get out of his restaurant. I was happy to oblige and did so with alacrity. By the time I caught up with the group I had smoothed my ruffled feathers and assured them that the bill had been settled without any problems.

Another new experience awaited me the next day – the thrills of an aqua park. After breakfast I set off to hire some cars from Vangelis. As I walked through the village it soon became clear that news of my eviction from the best restaurant in town had done the rounds. I was 'courted' by every restaurant I walked past. It took me a long time to get to Vangelis's office by which time I was brim-full of coffee and white wine. They had all assumed I was looking for another restaurant for my group but I had already decided I would take them to Le Gourmet, my personal favourite. Their food was good and the prices were reasonable – I did not want to repeat last night's fiasco which had cost me a day's pay. I had also learnt, the hard way, that I should always make people pay up front and deal with cancellations according to the policy of the restaurant concerned.

Our aqua park outing was a great success. On arrival I had felt intimidated by the sight of the huge slides, some nearly vertical and others snaking round like giant helter-skelters. I said I would watch from the side lines, well, the car park. An enthusiastic member of staff offered me free entry as I was the guide and insisted I went inside. I agreed – just to have a look. Once I was inside I was prey to the group's enthusiasm and I agreed to try one ride – which lead to another and then another. It was amazing and I was soon racing up ladders to plummet down near vertical slides clinging on to my swimsuit when I smashed into the water at the bottom. I floated down a pretty water course on a huge rubber ring and then dragged the rubber ring to the top of a water slide and bounced down to the bottom through a dark tunnel at a frightening speed. Two of us decided to repeat the experience on one ring and it went even faster than usual and we screamed all the way down – much to the amusement of the rest of the group who claimed they were seeing me in a new light. I was seeing me in a new light as well – bronzed, enthusiastic and happy.

After returning the hire car I skipped back to the hotel from the village just in time to get ready for the hotel's Greek evening in their taverna on the beach. It was a great evening with a fabulous buffet, unlimited wine, a show and communal Greek dancing. A very portly waiter was the star of the show because, despite his size, he was very light on his feet. It was amazing how the removal of his black jacket and the addition of a red cummerbund round his waist transformed him as he whirled and twirled like a professional dancer. After the show all the guests were invited to join in Zorba's dance which got faster and faster and very out of hand. I did have a go but the straps of my dress started to fall down and as I was not wearing a bra I did not want to prove to everyone that I had acquired an all over tan. I extracted myself from the tangle of bodies and went outside to cool off. As I emerged from the restaurant I spotted Eliza and Megan huddled together outside the ladies' toilet.

When Eliza saw me approaching she screamed at me to leave them alone. Megan was cowering behind her, crying. I was concerned and gently enquired if there was a problem. Between sobs Megan told me she had a crush on Jason and he had refused to allow the 'official' photographer to take a picture of them together when they arrived at the taverna. They asked me to intercede on Megan's behalf. I refused, politely. At her age she should know better – she was not a teenager. They both went off to their rooms and I went back inside. A little later Megan rang the taverna to tell me she had lost her room key. I got a pass key from reception and let her in to her room. She then decided that she had lost her purse and her key was inside it. I went back to the taverna to look for it. Everyone had gone by then and they were clearing up but the purse had not been found. The next morning I discovered that the purse and key had been in her room all the time. Megan had not called to say she had found them. She could have saved me from the joys of poking around in the ladies' toilet looking for an item that had never been lost.

I was delighted when four people in the group asked me to join them when they hired a car to explore further afield. I felt as though I was playing truant even though the group had assumed I was entitled to a day off (I was not). We were also supposed to stay with the majority but as they were going to sunbathe all day it seemed pointless. I persuaded myself that any difficulties that may arise were more likely to be with the explorers so I left my mobile number with reception and went off with them. It was a lovely day out and so nice to see another part of the island. Chania has a fantastic Venetian harbour and Rethymnon has a very pretty port surrounded by fish restaurants displaying their fresh fish on beds of ice. I dropped subtle hints about staying out for dinner but I should have known better, after all they had already paid for dinner in the hotel.

Danny and Karl had already had dinner when we joined the rest of the group in the hotel restaurant. I had seen them at breakfast and both of them had assured me that they were enjoying their holiday – without the group. Eliza had calmed down and seemed to have accepted the presence of families in our hotel. During dinner when we discussed our planned walk through the Samaria Gorge the next day Eliza exclaimed, "How lovely, are you going now?"

When a small group of us set off the following morning to walk through the Samaria Gorge I had no idea what to expect but I was ready to face the challenge. Soon after we started Megan, despite having trained by walking through the streets of London, began to struggle. The first section was very steep and she winced and whined all the way and then, after only two kilometres she said she had to sit down as her knee was hurting. I had been very happy when I discovered that Corea was our local guide again. She came to the rescue and strapped Megan's knee. Our three companions had stayed with us at first but they were all experienced walkers so I had told them to go ahead. I stayed with Megan but I found crawling along at snail's pace extremely difficult. I hoped my flimsy plimsolls would last the course, which was proving much tougher than I had been led to believe, but I was sure they would do better than the Scholl sandals that had just clumped past me. I had shouldered Megan's rucksack as mine was nearly empty. Everyone seemed to carry rucksacks all the time but I had no idea what they put in them and in particular Megan as hers was so heavy.

I had a quick peek when we had another enforced stop so Megan could fill up her water bottle. She had half bottles of vodka, gin and whisky and three packets of biscuits. I was sitting under a sign that said alcohol was not allowed in the gorge! Maybe she was thinking of holding a party when we completed the walk. Corea had offered to stay with Megan so I could walk at my own pace for a while. That would have been a treat but I declined as she was my client and my responsibility. After making her generous offer Corea jumped off the rock she had been perched on, like a leprechaun, and bounded off again. I knew that we would find her waiting for us again further along the path.

When we met up again Corea expressed serious concerns regarding Megan's slow progress and suggested that Megan took the only other way out of the gorge, on the back of a donkey. Megan was having none of it and fiercely resisted this plan. It was her ambition to complete the walk. I would have happily jumped on a donkey to finish the trek. I was fed up with scrambling along the dry river bed skidding over slippery pebbles. Corea had agreed that Megan could continue for now but I knew she was really concerned as she had the ferry tickets for a bus load of sixty people and if she did not get back in time we would all be stuck there overnight.

We made it! Well nearly. A truck picked us up at the park gates – Megan was not convinced we had walked the whole gorge and wanted to continue on foot. It was exasperating. Even the normally cool Corea was nearly shouting in her frustration as Megan demanded proof that she had completed the 'official' walk through the gorge. I had failed to convince her as I was only the 'rep' and I knew nothing. I was sure Corea was going to give us our ferry tickets, wish us luck and leave us there while she raced back to the port in the truck. I was itching to pick Megan up and throw her on board. She capitulated when she realised that Corea was serious and really would have abandoned us.

On the ferry we were reunited with our companions who had completed the walk in three hours. It had taken us nearer eight. They had spent the last four hours in a pizzeria drinking beer and were glowing as a result. Megan was radiant with the success at having completed the walk. I was exhausted but happy because I had helped Megan achieve her goal.

When I stretched as I got up the following morning my calf muscles went into a vicious cramp. I hobbled across to the restaurant for breakfast assuring everyone that I was not really suffering any ill effects from the walk. Soon after I sat down we were swamped by torrential rain and we were all moved inside to finish our meal. Water was gushing down the paths and we had to shelter in the main building for an hour before we could make a dash for our rooms. I retreated to mine while it was still raining as the group were suggesting card games or line dancing. I was ready to accept the challenge of organising the latter having attended some classes a few months earlier. I was not very good as I was not always sure which was left and which was right and often ended up facing the whole crowd as they galloped towards me. I had written down some easy routines we could try. I just needed to find some music – I was sure the Animation Team would be able to supply some.

The rain stopped before I had to don my party entertainer hat and the group was soon dispersed around the pools or on the beach. As the holiday was drawing to a close they were happy to spend their last two days chilling out so I had time to sort out my paperwork and confirm flights and transfers. My first departure was the next morning as Jason was going home a day early for business reasons.

I was not the only one to get up early to see Jason off the following morning. Tasha was also there, still wearing the same dress she had worn at dinner the previous evening. I did not comment but Karl had no inhibitions and was happy to point this out during breakfast. I left before the tears erupted again – I was not practised in the art of lending my shoulder to cry on. I had to start packing as I would be leaving with the group the next day.

Everything was spread on my bed when a note was pushed under my door requesting me to call Aimee. I did so immediately. After suggesting I sat down, Aimee asked me if I could stay on Crete for another two weeks. My replacement was ill and unable to travel. My only real concern was that I had run out of clean clothes and Aimee promised that my laundry bill would be paid. I agreed to stay – I had no work in the near future and I was enjoying my time on the island. I was freelance now and could work where and when I chose.

After the Manchester group had departed the following morning I took most of the Gatwick group to Le Gourmet for lunch. As we left his taverna Kostos asked me if I wanted him to organise a meal for the same group that evening. I just laughed off this suggestion as they would be airborne by then. But they would not. A fax from Aimee informed me that there was a six hour delay on the incoming flight so I did need to arrange a meal that evening. I raced back to Le Gourmet and did the deal with Kostos. The local grapevine was very efficient.

Next I had to tell the group about the delay. They thought I was joking. I still had the fax in my hand so they were soon convinced and happy to have some extra time in the resort. They settled back on their sun beds and I went off to find Danny. He was distraught when he heard the news as he was due to start work in the early hours of the following day. I agreed to call his boss to explain the situation and we went to my bungalow. I started my conversation with his boss by saying, "Danny is sitting on the bed next to me …"

I spent that evening running between Le Gourmet and the hotel. After taking the departing group to Le Gourmet, I ran back to the hotel to meet the new arrivals from Manchester. We had a drink in the bar before I took them into the restaurant where I had to leave them. I sprinted back to Le Gourmet to make sure that group would be finished in time for their transfer to the airport. I had told Kostos I would just have a glass of wine but when he put a juicy steak in front of me I could not resist. I ate as quickly as I could before herding the group back to the hotel and on to the bus. We could have lingered for another two hours because the flight was delayed for a further three hours. I bade them all a fond farewell and settled down with a book in Arrivals. The words danced before my eyes as I struggled to stay awake – I had partied until the early hours with the departing group and now it was catching up with me.

I had no sleep at all that night. As soon as the new group was checked in the duty manageress invited me to have a drink with her. It was three in the morning and not an appropriate time for my first complimentary drink from the hotel. I allowed myself to be persuaded and listened in horror as she told me that two of my single travellers had been put in the same bungalow. I knew the hotel had an overbooking situation that week but I had been adamant that my single travellers were strangers and would not be prepared to share. The hotel had found their own solution and I was outraged at their subterfuge. The excuses came thick and fast. It was a deluxe bungalow and each person had their own room; she was complying with the wishes of the women concerned as one of them, Miss Marples (the resemblance was uncanny), had requested bungalows next to each other. But the other one, Mabel, had requested a room in the main block rather than a bungalow (the hotel had missed or ignored that request). Maybe it would work out. I would find out at breakfast the next morning – or maybe even before that.

Mabel was waiting for me in reception when I passed through on my way to breakfast. She was distraught. Slim, dark and prone to bad headaches she screamed at me for five minutes and then, her anger spent, she collapsed in a weepy heap on a chair. She told me that Miss Marples – the friend who was no longer a friend – had grabbed the best room and had no intention of giving up their deluxe accommodation. Mabel would not have minded if there had been a proper bedroom for her but there was not. She had camped on a put-you-up in the vestibule. There was nowhere to store her belongings and her bathroom was basic and tiny. Miss Marples could only access her superior bedroom by walking through this vestibule.

Between gulps Mabel told me that she and Miss Marples had met at an art class. Miss Marples had persuaded Mabel to book this holiday but did not tell her that she had requested neighbouring bungalows. Miss Marples was very happy with the current arrangement and had informed Mabel, through her bedroom door that she intended to stay where she was. Mabel said the bungalow was certainly luxurious and close to the headland swimming pool but it only had one bedroom. She was adamant that she wanted a single room in the hotel. The manager responsible had gone into hiding so I turned to the director I had met during my first week in the hotel. He confirmed that the main block was full but he did offer the women two separate bungalows and we went off to look at them, collecting Miss Marples on the way. They were right on the perimeter, near the rubbish dump so I was not surprised when Miss Marples refused to consider it. Mabel was appalled and still adamant she wanted a room in the main block. I did not blame them. I offered to take one of the bungalows if Miss Marples would take the other one. Mabel could then have my bungalow. Miss Marples would not entertain the notion so it was stalemate again.

Mabel was weeping once more when Miss Marples announced that she had the ideal solution. Mabel could have my bungalow and I could move in with her. She had forgotten that Mabel did not want a bungalow. Miss Marples decreed that the matter was not up for discussion and rushed off. I suspected she had gone to guard 'her' bungalow. It was time to refer the matter to Aimee as Mabel was now demanding her money back and a flight home.

Aimee was surprisingly sympathetic and gave me a 'name' from the hotel's head office. It worked a treat and Mabel was offered a very nice bungalow close to reception. Miss Marples could keep the deluxe bungalow for five days. But on day five I would move in with her for one night and then the next day we would both be re-located. Everyone agreed to this solution and I settled Mabel in her new bungalow. She had one of her bad 'heads' which was not surprising after all the sobbing that had been going on. I was exhausted but immediately set off to find the rest of the group to remind them about the Welcome Drink and Information Meeting that had been postponed until that evening. I felt I had lost touch with them.

Most of the group were sunbathing round the headland pool and Miss Marples, who had emerged as a natural leader, was regaling them with the story of her 'victory' over me and the hotel management. She must have seen me approaching but she continued with her tale. She was not very complimentary regarding my role in the proceedings. I waited until she had finished her tale and then confirmed the arrangements for that evening. I retreated to my room. I was not used to being labelled the villain and especially when I had brokered a resolution.

The Welcome Drink and Information Meeting passed in a bit of a blur. There was more enthusiasm for the sun beds around the headland pool than the optional excursions. Night life was also at the forefront of some of their minds. Two attractive, vivacious blondes in the group, Sandy and Shirl, quizzed me regarding the night life in the village then knocked back their complimentary ouzos wished us 'bon appetite' and vanished into the night. Hamish, a high-powered executive, informed me that he was so stressed out he was incapable of making conversation but he said he might have found his tongue by the next evening when he may or may not join us for dinner.

The main topic of conversation at dinner was Miss Marples and her bungalow. She and Mabel were not speaking to each other so the atmosphere was a bit frosty. I tried to move on to other subjects and told them about Le Gourmet and suggested they might like to go there for lunch the next day. No one was interested. Tommie wanted to know more about Sandy and Shirl – he had been devastated when they left earlier and told me that I should have kept the group together. I said I would do my best to persuade them to join us for dinner the next evening but that was as far as I could go. Tommie was clearly in awe of the two girls but not brave enough to make a direct approach.

I spent the next day trying to inject some enthusiasm into the group regarding their surroundings but without success. Immediately after breakfast they went to the headland pool and queued until the sun beds were released from their padlock and chain. They arranged them round tables (already 'saved' with a pile of towels) under sun umbrellas. I went back there at mid-morning and asked if anyone wanted to join me for lunch. They did not. They were going to eat in the pool bar. When I stopped at the pool on my way back from the village they were all fast asleep. I suspected they would be there until the sun beds were collected and locked up again at six that evening. I decided to do some snorkelling and swam round the headland from the hotel's private beach to the public beach. Looking down I felt as though I was cruising over a mountain range, one minute brushing against the coral on the peaks and the next floating above a profoundly deep valley. It was daunting but also very exhilarating.

Before dinner that evening I took the whole group to Manolo's bar. The small area outside was packed with people but after manoeuvring furniture and customers Manolo created sufficient spaces for us to sit together. But this group, that is the dominant female, did not like Manolo's and after one drink Miss Marples led the charge back to the hotel bar. I had just settled down in the restaurant when Mabel approached me with a glass of white wine in her hand. Fleetingly I wondered if she had bought it for me as a thank you for sorting out her room. But I should have known better. She did not like the taste of the wine and asked me to deal with it. I took the offending glass to the bar, explained the problem and extracted a promise from the barman for a replacement glass of wine the following evening. Mabel claimed that having drunk half the wine before realising it was 'bad' she could not manage another full glass. I did not feel comfortable doing this as there was nothing wrong with the wine but the client was always right, a fact I had to keep reminding myself that must be accepted.

During breakfast the next morning several people expressed an interest in visiting Knossos but not on the advertised day, Monday. I called the agent to see if we could go on a different day but he said it would have to be Monday as the English speaking trip was always on Monday. I knew that but pointed out that last week the English speaking trip was actually in Hungarian as they had held the majority. He could not be persuaded. I would have to book a taxi and find a guide when we got there. I could not face the walk to Le Gourmet for lunch because my calf muscle was still really painful so I stayed in my bungalow and had a cold beer with some pretzels lying on a lilo (donated by Tasha) on my balcony. It was my last chance to enjoy its seclusion because I had to move rooms the next day.

That evening, after dinner, the group invited me to join them for a cocktail at their regular haunt, Chequers. I was delighted to accept the invitation. Mine was a difficult role as I had to tread the fine line of being available without being intrusive. When we arrived we received a warm welcome from the owners, Anna and Andrew, a young couple from London. It was a very English bar with wood panelling, old-fashioned beer pumps and high backed stools along the length of the bar. The cocktail menu was a throwback to my University days and I selected a snowball. This yellow fizzing cocktail had been my first taste of sophistication. I was startled from my memories when my miniature parasol burst into flames due to the close proximity of a sparkler Andrew had thoughtfully added. Our amusement at this small incident drew us together and I felt that at last the barrier created by the problems at the start of the trip had been removed. No doubt the generous measures in the cocktails were a catalyst. Morag, who to date had hardly spoken to me had discovered a very dry sense of humour at the bottom of a tumbler of neat vodka.

Despite my entreaty for a last minute reprieve the next morning I found myself temporarily homeless. I dreaded spending that night in an airless vestibule on a put-you-up with my clothes hanging in a wardrobe in the bedroom of a host who clearly found my presence a nuisance. I would try and stay out of her way. The situation had arisen because the hotel was hosting a huge conference over the next few days attended by one thousand delegates. They arrived from Athens that afternoon and brought the whole of Agia Pelagia to a standstill as an endless cavalcade of shiny black cars blocked every road into town and every entrance into the hotel. I watched the whole fiasco on my way into the village to visit Vangelis and then on to Chequers to borrow some books.

It was a struggle to walk there as I was still hobbling after my Samaria Gorge experience. One calf muscle had recovered but the other was getting worse. This was probably caused by the flat leather sandals I had purchased as it was not possible to do this job wearing high heels all the time. I probably walked around five miles a day trotting around the complex and down to the village which was not helping.

I lingered in the village to give Miss Marples some space but the 'Do not disturb' sign was still in place when I returned. I stretched out on a sun bed by the pool to read. A few minutes later the pony arrived. It dumped a pile of manure right next to me. It kicked a guest who tried to shoo him away and then sauntered into the bar area and stole some food from a table. The mule arrived soon after and it was mayhem until a member of staff enticed them away with a bucket of water. It was not long before the pony returned and I retreated. Back in my vestibule I had a shower and then tapped timidly on the door of Miss Marples' room. No answer. I was already dripping with sweat from the oppressive heat. My clothes were all hanging in the wardrobe next door and inaccessible. Desperately I delved into the bottom of my holdall, found a crumpled dress and pulled that on. I set off for Manolo's bar intending to have several tumblers of ouzo to dull the pain in my calf muscle.

I was sipping the first one when Shirl limped into sight. She had twisted her knee and wanted me to go to the pharmacist with her as she was convinced he would have an instant cure. Off we went – both limping. The pharmacist sent us to the doctor who examined Shirl's knee and announced, in English, that he could only explain the problem in German. He gave her a prescription and two receipts: one for the consultation and the other for writing the prescription. At the pharmacy she paid a very inflated price for painkillers and anti-inflammatories. I had considered requesting a consultation but as the doctor looked more like a road sweeper than a physician I did not bother.

When Shirl and I finally arrived at dinner there was total chaos. We had been moved to a makeshift dining room half way between the main block and the headland pool. Eleven of us were squashed round a table for eight in the gloomy, steamy interior. Miss Marples had been and gone but had left a message for me – she had decided she would not be moving out of her deluxe bungalow the next day as she was fed up with moving around. She had been in the same room since she arrived! My gloom at receiving this news was deepened by our appalling meal. The 'restaurant' was hotter than the food – slabs of congealed pizza. The scraps off the conference tables no doubt. I complained and was told Restaurant Makeshift was the best restaurant in the hotel. I knew that it was really a meeting room with a patio outside and that the food was being carried down there from the main restaurant. I was not in the mood for this helping of Cretan humour and said I would pursue the matter the next day.

That night sleep evaded me entirely – it was even worse than I had imagined it could be. The vestibule was airless and the pain in my calf muscle was excruciating. As soon as daylight began to creep through the crack in the front door I got up and went for a swim. The closeness of the pool was my only consolation and after a few lengths my calf had eased sufficiently to walk up to Restaurant Makeshift to save tables outside for breakfast. As soon as I had arranged our tables the pony and the mule appeared and rearranged them. They terrorised the guests as they snatched food from the tables until they were captured by several members of staff and marched off to a secure paddock.

At breakfast Miss Marples, having accepted her fate, told me I could find her on the beach when our rooms were ready. I had promised her first choice and as soon as I had the room numbers I tracked her down and gave them to her. She was not impressed because I did not have both room keys with me. She announced that she would check the rooms 'soon' and turned back to her book. I found a vantage point and settled down to wait. Miss Marples sat on the beach apparently engrossed in her book. She showed no sign of moving. I watched and waited. It was a full hour before Miss Marples left the beach. I waited another half an hour before I went to claim my room. I was in the main block and my room had a spectacular sea view.

At breakfast the next morning Miss Marples grumbled that her new bungalow was akin to Piccadilly Circus. I sympathised and said that my room was also very noisy and then asked her if she had any plans that day. She and Mabel (the friendship had been rekindled) were planning to visit the villages of Achlade and Fodele (birthplace of El Greco). She invited me to join them – a gesture of friendship or a contribution to their taxi fare? Whatever the motive it was an interesting trip. Achlade was small and pretty with an elderly population that was fascinated by our presence. They cackled and pointed at us and one old woman insisted on pummelling my rather ample bosom but I had no idea why. Fodele was more picturesque but touristy. The streets were lined with small shops selling tablecloths and other items made in macramé and crochet. Old women sat outside their houses knitting and weaving and trying their best to entice us inside the shops with sprigs of thyme, a biscuit and unfulfilled promises of slashed prices.

I was back in time from our village tour to join the sunbathers round the pool. Their routine had not changed since day one but the topic of conversation had.

They were dissecting the rumour that Sandy and Shirl had both found love interests among the locals. Tommie was distraught as he claimed to have fallen in love with both of them. He was such an innocent that he did not stand a chance. I had not realised people like him still existed and his frail vulnerability made me feel very protective. He went into the toilet to apply his sun cream and sunbathed wearing white socks. I knew I should avoid gossiping with the group but curiosity overrode caution. I had to drag myself away to negotiate tables on the patio of Restaurant Makeshift for dinner that evening. The food was no better but the setting was cooler and the hotel had finally accepted that several small tables could be pushed together to make one large one.

Breakfast was no better than dinner. The coffee was dreadful, it was put on the tables in vacuum flasks and tasted as though it had been made the previous night which it probably had. That second morning I asked for tea. Several minutes after placing my order the waiter arrived with a vacuum jug of hot water and filled my cup. He went off again and returned with one tea bag and one slice of lemon. The water was tepid by then. I drank the tea very quickly and requested a second cup. The process was repeated. Apparently he was not allowed to leave a flask of hot water, several tea bags and a few slices of lemon on the table.

The sunbathers were very late and hung over. The usually timid Morag had found her tongue and told us that she had carried a full glass of vodka back to the hotel and stored in her fridge to drink later. I left them giggling at the table and walked down to the village to see Vangelis and allowed him to serenade me on his accordion. I had lunch and dinner at Le Gourmet that day as the group had decided to eat out that evening. Everyone except Mabel was there. She had opted out as she was not a 'group' person. Sandy and Shirl were very coy about their new boyfriends; all we knew was that they were Greek.

When everyone moved on to Chequers I went back to my room and read for a while on my balcony. It was very pleasant listening to the soft murmur of the sea. I was well into my fifth book – a light read about a cruise ship in the 1920s. Earlier, at dinner, in an effort to introduce a new topic of conversation, I had mentioned the existence of flappers during that period, the Roaring Twenties. I was quite shocked when I discovered that none of them knew what a flapper was. When asked to explain I said they were good time girls and supposed that in those days our two lively blondes would have been referred to as flappers. That was a mistake as Miss Marples immediately informed the girls that I had referred to them as slappers. It had seemed an appropriate time to leave.

That evening also saw the end of the conference and by the next morning all the delegates had moved out and we were back in our usual restaurant for breakfast. During the meal I persuaded some of the group to venture into Iráklion with me. We went on the public bus and thanks to a tip from Corea I was wearing my badge and got a free ride. First we visited the market by the harbour. Apart from the fresh fruit and fish stalls it was mainly 'tat' and resembled one huge car boot sale – all the clothes were just thrown on a table and people rooted through them. After coffee in a taverna by the harbour to cool down in the sea breeze we tackled the shops in the town and then met up again for lunch.

Getting back was complicated by confusion regarding the right bus stop. When the bus had not arrived five minutes after the appointed time we were directed to another stop. A bus arrived there soon after we did and I asked the driver if we were in the right place but he did not speak any English and drove off. Then I tried a Swedish tour guide but she had no idea so I went into a large hotel nearby. The receptionist said it stopped outside that hotel but that we had 'lost' it. Undeterred I ran outside where I could see our bus working its way through the heavy traffic. I waved to the others across the road but they were chatting and did not see me. I jumped on the bus to stop it moving off and stood in the doorway waving and yelling at the top of my voice to attract their attention. Finally they saw me, ran across the square and scrambled onto the bus. The conductor was very cross by then and muttering about the 'English'. He refused me free passage.

I had invited everyone to join me that evening for pre-dinner drinks on my balcony. In anticipation I had several bottles of beer cooling on my air conditioning unit as this was more effective than the fridge. Miss Marples decided that she would have a drinks party on her terrace at the same time. Forewarned by another member of the group I did not splash out on nibbles as well as the beer. I took the latter to Miss Marples' soiree but discretely drank some white wine donated by Sandy and Shirl who had subsequently melted into the night. Miss Marples was in her element and grabbed an expensive bottle of red wine that Hamish had brought and poured it straight down her throat. Morag brought the glass of vodka she had liberated from Chequers three nights earlier. Whatever the technique a good time was enjoyed all round.

The following morning I went into the village to say my goodbyes. I started at Chequers and Anna asked, with a wicked grin, if I had seen Sandy and Shirl that morning. I had not but that was not unusual. Anna eagerly updated me on the latest gossip. The girls had been involved in a punch up in a nightclub and then moved on to indulge in some floodlit sex on the beach. I hoped this gossip would not reach the group but realistically it was only a matter of time as Chequers was their local. They would not hear it from me – I was too embarrassed. I blushed at the thought of meeting either of them but it was not until that evening that Sandy floated into the bar as I was organising our farewell cocktail. Her attire, a skimpy bikini with a colourful sarong encircling her waist, suggested she was not staying. She grabbed a cocktail, exchanged pleasantries and then left.

I had hoped we would all have dinner together that last night. Hamish had promised he would join us and just as I had given up hope he rushed into the bar. He claimed he had been forced to take the long way round to get there because Sandy and Shirl were 'at it' on their patio. The girls became the topic of conversation but they did not get the whole story until we went to Chequers. Anna wasted no time telling them about Sandy and Shirl and the ensuing discussion got very bawdy. I moved on to seek out Vangelis to say goodbye. I was really shocked by the behaviour of the girls but "trying hard not to show it" (Vangelis was getting to me).

Two days after getting home from Crete I was roused from a luxurious lie in by Aimee. She had called to inform me that they had received a five page letter from Sandy and several phone calls from Shirl demanding an apology from me for referring to them as slappers. Apparently this slur on their characters had provoked their outrageous behaviour. I had not even filed my report so I had to get to work immediately. The last time I spoke to Sandy and Shirl was at breakfast on departure day. They arrived very early and seemed surprised to see me. Sandy was still wearing the same bikini and sarong that she had been wearing the previous evening. We had a rather stilted conversation – I really liked both the girls and I had tried very hard to be broadminded but my face had reflected my disapproval. Now both ladies were demanding an apology from me on the grounds that had I made them stay with the group they would not have been bonking Greeks on the beach! After careful consideration I penned a letter which began "I thought you were two very attractive ladies having a wonderful time ... I now discover the reverse to be true".

* * * * * *

Aimee had said I was welcome to call in to the office any time so I delivered the letter and my report personally. As I was standing by her desk a piece of paper floated down on to the cluttered surface between us and a loud voice demanded to know what it was. I looked down and stuttered that it was my laundry bill from the Capsis Beach. Yes, he knew that but why was it so high? I had to agree that it was outrageous. How could they justify charging £77 for laundering eleven items? I remembered that the items had all come back starched and stiff as a board so they had to be rinsed through before I could wear them. I suspected I may have ticked some boxes in error. I apologised profusely and promised that it would never happen again. I was making history as my first trip had produced the best set of feedback forms ever received and my third the most controversial claim for expenses. Aimee told me that the other girls usually paid a sympathetic chambermaid a small sum to do their washing.

This advice came as a big relief as it indicated there would be a next time.

* * * * * *

I was offered a weekend walking trip on Derwent Water in the Lake District. I had claimed to be an experienced walker on the basis of having done two walks in the Samaria Gorge. Knowing that I needed to look the part I splashed out on a pair of Clarke's lace up boots that the shop assistant assured me would cope with all terrains. A few days later, full of confidence I set off in my little red sports car.

Disaster struck as I was speeding along the motorway. A stone flew up and cracked the windscreen. I had no chance to deal with this catastrophe because as soon as I arrived at the hotel clients began buzzing around me complaining about their rooms. Melissa wanted a cooler room for her dog and everyone else wanted larger rooms with a view of the lake. The manager was not happy as they had to clean several rooms for the second time that day. I offered my room as an alternative and changed rooms twice without seeing either of them.

During these changes I acquired a master key which opened the door of what I thought was my room. When I saw a black leather holdall on the floor and a man sprawled on the bed neither of which belonged to me I realised I was in the wrong room. I withdrew apologising profusely, my face a beetroot red. The hotel was unrepentant regarding the master key but at least they had kept track of the room changes and could tell me which room was mine. It was a cupboard. The wardrobe was so narrow a coat hanger would not fit on the rail so I rolled up my clothes and squashed them on to the shelves – there were no drawers. When I moved the trouser press to open the bathroom door it collapsed so I pushed all the pieces under the bed and doubled the floor space. On the way to my meeting with the manager I put my suitcase back in my car to give me a little more space.

The manager kept me waiting so I browsed the hotel shop where I found a leaflet about the boat trip we were doing the next evening. The trip started an hour earlier than stated on our itinerary as the times changed with the advent of autumn. I needed to sort that out with the manager as well. When he finally arrived he was still aggrieved about all the room changes and determined never to host one of our groups again. I requested a late dinner the following evening but he said we could eat early or not at all. I passed this information on to the group – more politely than I had received it. Some people decided to forego the included boat trip rather than have an early dinner.

I was taken aback by this decision but having already witnessed the fervour for 'wine included with dinner' it should not have come as a surprise. Each person was entitled to a half bottle of wine but the choice of wine was the prerogative of the hotel and each of the three nights would feature a different wine. At our first dinner the selected wines were not a success and the white wine was deemed to be 'undrinkable' and everyone wanted the red wine. I tried to swap the white wine for more red wine but all the bottles had already been opened and the manager was not prepared to change anything. Most people did not manage to consume their allotted amount and complained bitterly but finally forced themselves to consume the remaining white wine. After dinner we went into the conservatory for coffee and a game of Dingbats. I was not familiar with this game but Melissa fell on the cards with whoops of delight and the game was soon under way. I sat back and watched them wondering how I was going to sleep on a single bed that was two feet wide and six inches shorter than I was.

Chapter 3 – September

I lost the first battle with my tiny bed but I did win the war. When I crashed to the floor the bed clothes came with me so I stayed where I was. I slept like a log and felt refreshed and ready to deal with any renewed grumbling. As I made my way to the restaurant I caught sight of Derwent Water sparkling under the early morning sun beyond the hotel garden. We had a walk in beautiful countryside to look forward to. How could anyone not be happy?

Some of my guests were still unhappy. Agatha was in a huge ground floor suite that she hated because it was too big and Cynthia and Cedric were in a small double room that they loathed. I had already suggested that they swapped rooms but I was told it was too much bother for two nights. Yet they were still pursuing the possibility that the hotel would give them better rooms. Then they would be willing to move. The hotel would be happy to give them better rooms but on payment of a supplement. This notion was dismissed with scorn and the matter was finally laid to rest. No doubt it would see a revival in the feedback forms.

When I turned their attention to our walk that morning Melissa declared herself a non-starter as she did not walk. She was disappointed that no one else dropped out to keep her company. I offered to take her dog with us but the dog did not walk either. I suggested that she joined us for lunch at a local pub because she could drive there and she went off to get directions from reception.

It was time to meet our local guide Joseph. Outside I found a large bus blocking everybody's way. The driver greeted me and said he was ready to go when we were. I was taken aback as our bus trip was scheduled for the following day so one of us must be wrong. The driver just shrugged and said the next day would be just as good for him. He nearly knocked Joseph over as he reversed back down the drive. Joseph seemed unsurprised by both his narrow escape and the presence of the bus. He gave the driver a cheery wave as he extricated himself from a hedge. Joseph did not query the presence of the bus and as he was dressed for walking I did not think an explanation was necessary.

When everyone had gathered we set off on foot. The walk did not go entirely to plan. Joseph was a very amenable character and raced up and down the line introducing himself to everyone. At first the terrain was flat and we kept together. I brought up the rear accompanied by Cedric (portly plus angina) and Cynthia (stout and asthmatic). This was the first 'proper' walk I had ever done and I hoped that ambling along at the back I could hide my inexperience. I felt like Minnie Mouse in the long tailored shorts and Clarks lace up ankle boots with their thick, shock absorbing soles. There was not much conversation as neither of my companions could walk and talk at the same time.

When we began a steady ascent the group were soon strung out but Joseph continued to race up and down the line imparting information about the hills that surrounded us. He did not notice that the leading group had drawn their own conclusion regarding the route to take when they reached a junction. They chose the wrong path and Joseph had to chase after them. He instructed his companions to remain where they were and when the others caught up to tell them to wait as well until he returned. We were so far behind by then that Joseph and the stray walkers were already in sight when we joined them.

Once the group was reunited we continued to the top of a hill where we paused to enjoy the scenery. When Cynthia spotted our objective, the Farmers Arms pub, she got a second wind and had soon left Cedric and me behind. She overtook everyone and was the first to arrive there. I found her outside, half way through her third cigarette and wheezing contentedly. It seemed everyone was happy as they chatted over our pub lunch – even Melissa who had managed to find her own way there. It was amazing how the walk had drawn these strangers together.

We split up after lunch as Melissa's offer of a lift back to the hotel proved irresistible to some of us. Before we could set off I had to wait fifteen minutes while my fellow deserters queued for the toilet. The journey back to the hotel only took ten minutes. I had pleaded paperwork as an excuse to stop walking but in reality I was just too tired to continue. I had enjoyed the walk and felt a great sense of achievement at having completed it without any problems. I would have welcomed a soak in a bath to ease my stiff muscles but I had to be content with squeezing into my tiny shower and standing to attention while rotating under the spurts of water.

Our boat trip that evening was excellent but I had to work hard to get everyone aboard the transfer bus on time. I raced around the reception rooms like a sheep dog herding its flock. First I had to drag the early diners out of the bar and into the restaurant. Then I had to round up some waiters to serve us. I only had time for a few mouthfuls of food myself but I hoped I could make up for that later as we were going to be 'allowed' back into the restaurant later for our dessert.

We boarded the launch (the ferry in disguise) at Keswick and circled the lake. We were seeing the lake in its best light, the last hour before dusk. The commentary by Frank, our guide, was an entertaining mixture of history and humour. We were still laughing when we joined the rest of the group in the restaurant. But my companions failed to see the funny side when they realised all the wine had already been drunk. I had not expected anything else and to end the fair share debate I moved everyone out of the restaurant as soon as possible. I tried to distract them with some leaflets I had collected about the places we would be visiting on our coach trip the following day.

Melissa waylaid me as I was leaving the bar to tell me that she did not 'do' coach trips so she was not joining us on that trip either. I expressed my concern and wondered, aloud, if she had been misled regarding the programme for the weekend. She had not been under any misapprehension regarding the events of the weekend but she had assumed that others would drop out of the activities so she would have had company. I nearly offered to spend the day with her but then the thought of the other twenty guests let loose in the Lake District soon made me see reason. Anyway the rule of thumb was that I should always stay with the majority if a group split up. I suggested some places she might like to visit in her car but she was not interested in some independent sightseeing.

Joseph also accompanied us the following day. He was certainly a Jack of all trades but with only one outfit. It soon became clear that coach tours were not his forte. He could not figure out the public address system on the bus so he ignored it and abandoned any attempt at a commentary. He had switched the microphone off when he started to talk and then switched it on again when he had finished speaking. It sounded as though there was a large bluebottle loose in the bus. He chatted to the people around him and they passed the information back down the bus by word of mouth. When we arrived at Ullswater he passed the microphone to me so that I could tell everyone what time we had to be back on the bus. This was my first experience of using a microphone and I was no better than Joseph when it came to timing my comments with an open microphone. Instead of relaxing over a cup of coffee I flitted from table to table checking everyone knew what time they had to be back on the bus.

We drove on to Hawkshead where I followed in the footsteps of Beatrix Potter and William Wordsworth who had both attended the school here. It was a very pretty village and I enjoyed exploring but all too soon it was time to get everyone back to the bus. We continued to Coniston Water, our last stop, before making our way back to the hotel. Some of us got off in Keswick. We had a stroll around the town and then walked back to Portinscale where we were based. It was nice to be in the fresh air after a whole day on a bus. I did wonder if I should call the manager of the hotel to discuss the choice of wine at dinner that evening. Everyone had enjoyed the two South African wines he had chosen the previous evening. There had been a consensus that I request the same wine again. I decided there would be plenty of time to sort it out when I got back to the hotel.

I was wrong as the decision had already been made. Cedric and Cynthia had dined very early and then left. Their legacy was half a bottle of Liebfraumilch and half a bottle of Mateus Rosé on one of the tables. Full bottles of the same wines graced the other tables. I was sure I detected a slight smirk when the manager insisted it was too late to change this selection. He also had a message for me from Agatha who had called reception to say she was sick and would not be joining us for dinner. I went off to deal with this new crisis. Agatha was suffering from an upset stomach and all she needed was some water. I organised a bottle of mineral water to be sent to her room.

There was uproar regarding the choice of wine. I asked the waiters not to open any more bottles while I pleaded for a third choice, a red wine, as rosé was an unusual choice. After much discussion the manager replaced some bottles of rosé with a red wine. I suspected the manager's attitude had softened because he was desperate to find an audience for the hotel entertainment that evening. It was a slide show – 'A Walk Round Derwent Water'. This should have taken place while we were having dinner as my group had refused the invitation to dine early in order to attend. When they only had an audience of two the manager delayed the start so my guests could also attend. I had already promised to organise a quiz and the group wanted to do both. We started the quiz so late that I was nearly falling asleep over the question sheets. Melissa complained about the questions, the answers and the prize – a bottle of Liebfraumilch.

At six the following morning I was trying to reassemble the trouser press in my room when my telephone rang. Agatha was calling to tell me that she still felt ill. I sympathised, thanked her for letting me know and asked her if she wanted any more water. She did not. Trouser press back in place I went to breakfast – a full cooked English and time to enjoy it at my leisure. Soon after I finished Autoglass called me and said they would be at the hotel later that morning to repair my cracked windscreen. That was perfect timing as I could not leave until all my guests had checked out. I settled down in reception to wait.

It was a long morning as everyone left at different times. By the time my windscreen had been repaired and I was ready to leave all the guests had checked out except one, Agatha. I had called her several times that morning and each time she had informed me that she was not getting any better. It was time to consult an expert and the doctor was summoned. The doctor pronounced her fit to travel and the manager immediately sent a porter to her room to help her with her luggage. While I waited for her I broached the subject of the mineral water Agatha had had for supper last night – that was all she had but she was being charged a hugely inflated price for it. The manager would not relent. He pointed out that as the food had already been prepared (and paid for) it just went to waste. Mineral water was in a different category and had to be paid for. Our group had pushed him beyond gestures of good will.

* * * * * *

I was delighted when I received my next assignment. I was hosting an activity weekend at the Haven Hotel in Sandbanks near Poole. I was not sure about the activity aspect but delighted with the venue. I had stayed there before and I knew that it was right by the sea. I decided to get there early so I had time for a walk along the beach followed by a leisurely lunch on the patio outside the hotel restaurant. When I set off the sun was shining so I took the roof off my sports car and bowled along the motorway singing at the top of my voice. I decided, as a matter of courtesy, that I would go into the hotel first to tell them I had parked my car in their car park.

As soon as I introduced myself to the reception manager I was hijacked by some of my guests complaining that they had not been able to check-in. It was only midday and our information said they could not check-in before two thirty. I sent them off to find something to fill in the time but within minutes they were back raising another issue. It was an activity weekend and all the activities were pre-booked. They wanted a schedule of events. Aimee had told me that these would be given to the guests when they checked in so I referred them to reception. Reception sent them back to me. The hotel had assumed the schedules would have already been sent to the guests. I had to abandon my own plans and find the Duty Manager. He was charming and said he would get the schedules copied in time for our Welcome Drink that evening. Despite relaying this information to my group I was still inundated with repeated requests for the schedules. It seemed prudent to make myself scarce.

Luckily my room was ready because it was on the very top floor in the attic beyond the limits of the lift and therefore not very popular. I made my way up to my retreat. I loved it. It was a small double room with a sloping ceiling and a fantastic view of the sea although I had to stand on tiptoe to see it. It was like being on the prow of a ship. My reverie was interrupted by a call from reception to tell me the copies of our programme were ready. I collected them and distributed some to those guests I could find in the bar area. Then I sat in reception greeting the new arrivals and checking the programme for the next day. It did not match the copy of the programme Aimee had given me as agreed with the hotel. I needed to speak to the leisure centre manager but he had already gone home. I would have to see him as soon as he came on duty the next day.

There was an excited buzz at our Welcome Drink that evening as people consulted their schedules. The hotel had done a good job and the comprehensive timetable included lists of participants. This was a useful way to introduce people to each other and some took advantage of mutual interests to arrange activities during their free time. It seemed this group was going to look after itself as they sorted out their own seating arrangements in our private dining room. Dinner was followed by our own disco in the same room. My guests needed no encouragement to get up and dance. The music was really good – so good that it attracted the attention of other guests in the hotel and an entire wedding party tried to gate crash our small disco. They would not be deterred and I spent the rest of the evening on the door.

The next morning I was the early bird who caught the leisure centre manager, Max, to discuss our programme. He was a very likeable young man and anxious to find a solution to my problem. Due to the rearranged schedule some people were now free that morning. They could not join any of our programmed activities that morning due to limited equipment for the mountain-biking and scuba diving. Assuming that everyone would want to be active the entire weekend I needed to fill the gap. Max gave me a list of pursuits organised for all the guests in the hotel so my group could join those if they wished. Problem solved I made my way to the restaurant for breakfast. I found some of my guests still drinking in the lounge. They had been up all night and said they would join me for breakfast when they had finished their bottle of wine. Then they were going to bed.

Most of the group had stayed up very late and were in no rush to be active that first morning. The sun was shining and it was already hot so they were glad to have some free time to swim in the large outdoor pool and lie in the sun. Some abandoned their selected activities but as most of them were included in the package this was not a problem. Max helped me to get everyone organised and then, as there was a bike available, he persuaded me to join in the mountain biking. I feared that I might disprove the old saying that you never forgot how to ride a bike as it was many years since I had used one. Then I only had to worry about three gears now there were at least twenty-one combinations. Fortunately we had a practice before we set off. The gears were quite tricky to master but once I got the knack I was amazed how easy it was to cycle up hills and also to get some speed up on the flat. We cycled along a narrow track to a headland and then turned round and cycled back. It was very bumpy at times and I was glad that this, like all the other activities, was limited to two hours. By then I was getting saddle sore. I envied Max the padding on the seat of the cycling shorts that encased his lean, athletic figure.

My cycling group were anxious to do some more exploring – on foot. We took the ferry from our hotel to Poole harbour. Before docking we had a tour of the harbour accompanied by an interesting commentary. After a stroll around the old town we returned to the harbour where we had a late lunch outside a small pub before boarding the ferry for the return journey. As we approached our landing stage the captain's voice boomed across the deck requesting that we all stood on the right side of the boat. No one moved. It sounded as though someone was playing a trick on us. A second announcement assured us that it was not a joke. It was low tide so it was difficult for the boat to dock in the shallow water. It was a while before the captain was able to edge the tilting boat close enough to the shore to allow us to jump off.

I had promised myself a relaxing dip in the hotel's American hot tub before changing for dinner but several other people had the same idea. Desmond suggested it would be more hygienic if I removed my swimsuit. I was embarrassed but assumed he was kidding and behaved accordingly. I slid into the warm, foaming water as far away from him as possible. But I could not relax and I got out soon afterwards in case he had taken his own advice! I had to move on to my next task anyway as we were eating in the main restaurant that evening so I needed to check our tables. We were also joining the hotel disco after eating so I would be relieved of my role as bouncer.

My wake-up call the following morning was an hour earlier than I expected. It was an angry instructor wanting final numbers for the horse riding that afternoon. Three people had cancelled already and now he wanted definite final numbers. This activity was the only one that involved a cancellation fee but it was not just the money, it was a popular activity with all the guests in the hotel and the stables had a waiting list. I had to catch everyone on their way to breakfast and with one exception they confirmed their bookings. Silas was proving to be a thorn in my flesh. He was the youngest in the group and did not seem to be mixing well with the others. He had dropped out of all the activities he had signed up for so far and he was on the list for the horse riding that afternoon. When I tried to confirm his booking he said he was a definite maybe. He found this response a lot more amusing than I did. I did not know whether to cancel his booking or not. I had told him several times that he would incur a cancellation fee if he did not turn up and he said he understood that but he still avoided making a commitment.

I was mulling over the problem of Silas when I absent-mindedly agreed to join some of the women for an aerobics class that morning. I immediately regretted it. I had never been to an aerobics class and I did not have any suitable attire with me. But this was not a good enough excuse, they insisted I take part. I raced back to my room and slipped on the oversize T-shirt I slept in. A fluffy kitten lying on its back adorned my chest and it was inscribed 'I don't do mornings'. I pulled on some baggy tracksuit bottoms, a relic of my tennis playing days, and raced off to the gym. Everyone else was wearing skin tight leotards with co-ordinating footless tights and I felt really out of place. There was no introduction to the class. Our instructor arrived, switched on the music and started shouting instructions that everyone else found easy to follow. Despite her exhortations I was always half a beat behind the others. Within minutes the sweat was pouring off me and tendrils of my damp hair snaked across my red face. It was relentless and just as I decided I could not struggle on any longer the music stopped and I was free to sit down and catch my breath. Never again.

After a swim to cool down I called Silas to check he really was going to turn up for the horse riding. He was not in his room. I had introduced him to Desmond and Drucilla who were taking him in their car so I had done as much as I could. Silas did not turn up at the appointed time and the others had to leave without him. I called his room before they left but there was no answer. I tried again soon after they had gone and he was there. When I told him the others had waited for him but then had to leave for the stables he was very angry. I was not sure why because he was the one who was late. I reminded him he would have to pay a cancellation fee. Silas insisted that it was the hotel's fault that he was late. There was no logic in his accusation as none of the hotel staff had been directly involved. He decided he would appeal to Max to waive the cancellation fee.

Max led the walk on Brownsea Island that afternoon and while we were on the ferry he told me that Silas was refusing to pay the cancellation fee. The charge would be put on Silas's account but it would not make any difference. It would simply defer the argument until he checked out. I offered to pay it myself and try to claim it back on my expenses. Max decided he would rather the hotel billed my company directly and then they could decide whether or not to pass the charge on to Silas. I let the matter rest as we had arrived on the island and Max had to organise everyone. It was a lovely walk and we all enjoyed it. Even Silas. Max had persuaded him to join us and I really appreciated this gesture. It was the first time Silas had been part of the group. We were all unanimous in our joy at seeing the rare red squirrel that inhabits the island.

On our return to the hotel I went straight to the American hot tub hoping no one else would be there yet. I was out of luck and Desmond was already in the tub but Drucilla was there as well. Desmond told me that Drucilla used to tour England and the world giving recitals of eleventh century nuns' songs. He encouraged her to sing for me. It was bizarre sitting there in the foaming water while Drucilla trilled away next to me. One of the joys of my new job was meeting interesting people and learning about their unusual jobs and experiences. Desmond was also an entertainer. At dinner that night he tried to set fire to his Sambuca which, I was assured, they do in all the best Italian restaurants but he only succeeded in setting fire to his shirt cuff.

A sea gull tapping his beak on my window was my very early wake-up call the next day. The sun was shining and it was the start of another glorious day. We decided to profit from the good weather and delay our departure until the afternoon. I joined some of the women in the water aerobics class hoping I would succeed in the water where I had failed on the land. It was more fun and we certainly entertained the men who watched us from their sun beds. I felt like a penguin as I found it very difficult to keep upright because my legs kept slipping away from me. When we circled I was constantly being jostled by the person behind me as they caught up with me but the harder I tried the slower I got. We lunched on the terrace before going our separate ways. I was exhausted and still saddle sore from mountain biking. But I was glad I had done it as my next trip included this activity but for real – in the mountains. I was off to the Sierra Nevada in Spain.

****

I trained for my sojourn in the mountains by taking the stairs whenever the opportunity arose rather than using a lift. I was excited by the challenge ahead of me. Before I left I had another trial to face – explaining to Aimee why I had allowed the hotel to bill them directly for the cancellation charge relating to Silas's failure to honour his booking to go horse riding. I was told I should have settled the charge myself and then persuaded Silas to pay me back. I suggested that his resolve not to pay the fee was unlikely to be shaken by my plea to reimburse me as my company would not cover it as a legitimate expense. I promised to try harder should a similar situation arise in the future. Being a rep was proving to be a long learning curve but there was excitement round every corner and this was certainly true of my next destination.

Bubion is a small village high up in the Alpujarras Mountains, part of the Sierra Nevada. We arrived there very late after a long transfer from Malaga airport. Phillippe, our local agent, was waiting for us and took us straight into dinner in the Café Artistas. At first sight, due to his small and slight stature, I thought he was very young but in fact he was in his forties. He was French, very French, and charming with his mischievous smile and crisp, curly black hair. One to hold at arm's length I suspected. This would not be difficult with his Spanish partner Imelda glowering in the background. When we compared rooming lists I discovered that Phillippe was working from an out of date list. We did have an odd number, an extra woman, not an extra man as Phillippe had anticipated. He just shrugged and said "we will 'ave to start again" in an accent that made all my hormones teeter on the brink.

As we discussed the various options the problem was further complicated when Hetty and Trixie, who had booked a twin room, made an eloquent plea for two single rooms. Phillippe was clearly a man who could not say no to a woman, even a comfortably maturing one. This, of course, was part of his allure. He agreed to accommodate their wishes – subject to my taking a room in a hotel in the village. As this request was made in front of the women concerned I felt I could not refuse. I could only hope that the hotel was not too far away.

My hotel was at the other end of the village and I had to wait until Phillippe was free to drive me there. While I was waiting two clients came back to the café with complaints and Phillippe went off to deal with them. Bruce was unhappy with his accommodation as he had the smallest room in the 'Brown' apartment and he had to share a bathroom. He was adamant that 'single room' meant en suite facilities and he said he would write to my company to explain this definition to them. He was offered a room in my hotel but he declined. Hetty, who had come back to complain about the lack of coat hangers in her room, heard him turn the room down. I made a note for my report. We had to record every detail if someone made a complaint during a holiday.

Phillippe abandoned me again to find some coat hangers, Imelda went home and I sat down on one of the settees on the balcony of the café to await his return. This small rustic café would be our meeting place as well as the venue for all our meals. These would be cooked and served by Lolita, Christina and Mercedes and I could hear them chatting as they tidied up in the kitchen. They finished before Phillippe returned and, after apologising profusely, they moved me and my luggage outside, turned off the lights plunging me into darkness and then left. My repeated thanks for an excellent dinner fell into the widening void between us.

Left on my own my thoughts turned to the walk the next day. I had gleaned from the conversation around the dinner table that I was the only complete novice in the group. Rather than expose my ignorance I had smiled and nodded knowingly when terms that I had never encountered before like extending walking poles and Gore-Tex clothing were bandied around. I did not want to be puffing along behind them clutching my empty rucksack – maybe I could excuse myself on the grounds I had paperwork to do.

Finally Phillippe reappeared and drove me to my hotel in his battered old Renault. We seemed to be driving up and down narrow, winding lanes for a long time before we got there. He collected my key from the rack behind reception and pointed me in the direction of my room before rushing off into the night. My room was small and basic and totally devoid of shelves and cupboards. It had a bed, a wooden floor partially covered by a rug and a few hangers on a coat stand. It was so late I didn't care I just wanted to curl up and go to sleep.

But sleep evaded me as there was a party taking place on the patio outside my window. This continued until the early hours when I dozed off. Then two hours later, at five in the morning, everyone went out. They must have been aspiring mountaineers as a lot of heavy gear was dropped on the wooden floor in the corridor right by my door. My room was next to the rear entrance and, I had been assured, was especially selected for me as it was convenient for me when entering and leaving the hotel. Everyone else used the same door and I was subjected to a steady stream of stamping feet.

There was no point in trying to get back to sleep so I got up and prepared for the day ahead. I waited until ten minutes after the time Phillippe had said he could collect me and then set off on foot. As I had arrived at the hotel in the dark I had no idea how to get back. I did not even know the name of the place where the group were staying. I knew it was somewhere on the main road so I worked my way up the hill through narrow cobbled streets that all looked the same. Once on the main road I walked along until I found the café where we had eaten the previous evening and where we would be having breakfast. The girls were already there, bustling around making coffee and putting fresh croissants on the table. The aromas were driving me crazy but I had to be patient and wait until the first guests arrived.

Breakfast tasted as good as I had anticipated. While we were eating our walking guide, Shamus, arrived and I joined him on the balcony to discuss the programme for the week ahead. Shamus was Irish and despite living and working in the area for many years he barely spoke a word of Spanish. His tall, lithe frame was topped by wavy, auburn hair and his face was half hidden behind a bushy beard. I loved the sound of his lilting brogue as he described the walk we would be doing that day. I snapped to attention when he gave me instructions regarding my position as back marker. It had finally dawned on me that it was compulsory to walk with the group. I had anticipated waving them off and spending the rest of the day catching up on some sleep. As he spoke I followed his eyes to my sturdy new boots that he was viewing with suspicion. The twinkle in his eye told me he knew exactly how inexperienced I was but he said nothing.

I thought the morning walk was quite demanding. It was mostly uphill following narrow paths that sometimes edged steep drops. Occasionally a local would brush past us on his way to work in one of the small fields marked out on the slopes. When we emerged from our cover of trees or buildings we had spectacular views of the snow-capped peaks around us. Hetty was having trouble breathing due to the altitude so we had to walk slowly at the back. This suited me and gave me a chance to drink in the spectacular scenery. Everyone else seemed to find the walk very easy. We meandered through the countryside and traversed a few villages before flopping down by a river to eat our picnic lunch. The setting was idyllic and our simple picnic was scrumptious. We harvested some watercress from the river bank and added this to the cheese in our crusty rolls.

Our lunch box included a small bottle of water and Shamus told us to keep the empty bottle. Before we set off again we refilled our bottles with cold, fresh water from the river. The afternoon walk followed a road most of the way and was much easier. Hetty had acclimatised to the height and we kept up with everyone else all the way back to Bubion where Shamus steered us into the first open bar we came to. Our table was soon littered with foaming jugs of beer and little plates of tapas. It was a great end to the day and an opportunity to get to know Shamus. He seemed to do everything from guiding walkers to importing Red Label tea for expats. I went straight from the bar to the café to wait until it was time for dinner. Some people joined me still glowing with enthusiasm for the walk we had just finished. I longed to tell them how proud I was that I had completed it without any problems but I did not dare because in their eyes I was the rep and therefore experienced in everything I did. After our evening meal I walked back to my hotel and I still had quite a way to go when I could hear the noise of a party and a second sleepless night loomed ahead of me.

As I struggled out of bed early the next morning I told myself I only had to keep going for a week. The exhilaration of being in the mountains was acting like an intoxicant and there was soon a spring in my step as I made my way to the café for breakfast. I was looking forward to our walk that day as we were heading for Mulhacen, the highest peak in the Sierra Nevada. We were doing most of the ascent in four by four vehicles and then the final part would be on foot. Hetty dropped out because she had an upset stomach. This made room for the Spanish couple that Phillippe had, without my knowledge, included in our party which meant twenty-two of us (including Shamus) had to cram ourselves into three four by fours. We also had to take lots of extra water because we would be above the water table so there were no natural sources of water. Shamus constantly encouraged us to drink and pee a lot – several of the men were happy to oblige but not with water.

We got out at four hundred metres which meant we had another two hundred metres to walk to the summit. It was the highest I had ever been and I felt light headed. It was going to be a challenge to make it to the top. But I soon discovered it was not one I had to face. Four women in the group decided it would be too much for them so they were put in my charge and we took our picnics and set off on an easier walk to a nearby lake. It was much further to the lake than Shamus had thought and we never got there even though we walked for two hours. We decided to have our picnic and then walk back to the meeting point. While we were eating the clouds rolled in, below us. It was surreal – perched up there above a sea of cotton wool.

It was eerie descending through the clouds and we had to go slowly but we got back to our vehicles before the rest of the group. We were cold and huddled inside one of the four by fours until the others appeared out of the gloom around us. They were glowing with their success in having reached the summit but their descent had also been hampered by the mist. We were all ready to celebrate with a few jugs of beer when we got back to Bubion. We were fortunate that Shamus was an expert on bars in the area. As the season was coming to an end the bars were taking it in turns to open each day and Shamus always knew where to go.

When we lurched back to the apartments we discovered that the office was locked and all the keys were inside. Phillippe had been called away on business and had forgotten to inform anyone other than Imelda and she was at home. I called her and she arrived a few minutes later clearly not happy that I had interrupted her siesta. They had insisted we leave the keys with them when we went out but then forgot to make sure we could get them back when we returned. I left Imelda scrabbling through drawers looking for spare keys.

The next morning I was up soon after my inbuilt alarm woke me – the stampede of guests along the corridor to breakfast. As it had been quiet when I got back to my room the previous evening I had taken advantage and gone straight to bed rather than catching up with my paperwork. I had to organise the optional activities available during our stay and deal with requests for horse riding, t'ai chi and a Tarot card reading. I knew there would be some mind changing and I was ready to deal with it. Once the lists were completed I walked up to the café for breakfast. My taxi service, Phillippe, had let me down yet again but I enjoyed my early morning walks watching the village waking up. I smiled sympathetically at anxious mothers dragging their reluctant children to the small village school. I paused occasionally to appreciate the splendour of the surrounding peaks bathed in the rosy glow of a rising sun.

That day we were doing a walking tour of the villages of La Taha. Hetty and Trixie were not very keen on doing this walk but Shamus persuaded them to come with us by describing it as a stroll from one village to the next. Shamus failed to mention the peaks and valleys in between these villages. It was a demanding walk and Hetty and Trixie kept reminding me that they were unwilling participants. I sensed a note of pride in their protests though as this walk was tougher than any they had tackled before. My walking was also improving although Shamus never missed an opportunity to comment on what he called my 'fashion boots'. He found lots of different places to fill up our water bottles and we had a water tasting. We all loved the naturally effervescent spring water but nobody liked the iron flavoured fountain water with its sulphurous undertones. When we stopped for our picnic lunch I sat with Bruce who spent the entire meal telling me that he still intended to write to my company to explain the definition of 'single supplement'. I just nodded my head as I watched two eagles riding the warm air currents above us.

We finished the walk in Pampaniera where we had a beer and then caught the local bus back to Bubion. Some keen people insisted on walking back along the road but I was happy to get the bus, especially as it stopped very close to my hotel. Had I been able to find a timetable for this bus I could have used it more often but it seemed bus times like the opening times of local bars was information that was only circulated by word of mouth. I was conserving my energy for the mountain biking taking place the next day. This would be another new challenge for me and I hoped I could rise to it. Some people had already opted out. Three were going horse riding and three were walking up to Capileira, the next village. Shamus had told Hetty and Trixie about a woman he knew in the village who would do a Tarot card reading for them.

After an early breakfast the following morning we were taken half way up a mountain where Pacho, our guide, was waiting for us with our bikes. He was gorgeous with long flowing auburn locks and slim athletic body. He chatted easily with the group as we selected our bikes and had a practice. The spare bikes were put on the roof of the support vehicle and we were off. We followed a route with a good variety of uphill and downhill stretches. I was the back marker and expecting to be left behind but some of my companions had to keep stopping to catch their breath on the uphill sections of which there were several. I felt like the tortoise chasing the hare and by pedalling slowly up the hills I managed to stay with them.

When Bruce jammed the gears on his first bike we all had to stop while a replacement was unloaded for him. We had just got going again when the chain came off his second bike and we had to repeat the process. This interrupted his monologue regarding the standard of this second bike which, apparently, was not as good as his first bike. Then he started moaning because he said someone should have told him that we were biking in the mountains!! This prompted several people to put on a spurt and race up the next steep incline. Bruce was reluctant to join them and suggested that Pacho call them back. Instead Pacho returned with a message to say they wanted us to join them 'up there' and assured us it would be worth the effort. It was a steep climb but not too long and it was a brilliant picnic spot. We seemed to be floating among the mountains on our own small plateau. Bruce missed both the scenery and the entertainment of a small fox chasing our scraps as he was too busy converting his rucksack into a ground sheet.

I was developing an interest in wildlife. It was wonderful seeing wild animals in their natural habit. But I was not so keen when a local wasp decided to investigate my cleavage. We were making our way back the way we had come – reversing the ups and downs. There had been some really tough uphill climbs and several of us had dismounted to walk for a while. This was when I got my unwelcome visitor and amused the group when I threw my bike to the ground and started screaming and writhing. They had no idea what was going on and watched my antics in amazement. Thankfully the wasp found its own way out before it became necessary to remove my top rather than risk being stung.

After pausing at a beautiful waterfall to re-fill our water bottles we had a final long descent. Bruce was the last to go and just before he set off he turned back and said "who looks after the back marker?" My response that the back marker did not need looking after was whipped away by his slipstream. I rolled down the hill behind him and then came to a shuddering halt when my chain fell off. I tried to put the chain back on but it was impossible. I knew it would be a while before anyone realised I was not with them. For the first time that day the support vehicle had gone ahead of us. I was on my own and had to find a solution. The wheels still went round so I stood up on the pedals and carefully rolled down the hill using the brakes to control my speed. Pacho had realised that something must have happened and was already on his way back up the hill when I trundled into view. By then we were nearly back where we had started and it did not seem worth unloading a replacement bike for me. Everyone was disappointed when they realised we had nearly finished so Pacho gave us the option of freewheeling the eight kilometres downhill to Bubion. This offer was greeted with such enthusiasm that I was soon on my replacement bike and whizzing down the hill behind Bruce. I suspected that he wore a wig and I was slightly concerned that it might fly off and cover my face so I would not be able to see where I was going.

Back in my hotel room my desire for a hot shower was thwarted because all the hot water had been used up. Not realising that the Spanish for hot was 'tepida' I engaged in a pointless discussion with the girl on reception who did not speak any English. There was no time to pursue the matter so I braved a cold shower and raced back to the café where the long promised t'ai chi session was due to take place. Phillippe relied heavily on his charm to conceal an almost total lack of administrative talent. I dealt with this failing by writing out daily instructions for him and leaving it with the girls in the café. I watched the group for a while but refused their invitation to join them. I was expected for pre-dinner drinks and nibbles organised on the patio of Hetty and Trixie's apartment.

This little soiree was my first opportunity to look around their apartment which was called 'Peter'. It had two en-suite bedrooms, a small sitting room and a large patio with a fabulous view of the mountains across the valley. Several other members of the group joined us and inevitably the conversation turned to discussing absent colleagues. My own perception had been that everyone was getting along with each other but it seemed I was wrong. They all resented the fact that when we ate in the café the same four people always sat together at a small table for four. They were plotting to usurp them. I was amazed how much falling out and backbiting could be crammed into a seven day holiday. They succeeded in their plan which resulted in open warfare and a request to create a second table for four. Having watched the debacle from afar I intervened and made a few swift table moves that allowed the four to sit together at the far end of the large table. No doubt they would be loitering even earlier before the next meal to grab 'their' table – just what their adversaries had intended.

There was lots of excited chatter at dinner that night as everyone had enjoyed their different activities. The horse riding had been very successful. They were complete beginners and I had been concerned about them. The last time I rode in Spain when we turned for home my horse had bolted and I had clung to his mane as he galloped flat out for the stables. The animal did not stop when we reached the yard but trotted into his stall inside a large barn and tucked into his manger of hay. I was still clinging to his back when the rest of the cavalcade got back. Hetty and Trixie had now discovered their fortunes but would not share this knowledge with the rest of us.

I had a very early start the next morning as I had to finalise the arrangements for the Granada trip. Some of the group wanted to stay in the city for dinner and although I doubted this would be possible I had promised to discuss it with Phillippe. That was if I could find him. He had vanished, 'away on business' again. I did receive a message to say that the flamenco show would take place the same day as the Granada trip. Imelda had told me he would be back the previous day and then at dinner she announced he would be back the following morning. She was right and a very dishevelled Phillippe appeared while I was waiting for breakfast to start. He summoned me to his office to discuss the Granada trip leaving an hour later. I managed to negotiate an extra hour in Granada. Phillippe then gave me a map for each person. He had marked the pick-up point on one map and I had to mark the rest before giving them out. There was no time to do it before we left as the bus had already arrived – it would have to be done in transit.

I spent the first part of the journey, as we lurched down winding roads, marking the pick-up point on each map. I then had to go round the bus giving each person a map and explaining how to get to the place I had marked. I was very relieved when we turned on to the main road and our passage was smoother, nevertheless the damage was done. On arrival in Granada we were set down in the old Moorish part of the city and I made a run for the nearest bar and the toilet at the back. A bewildered group were still waiting on the street when, white as a sheet, I joined them and apologised profusely before leading them through the narrow streets towards the bustling main piazza where I pointed out some landmarks. I was following the script given to me by our absent guide – Phillippe. I showed them the road up to Alhambra and the stop for the local bus if they did not want to walk. We had to meet our palace guide at the entrance that afternoon.

Three of us decided to walk up to Alhambra. We followed the signs but when they petered out we took a wrong turn and went a long way in the wrong direction. We re-traced our steps and then had to race up two flights of very steep steps so we were very hot and sweaty when we arrived ten minutes after the appointed time. As I scanned the crowds for our guide some of my group whizzed past in a taxi waving merrily – I tried to flag them down as they sped past the meeting point with no sign of slowing down. They waved back and carried on. In my flustered state I mistook a tourist for our guide much to the amusement of those members of my group who were already clustered round Jose, our guide.

Jose was not amused. He was getting very anxious because the entrance tickets were timed. We did have some time to spare but he had planned to use it to give us some information before entering the palace. I felt stupid for being late but owned up to getting lost before we began our tour. Jose was excellent, Alhambra is wonderful (most of it is still original) and the gardens are superb. After Alhambra we returned to the city centre, where we did some shopping and had some sangria in the main square. We all met up on time at seven o'clock and found our way to the right square but the bus was late.

Dinner was delayed until nine thirty that evening and consisted of home-made paella with salad followed by bunches of fresh grapes. After dinner we watched some genuine flamenco dancing. Lolita, Christina and Mercedes our erstwhile cook and waitresses were transformed as they sang, palmed and danced for us accompanied by a talented young guitarist, a local boy. I had not realised that flamenco was not just a dance but also palming and singing, a whole culture. It was a brilliant performance and much appreciated by the group who said it was a unique experience and a highlight of the holiday. Bruce would not know as he sulked outside claiming it was not a 'proper' show. I was cross with him for failing to show any appreciation at all for the girls' efforts. Due to lack of sleep I was getting very irritable and it was difficult to remain patient with some people. Phillippe had promised that I could move to one of the apartments the following week.

There was a mass exodus from my hotel at five the next morning so I got up and began gathering my belongings from the floor and squashing them into my holdall. I would be moving into an apartment when the new group arrived the following day. That day it was our last and longest walk. Harris had an upset stomach and had been awake most of the night but he still intended to walk. I was very concerned as I knew this walk would be through a remote area with no vehicle access should he find it too much for him. The group did not support me but rather encouraged me to let him do the walk. Harris had presented himself as a macho man all week, never using sun cream, drinking more beer than water and finally shrugging off an upset stomach. He took no notice of me and also brushed off Shamus's concerns. I had to leave Shamus to deal with the problem as I needed to find a public phone to reconfirm the flights for the following day. Phillippe's office was empty and locked. When I got back Shamus said Harris was coming with us. We had to concede that we could not force him to drop out as he was an adult and could make his own decisions.

When we set off Harris marched briskly at the front. I was in my usual place, bringing up the rear. We could see our destination, a Buddhist garden – a tiny dot on the far side of the valley and a lot of down followed by a lot of up. We left the road just outside Bubion and began working our way across the countryside. It was very hot day and we were fighting our way through overgrown brambles that straddled the path pushing through gaps that Shamus was creating with a pair of garden shears. It was not long before Harris dropped to the back to walk with me. I could see him getting weaker with every step and hoped that he would not collapse as he was a big, well-built man and I would not be able to lift him. He stumbled along for another hour and then slumped at my feet claiming he could go no further. Shamus was two hundred metres above me and the group was strung out between us. A message was passed along the chain to him as we started the final ascent to the Buddhist garden. Harris said he would wait in the shade of a tree where we could collect him on our way back. He had not appreciated that the walk was circular but now we would have to go back the same way as we could not abandon him.

I had just settled Harris under a tree when a car appeared on its way down from the top! Shamus stopped and spoke to the occupants. While the car was still winding down the road between us I shouted up to Shamus to ascertain whether he had asked them to take Harris back to our village. He had not and galloped back down the mountain while I stopped the car. My feeble attempts at Spanish were so poor that I nearly got myself bundled in the car and taken back to Bubion. Shamus arrived just in time and between us we persuaded them to take Harris back. What a relief it was to get that problem resolved. Now we could all relax and enjoy the rest of the day. At the retreat we were invited inside to have a look around. It was very simple and very peaceful and so deeply moving for some people that they actually cried. As we left one of the nuns enveloped me in her arms and whispered in my ear that I had made the right choice. I could only think that she meant the career change I was already planning.

The path we followed after walking through the Buddhist garden was very stony and I could feel every one of them through the soles of my boots that were wearing thin already thereby fulfilling the unvoiced predictions of Shamus. We stopped in Pampaniera for a beer and some shopping. I tried to find some proper walking boots but without success. Bruce came with me to offer his valuable advice. He and I then walked back to Bubion while the others went on the local bus with Shamus. Back in Bubion I was walking along the road when I met Shamus. He invited me to have a drink with him – he wanted to reward me for my quick thinking on the mountain earlier. He was also curious regarding my appearance in Bubion just after he had arrived on the bus. He asked me if we had changed our minds and sneaked on to the bus. We had not but nor had we followed the road that wound round the mountain as we had found some steps that went straight up it. I was pleased he was impressed as initially he had viewed me as a city girl who did not have a clue about walking in the mountains. He was right – of course I was a city girl overwhelmed by the mountains but suddenly it was very important to dispel that image.

We had a party after dinner and Shamus came along and entertained us playing the spoons while vast quantities of sangria were consumed. Harris skulked in his room. I spoke to him through his bedroom door and tried to persuade him to come out of hiding. Bruce, now that occasion demanded, revealed himself as a charge nurse. He checked Harris and assured me that he was fine. After dinner as I set off for my hotel Bruce appeared and steered me into his apartment. He was determined I should see his room. It was tiny but the apartment also had a sitting room and a kitchen (with a fridge full of beer) so he only had to sleep in it. I was not in the mood for a long conversation about rooms so I suggested he walked with me to the hotel so he could see where he could have stayed. He was not interested and went off to join the others in a local bar.

That was the last night of my first week in Bubion and the following morning I accompanied the group to the airport. I had hoped we could go along the coast road and find somewhere nice for lunch on the way. The driver said this was not possible so I agreed to go via Granada. As we got close to the city the driver said there was a fiesta in the city so we had to take another route and we stopped for lunch at a roadside café in the middle of nowhere. I was sure it was all a ploy on the driver's part to ensure he got a free lunch. On seeing the driver in the restaurant with a plate piled high with food some of the group went in there to eat. They had not realised that the driver was given priority. It was a long time before they finished their three course meal and the rest of us had to wait for them. I spent the time mediating between the waiting group, the eating group and an impatient driver.

Despite this delay we still arrived at the airport in plenty of time. After checking everyone in I said my goodbyes and set off to Arrivals to meet the new group. I could not find Arrivals. I found signs to Arrivals and then they disappeared and the next sign I found took me back the way I had come. I was getting so desperate I even went outside and tried following the signs on the road but they always brought me back to the same place, Departures. Nowhere did it indicate that Arrivals was THROUGH Departures. I asked several people and finally got there just as the flight arrived. I gathered together this second, smaller group and we were soon on our way. I was confident there would not be any problems when we checked the group into their apartments as I had already made sure that Phillippe and I were working from the same lists.

When we got back to Bubion we had dinner first and then everyone went to their apartments. I had put myself in 'Peter' in a pretty en suite room but not too luxurious to avoid adverse comments from my companions. I was sharing the two-bedroom apartment with Donna. After we had settled in I decided to explore my new surroundings. As I strolled around the patio I glimpsed a partially open door beyond which I could see a gleam of white. Assuming this was the washing machine and desperate to get some washing done – even at midnight. I stepped through the door – into a void.

Chapter 4 – October

I felt like an advert for personal injury solicitors when I hobbled into breakfast the following morning. My right leg was heavily bandaged and my left hand was in a splint although I had already discarded the sling. From the look of puzzlement on the faces of my guests it seemed they thought it was some kind of a joke – a ruse to get out of walking maybe. The last time they had seen me I was bidding them goodnight as fit as the rest of them.

A sudden desire to launder seven days' worth of dirty clothes had been my downfall. When I finally came to rest and put my hand out to push myself to my feet there was just fresh air and I went into free-fall again. I had banged my head but I was still conscious when I came to a shuddering halt. Cautiously I felt around me. I seemed to have reached solid ground. I managed to crawl back up the stairs and across the patio. As I collapsed on my bed I shouted for Donna. She immediately took charge and after mopping up the blood – my right hand was bleeding profusely from gashes on the knuckles – she had fetched the girls from the café. They found Phillippe and insisted he took me to the local hospital at Orgiva.

At Orgiva I was immediately given a tetanus injection (my second that month), filled with painkillers and referred to a bigger hospital in Mottrill for X-rays. When I discovered what the injection was I was concerned that I might be suffering from an overdose and could end up with lockjaw. Phillippe patiently listened to my nonsensical ramblings but in reality his mind was on other things – mainly the dinner he had just left behind. When he drove through a village that was celebrating a local fiesta he pulled up near a small stall laden with food and asked me if I wanted anything to eat. I thought he was joking and giggled in disbelief so he drove off again.

My head, back, knee and hand were X-rayed and then we had to wait for the results. Phillippe disappeared and I suspected he was looking for something to eat. He reappeared when the doctor arrived with his verdict. A fractured finger and damaged knee ligaments. The doctor recommended I spend the night in hospital being observed but I said I could do my own observing back in Bubion. As soon as I had been bandaged up we set off with me clutching a list of symptoms to watch out for in case I was concussed. Through a painkiller induced haze I repeatedly thanked Phillippe for his help. He had been great and had sorted everything out and would fax the hospital all the relevant details regarding my European Health Insurance Card the next day. It was all a good learning experience for the future but my immediate concern was how to cope with the present situation. I babbled away throughout the entire journey aware that Phillippe was struggling to keep awake.

When Shamus arrived to lead the walk that day the tale had to be told again. He went and checked the door I had fallen through and reported back to Phillippe that it should have a lock put on it immediately. I doubted that would happen as immediate was not in Phillippe's vocabulary. I did appreciate Shamus' concern and his assurance that there was no need for me to inform my office and ask them to send a replacement. The group were also very supportive and agreed with Shamus. As soon as everyone had set off on the walk I collected my picnic lunch and went back to the apartment to try and get some sleep.

The girls woke me up when they came in to clean and then Phillippe came in to check on me but I was barely aware of any of them and just wanted them to go and leave me alone – even Phillippe now that the super-strong painkillers had worn off. I read and dozed until Donna came back. She told me that the walk had been quite testing but within everyone's capabilities. As Donna was around to rescue me should the need arise I eased myself into the bath, draped my bandaged leg along the edge and had a long soak before getting ready for dinner. Soon after we had finished our meal Phillippe joined us to check that everyone was happy. He walked back to my apartment with me. My daytime dozing had been seriously marred by a light that was permanently lit in our sitting room. He fixed it by unscrewing the light bulb.

The following day the group went off to walk up Mulhacen and I read and dozed until they came back. Donna assured me that everyone had enjoyed the day and those who had opted to go to the lake actually got there as they went in one of the vehicles. Her reticence prompted me to request more details. I learnt that only four had made it to the summit. Shamus always monitored the ascent very carefully and anyone who did not make it with him had to turn back when he met them on his way back down with the successful walkers. Aiden had refused to comply and had continued to the top and then, on the way down had taken a short cut and by-passed Shamus who was waiting for him. When a distraught Shamus had rejoined the group and discovered Aiden was with them he was too angry to speak and they drove back in silence. I could not imagine a quiet Shamus. It seemed the incident had upset him more than it did Aiden who was unrepentant. As it was a question of safety I thought Shamus was right. Aiden was taking the view that he had not come all the way to Spain not to reach the summit of Mulhacen.

I waited until Donna rolled back from a gin and tonic session in one of the apartments before joining the group for dinner. I had declined the invitation – even though I was feeling much better it still took me a long time to do the simplest things. Dressing was one example. I had struggled into my new tight white trousers for dinner as pulling them over my swollen knee was a real effort. My attire did not go unnoticed and during the meal Chloe commented on the cosy fit of my trousers and asked me if Phillippe had helped me into them! I was shocked but laughed it off and said, "I should be so lucky." Later, as I followed Phillippe to his office to discuss the programme for the next day I could feel Chloe's eyes piercing my back. I could imagine the spiteful comments being scattered in my wake. But there was no point in worrying as I had a job to do.

As we entered the office I noticed that the wooden sign outside the door was smoking and pointed it out to Phillippe. He just shrugged. As we were leaving the office a motorist stopped to tell him his sign was smoking and he got the same reaction. By the next morning a large hole had been burnt in the wood by the bulb that illuminated it. I suspected it would stay like that for many years to come or until the whole building caught fire.

At breakfast the following morning there were the usual mutterings about the lack of hot water, soap and sachets of shampoo. As I arranged my face to look as concerned as possible the words that had gathered in my brain were suddenly floating round me, "Where do you think you are? The centre of London?" Hayley did not mince her words and some of the complainers looked taken aback. Justified or not I promised to deal with all the issues that had been raised while the group were out mountain biking, horse riding or exploring the next village. As the office was empty I left the list with the girls in the kitchen. I had marked the hot water problem as URGENT in the hope Phillippe would deal with it as soon as possible. There was no sign of that happening when I set off for the village with Donna and Shamus a few hours later to join the bikers for a drink.

We were encouraged to try some young red wine mixed with lemonade which was very pleasant and cheap. When a local brought what looked like a baby boar on a lead into the bar I think we all felt that maybe we had over-indulged. But closer inspection revealed that it was a boar. It was so cute; we all tickled it and talked baby talk at it. I left them there as I had yet to resolve the hot water issue. Phillippe was still insisting there was nothing wrong with the immersion heater. He was right but when I asked if he had checked the gas that fuelled it he looked sheepish and admitted that he had not. As soon as the gas cylinder had been replaced hot water flowed again. One problem solved and another was dealt with as I took the opportunity of Phillippe's fleeting presence to collect the maps of Granada for our forthcoming trip giving me time to mark them before the journey down the mountain.

As soon as the group had set off on their walk the following morning I shuffled down to the village on a mission of my own – to find a present for the girls in the kitchen. In every shop hams hung from the ceiling and racks of red wine lined the walls. I settled for a bottle of good red wine and hobbled back to my apartment. My exertions had resulted in my bandage descending into a concertina round my ankle. I needed to rescue the situation with some strapping and it was a good excuse to visit Phillippe in his office away from prying eyes and enjoy some harmless flirting with him on the pretext of asking him to write down the word for bandage in Spanish. We had developed a good rapport and it was all harmless fun. The transient nature of my job – here today and gone tomorrow – encouraged it but I had learned that it was not wise to indulge in front of my guests.

The wine was a great success. After some wonderful paella for dinner the girls changed into their full skirts and produced a brilliant flamenco show. It really came from their hearts and we were drawn into the drama of the songs and dances. When I presented them with their bottle of wine they had opened it immediately, drank some and then began a spontaneous jamming session. It was a magical evening.

When we set off for Granada the next morning it seemed that our driver was determined to make us all throw up. He drove really fast and each bout of acceleration was punctuated with some hard braking. Several people complained but my requests to slow down fell on deaf ears. I spoke to him as loudly as I could so that everyone was aware that I was trying to slow him down even though my efforts yielded no reduction of speed. We were all very grateful to get out of the bus and walk through the narrow streets of the old town.

We avoided the fiasco of the previous week by taking the local bus up to Alhambra in good time for our guided tour with Jose. I did not join them but walked straight to the Generalife entrance to wait for them. People kept coming up to me and asking for directions just because I was wearing my company badge so I removed it and stretched out on the public bench. I dozed off and the group walked straight past my prone body. I woke up just before we were due to leave and found them all in a café on the way to the coach park. It was a much gentler journey going back. I guessed our driver had had an assignation in Granada but he was in no rush to get home.

When Phillippe discovered that I had not been able to get some strapping for my knee he became very concerned and suggested he should take me to the doctor in the next village the following day. I agreed as I also needed some more painkillers to get me through the journey home. Phillippe then had a second thought; we should go straight to the hospital as the doctor was bound to refer us anyway. I agreed.

Shamus cut it a bit fine for the walk the following morning. When he did arrive he needed to retrieve his stick from the office where he had left it the previous day. The office was locked and Phillippe was not around. Lolita had a key and as she was confident that the alarm would not have been set she unlocked the door. The alarm was piercing so Shamus grabbed his stick and raced off to join the group. Before I could make my getaway Phillippe appeared, summoned by the bell that rang in his house. I explained why we had been trying to get into the office but he was not at all concerned. I wondered if the girls used this technique when they needed his presence urgently. As he rushed off again I reminded him that he had promised to call the Buddhist monastery to tell them our group would be visiting that day.

Phillippe actually arrived on time to take me to the "'ospital" in Orgiva. Before we left I asked if he had called the Buddhist retreat. "Ah yes," he said, "I will do it now!" He raced off to the office. Then we stopped on our way through the village so he could say hello to his son. Finally we got to the hospital in Orgiva and they referred us to the hospital in Mottrill. I would have been happy to return to the apartments but Phillippe was determined I should see a doctor so off we went. On arrival at the hospital I was given an incredibly painful painkilling injection, a pain distracter, before they drained my knee. Throughout the process Phillippe flicked through a magazine he had brought with him.

As soon as I had been bandaged up again we headed for home taking a short cut over the mountains. The scenery was stunning with wonderful views right down to the sea. When we reached Orgiva Phillippe begged permission to stop there for a while so he could visit an antique shop he had never noticed before. It was such an eloquent plea I could not refuse. He was gone for ages and came back eyes shining like a little boy who had found a treasure trove of toys. We eventually got back to Bubion just in time for dinner, our last dinner.

When the bus arrived the next morning Phillippe spoke to the bus driver about stopping somewhere nice for lunch on our way to the airport. The driver took us to a good restaurant by the sea. While the group cavorted on the beach I dozed on the bus. The new painkillers the hospital had given me were so strong I could have floated home without a plane. As our flight was delayed I had missed my bus from Gatwick but Hayley came to the rescue. She bundled me into her car, chased it up the motorway and dropped me off at its next stopping point. I really appreciated this act of kindness and it underlined my good fortune that their support had enabled me to survive a difficult week.

* * * * * *

My next trip, Halkidiki, did not start well. On my way to the airport all the traffic on the M25 came to a halt because a car had burst into flames. My taxi left the motorway and followed some minor roads to Gatwick. Time was racing and so was my heart. I arrived as the check-in desks were preparing to close. No one was at the meeting point when I finally got there as the flight had been called for boarding. I found all of them at the boarding gate, bar one. We boarded the plane on time but did not go anywhere. The pilot finally announced that one passenger was missing but as his luggage was in the hold they had to either find him or his luggage to unload it. The former was the easiest option and they were searching for him. I wondered if this missing passenger could be my client. When he was found and dragged down the aisle to his seat it was not a good time to ask his name.

The drunken passenger, Gavin, did belong to me and by the time we landed at Thessaloniki he had sobered up sufficiently to introduce himself. We arrived at our hotel at five thirty in the morning. There was only one person on reception so checking in was a slow process. He handed out our keys and left us to stumble along dimly lit corridors and up flights of stairs searching for our rooms. Both light bulbs and porters were missing. I abandoned my own luggage in reception and escorted people to their rooms lighting the way with my torch. I reminded them that our Information Meeting would be at midday the next day. Our local agent had been a fleeting presence at the airport and told me that he was not attending our meeting. I was on my own and would have to cope with an information pack left by Ryan the previous Host. I would have to get up early to prepare for it.

I had a bumpy ride at the meeting but I did have some assistance. Sadie had already been in the resort for a week and when we met at breakfast she was a mine of information. According to Ryan I would have to book optional excursions through the Thomson rep in the hotel. Today was his day off. Ryan also suggested I collect the hotel tips in advance but the notion of tipping any of the staff was greeted with general hostility. My request (discretionary) brought all their grievances to the fore – slow check-in, no porters, and the terrifying experience of searching for rooms in dark corridors. The English generally did not like tipping and did not seem to appreciate how much it could smooth their passage. In large hotels, like this one, giving our waiters a little tip every evening after dinner would ensure their undivided attention at the next meal. I tried to move swiftly on but before I could introduce the topic of excursions Norris rudely interrupted what I was saying and told me to get on with it. I was shocked into silence by his abrupt manner. I stuttered my way through the rest of the meeting before escaping to call the agency to book the Mount Athos trip for the following day.

Bettina was waiting for me when I emerged from the telephone cabin. She was determined to get a room like her friend's room which had an uninterrupted view of the sea. I had already requested a change for her but reception insisted there were no rooms available on the sea front. Now she was claiming that her room was a threat to her health as there was a noisy black chimney belching smoke right outside her window. I was not allowed to inspect the offending smokestack as she marched me to reception and insisted I report this to the manager and demand a room change for her.

The hotel manager was not available and the reception manager was adamant there were still no rooms available that day but said that there may be one the following day. I had already offered Bettina my room but she had turned it down. I repeated my offer but she refused preferring to hold out for a sea view whereas mine was a pool view. I knew I had not heard the last from Bettina about her room but she did let the matter rest while we explored our environs. The Sani Beach Hotel was a large complex comprising not just our hotel but also the Sani Beach Club, the Porto Sani Village and the Porto Sani Marina. Everywhere was deserted as the season was nearly over. Some of the facilities were already closed and the shuttle bus service had ceased operations. When it began to rain we scuttled into the only bar that was still open.

During lunch Lucille and Bettina told us of their strange encounter with a set of false teeth on the plane the previous day. The teeth kept sliding along the floor under their feet and they had no idea where they had come from. They pointed them out to the stewardess who suggested they pick them up – they refused and the stewardess would not pick them up either so they remained where they were. They thought the owner must have retrieved them when they finally disappeared. I hoped he had as I suspected I knew who owned the errant teeth. Thinking of Gavin made we realise that I had not seen him that morning and I needed to know if he wanted to go on the Athos cruise the following day. I had until that evening to finally confirm numbers. He did not answer his phone so I went up to his room and shouted through the door. He said he was fine and did not want to do the excursion.

Due to our late arrival the previous evening we had postponed our Welcome Drink until the second evening but when I arrived in the bar nothing was ready and I had to remind the reluctant barman that the group would be there soon. He grudgingly began to prepare drinks and nibbles. He was not the first unhelpful person I had dealt with. Throughout the day I had encountered several members of staff who seemed to find the presence of guests a big surprise and an irritating inconvenience. Eventually our drinks were placed on a large tray ready to serve to my group. The barman then disappeared so I carried it to our table and offered everyone a choice of either ouzo or orange juice.

This arrangement did not suit Norris who made a big fuss because he said he did not like either of them. He wanted a beer and nothing else would do. I asked the barman if he could have a beer but he said no. This annoyed Norris even more and he snarled at me that it was my job to get him an alternative immediately. I was handing round the tray of drinks. I could not do anything else and I pointed this out to him. He got even crosser. I set the tray down and went to the bar. The barman refused to give him a beer but after some persuasion he offered a further alternative, pineapple juice. Norris refused this offer and stormed off to buy himself a beer. My apology was met by a tirade regarding the failure of my company to select a hotel that offered a decent welcome drink.

Norris forgot his grievances over dinner, a nice mixture of service and buffet – until we got to the buffet dessert which was empty. I pointed this out to the head waiter in the hope that he would refill it but he did not. He had also forgotten that it was Sadie's birthday that day even though I had reminded him three times. Finally he produced a tiny cake with a candle on it so we all sang Happy Birthday to a background of Norris muttering about my failure to produce a proper cake. I distracted him by suggesting we went to the Piano Bar where we could dance. While the others joined in the dancing Sadie revived her favourite topic of conversation: the table tennis table outside on the patio. She thought it should be inside. She was the only one who seemed to be interested in playing the game so it was unlikely to be used wherever it was. Nevertheless I mentioned it to reception who told me to speak to the Animation Team. I put the problem on hold but if Sadie found an opponent then I would have to renew my efforts.

It was more important to find Gavin who had not appeared at dinner. I went to his room and spoke to him through the door. He said he would be down later but he never appeared. I checked with reception regarding Bettina's room change and they said they had a room but she had to leave her bags packed ready to be moved before she went out the next morning. I reminded Bettina about this when I joined the group in the Piano Bar.

Before we left on our trip the following morning I asked Bettina if she had packed her bags. She had not but said she would do it when we got back that afternoon. That would be too late as there was a conference arriving during the day and they would need her room. Of course Bettina thought they were just being awkward and assured me that she could sort it out herself when we got back. I was not convinced but it was already time to leave for our trip and we drove off through a murky morning. It was so misty we thought we would not see Mount Athos and its famous monasteries. Then the weather began to improve and as it warmed up the clouds parted and Mount Athos appeared out of the swirling clouds. It was magnificent.

The cruise got better and better. We saw eight of the monasteries all perched at various levels on the hillside with their own jetties on the beach below. We stopped in Orunoupolis for lunch in a taverna and a wander round the shops. As we cruised back to Halkidiki peninsula the sun was shining so we lay on the deck and watched dolphins frolicking in the sea. We were late back so I suggested we went straight to dinner but both Ambrose and Norris were adamant that the meal should be delayed until eight thirty. Fortunately the restaurant agreed. Norris took the view that as the customer he was always right. He had found one supporter in the group, Ambrose, and this was fuelling his aggression. At least the delay gave me time to calm down Bettina who had discovered that the hotel had indeed given 'her' room to another guest.

We were the only guests in the restaurant that evening and both the food and the service were minimal. There was no sign of any delegates or a conference. They had not been in the bar earlier and they were not eating in the main restaurant. This made Bettina even more suspicious regarding her failure to secure a sea-front room. It had been impossible to convince her that there really was only a small window of opportunity regarding room changes. I was still trying and failing but I had to move on as I had other, more important issues to deal with.

I was getting very concerned about Gavin as this was the second evening that he had not appeared for dinner. As soon as everyone was settled at our tables I went to his room and knocked on the door. He mumbled through the wood that he was alright – he sounded drunk. He joined us in the bar after dinner and apologised for his bender which he claimed had been induced by working nights prior to his holiday. I introduced him to the group and then got him some bread and cheese from the restaurant. I left them to get acquainted as I had a trip and mountain biking to organise for the next day. It was a good excuse to escape Bettina who was still whining about her room without a view. I offered her my room once more but again she refused. Sadie was changing her room the next day because Gavin, her neighbour, was very noisy. It seemed he was a night owl.

I was woken at the crack of dawn the following morning when a neighbour's alarm went off – it must have been one of the mysterious conference delegates. I went out for a walk and did a full circuit around the hotel looking for a large chimney belching out black smoke but I could not find one. I had a solitary breakfast looking out at the dull weather and praying that it would cheer up later. The last thing I needed in this desolate resort was more bad weather. Gavin greeted me on his way to the bar and his first beer of the day. I followed him there and asked him if he wanted to go any excursions. It was my first good look at this character as to date he had been a shadowy figure flitting to and from the bar, drink in hand. He was short and slim and his shaggy hair flopped endearingly over his face. As he kept looking down his hair flopped even more and I could not see his features and I could hardly hear him as he mumbled at the carpet. He booked and paid for the Macedonian experience the following day. During breakfast I discovered that Gavin had woken a few people up as he staggered down the corridor trying to find his room in the early hours. As he was still in the bar I passed on these grievances and he promised to behave himself.

My list of complaints was getting longer. There had been no hot water that morning and more light bulbs had gone out. They had not replaced any of the spent light bulbs since we arrived. I reported these grievances to reception on my way to see Jules, the Thomson representative. I found him at his desk. After taking all the bookings for my group he offered me a free place on any of the trips they had booked. My next stop was the bike hire shop but as the bikes were all out that day I made a reservation for the following morning. As I walked back through reception I caught sight of Gavin lurching back to his room.

I had hoped to while away some of the afternoon soaking in a hot bath but the water was still tepid. Instead I had a walk along the beach and met Bettina who invited me to inspect her room. Finally I was going to see this room 'without a view'. In fact it had a super view, trees on one side and the sea on the other. It was a much nicer view than most. If you leant right out of the window you could see a small metal chimney on a roof two floors below. But there was no sign of it belching black smoke.

And so another day ambled slowly towards the evening entertainment, the only successful activity so far. This trip was proving to be an uphill struggle. The Piano Bar had become a favourite haunt of my group and they danced until the early hours accompanied by Nikos, the pianist. That evening Nikos was entertaining the conference delegates elsewhere but Lucille hung around until he had finished and then dragged him to the Piano Bar. I would add him to our tips collection, if I ever get one going. I had been opposite Norris during dinner and forced to listen to his current moan – the lack of men in the group. It was true there were fewer men than ladies but I was not sure why it bothered Norris so much. I think he just felt obliged to find a daily grievance.

The next morning the sun was shining and there were happy faces round the breakfast table. But there was no sign of Gavin who had booked the trip that was departing in thirty minutes. I had already called him twice so I went and hammered on his door. I managed to wake up Bettina who popped her head out of her room to tell me I had woken her. I gave up and the coach left without him. Four people had hired a car and they went off to catch the ferry to Athens. I set off with the mountain bikers to collect our reserved bikes.

But there were no bikes. As we approached the bike shop we could see a German group speeding away on 'our' bikes. The people in the shop had just watched them as they grabbed all the bikes. Our booking accounted for nothing. I tried to book them for the next day but was informed that the shop was closing that evening. I complained to reception but they were not interested. There were still some pedaloes on the beach so I hired a flotilla and we amused ourselves fighting mock battles using water as ammunition. Afterwards we wrapped ourselves in our towels and had hot chocolate in the bar to warm ourselves up.

Our high spirits were dampened by a dismal dinner that night. Our tables were right by the door and the dessert buffet had dwindled to a bowl of fruit. Gavin did not come to dinner and when I spoke to him through his door I got very little sense out of him. When he joined us in the bar after dinner he made no attempt to socialise as he gulped down several glasses of wine before staggering back to his room. This was my first experience of a heavy drinker and I suspected that a desperate relative had booked him on this holiday and was now enjoying some peace at home. After everyone had finally gone to bed I settled down in reception to wait for the four people who had spent the day in Athens. The night porter was tutting and saying they must have missed the last ferry. I kept telling myself they were adults and could do as they liked but as the hours crept by I did begin to worry.

I was half asleep the following morning as I had waited in reception until three in the morning when the four finally returned from their day out. After crossing back on the ferry they had decided to have dinner before driving back to the hotel. They got completely lost and it took them a long time to find their way. It did not occur to any of them to call the hotel for directions. They just kept driving round in the hope they would be the recipients of some divine inspiration.

Shopping and sightseeing in Thessaloniki was on the agenda and when we arrived in the city the first stop, by popular demand, was the market. Thanks to directions from the Thomson representative on the bus and despite counter suggestions from the group who had suddenly become 'experts' on Thessaloniki, we found it easily. It was a huge colourful market throbbing with locals doing their shopping from stalls loaded with fish, meat and household goods. As we searched for the exit we found a stall selling fresh Greek pasties and bought some for an al fresco lunch before boarding our bus for some sightseeing. The first stop was the archaeological museum. Due to a total lack of air conditioning it was hot and airless so we raced round on our own reading the labels and left the guide talking to herself. Next stop the Acropolis, the highest part of the city with fabulous views. Finally we visited the Greek Orthodox church of St Dimitrius. The crypt houses the well into which, legend assures us, St Dimitrius' body was thrown and then turned to myrrh. This well was reputed to have great healing properties but no one was tempted to lower themselves down in the bucket to test this theory.

As I changed for dinner I had a call from a very angry Norris informing me that the hot water was still in short supply and the number of spent light bulbs had increased by two. I assured him I had reported these problems on a daily basis and promised to renew my efforts to speak to the manager who was proving to be very elusive. I had asked to speak to him personally several times but he always seemed to be 'busy'. I went to reception and tried again. This time I was asked to wait. That was encouraging – it suggested that he did exist. I had to give up waiting as the time ticked by until it was nearly time to join the group for dinner billed that night as a Greek evening. Given the present rate of progress I suspected that they had probably run out of Greeks as well.

The Greek evening was great fun and everyone joined in including Gavin who was sober and drinking lemonade. I sat next to him during dinner and he was very honest about his drink problem and apologised for getting drunk at Gatwick and his subsequent four day bender. He had drunk the contents of his mini-bar twice. He said he would not drink again that week as he had to be sober when he returned to work the following week. I believed him. He then added that one of the reasons he had stayed out of the way was because he had lost his top set of teeth and he felt very self-conscious without them. He had not realised that they had fallen out on the plane. I suggested that might be what had happened and promised to contact the airline to see if they had found them. I was pretty sure they would have been swept up with the rubbish and thrown away but it was worth a try. During our meal we ate lots of delicious moussaka but when we moved on to the communal dancing I escaped and returned to reception again in the hope that the manager had not gone home already.

My patience was finally rewarded and I had a very successful meeting with the manager. He seemed really sympathetic and kept saying "Oh dear" as I listed the problems we had encountered. When I reached the end of my list he asked me to suggest something the hotel could offer by way of compensation. We were not leaving until after midnight on the day of our departure and I suggested that everyone should be allowed to keep their rooms, free of charge, until we left. He agreed. I skipped back to the restaurant to give everyone the good news and they were delighted. We had all been concerned at the thought of being kicked out of our rooms thirteen hours before we left for the airport.

The weather had deteriorated even more by the following morning but bizarrely the water in the pool was getting warmer which was probably due to the greater contrast with the air temperature. I decided breakfast would be a good time to start the tips collection. Most people gave willingly, except Norris, who muttered that he never volunteered his money. Our leisurely breakfast ended abruptly when the rain stopped and we decided to go for a walk. There were some interesting walks around the complex. I had hoped to join them after I had confirmed the flights for the next day. But when I discovered we were one flight short for Gatwick and had a surplus flight to Manchester I had to contact Aimee.

The rain really set in after lunch so we joined the afternoon entertainment – bingo in four languages. It was won by the bar manager, probably because the first language was Greek. By dinner time there had been no reply to the fax I had sent Aimee regarding the inbound flight. I feared the worst – being stuck in Greece with Nikos the pianist. He was short and bald and definitely not my cup of tea but he had been a godsend this week as the group loved him. Every night they had danced to his music in the Piano Bar. Ambrose was a ballroom dancer and he had danced with all the ladies in turn – except Lucille our most ardent dancer. He claimed this was because she was unorthodox! I suspected this was male talk for being scared because she was a better dancer than he was.

When I got back to my room after dinner that evening I found a fax from Aimee that had been pushed under my door. I had to fly back to Manchester. I had no idea how I was going to get home from there and suspected it would take a long time whatever form of transport I chose. Aimee apologised because she could not allow me to take a taxi as I would have plenty of time to get home. She sugared this bitter pill by reminding me that I was an experienced traveller and should be able to find my way around my own country.

Thanks to severe storms and heavy rain during the night the ground floor of the hotel was flooded and the walkways were awash so we had to paddle to breakfast the next day. It was still raining when we finished eating so it seemed the boules tournament that the Animation Team had organised for us would be abandoned. I was preparing to organise an indoor games morning when the sun came out. But the Animation Team did not. Undeterred I gathered together the equipment and the tournament was soon underway. As the hot weather continued all day we then swam and sunbathed by the pool. The pool bar was closed and we had to traipse inside if we wanted some drinks. A sober Gavin joined us and discretely reminded me about his missing set of teeth. I had called Monarch who had suggested that we ask at the Monarch desk at the airport. Despite his missing teeth he had clearly enjoyed the last two days with the group.

At dinner that evening we celebrated Lucille's birthday. This time we did it in style as the hotel manager had provided wine and a large birthday cake. The group were in a good mood and there was still time for one last dance in the Piano Bar before changing to go to the airport. The only problem was the lack of porters to help with the luggage and we had to trundle it along even darker corridors ourselves. I set up a relay system and guided people to the lifts with my torch. For most of them it was an adventure but for Norris it was another item for his list of complaints.

Just five kilometres from the airport our bus broke down. After cursing loudly our driver jumped out and started delving in the engine trying to fix it. He ignored my entreaties to call another bus. Time was getting on and we should have already checked in. Empty buses having delivered their passengers to the airport were thundering past us. I succeeded in stopping one of them and our luggage was soon transferred from one bus to the other. We left our driver still trying to fix his bus. I had time to get the Gatwick group checked in before boarding my flight. When I said my goodbyes most of the group said they would definitely travel with my company again although they would never go back to Halkidiki.

I was only half way through my first decent cup of tea for a week when the telephone rang. Norris had been busy and had already filed his complaints. My report was still in my head which was woolly from lack of sleep. I had to agree with Aimee that there had been a gentleman in the group with a drink problem but in my opinion this had not spoilt the holiday for anyone. He had spent most of the time in his room. When he finally emerged he did not drink at all and he was charming. I had not known that we really did have a black list and that Gavin was a serious candidate for inclusion. Personally I thought he deserved a second chance. If it had been up to me I would have suggested that Norris, as the more tiresome of the two, should go on our black list.

The conversation moved on to my next trip. The regular tennis hostess was having her own holiday and unable to take our next tennis week in Spain. I had listed playing tennis as one of my skills at my interview so now was my chance to prove it. I had not actually played tennis for several years and I had to scrabble through drawers and cupboards to find a racket and a tennis skirt.

* * * * * *

Our flight to Malaga would have departed on time but the lorry attached to the steps we had walked up to board the plane had broken down and the two were inseparable. We had to wait while they repaired the engine and it seemed to take forever. Timing was crucial regarding our departure as our transfer had been arranged to combine groups arriving from different destinations at approximately the same time. I could not call anyone as we had already been told to switch our mobile phones off. I knew from past experience that cabin crew had keen radar when it came to people making phone calls on board. I would just have to hope that the driver knew exactly how many passengers he should have and which flights they were on.

When we finally arrived at Malaga airport and there was no driver in Arrivals I thought my worst fears had come true. I told the group to stay put while I searched for our bus. I was very familiar with this airport and went straight to the coach park. Our bus was still there and the driver was standing by it casting anxious glances around him. The first arrivals were already on board so I boarded to say hello and apologize for keeping them waiting. The restless murmurings that greeted my explanation regarding our delay suggested it was beyond their belief but I would soon have twelve witnesses to substantiate my story and I rushed off to collect them.

While everyone was boarding a woman pushed her way to the open door. All I could see was a back bristling with anger but I heard the loud voice fiercely demanding "where is this hostess who is supposed to be meeting us". Arleen smiled and said "right here" and pointed to me. I feared I was going to be assaulted with a document that was being waved close to my face as a finger stabbed at the information typed on it. My adversary was beyond introductions and kept demanding to know why I had not been waiting for them when their flight arrived. She was adamant that according to her itinerary I should have been there. It was not a good time to point out that this was a physical impossibility as my flight had always been due to land later than hers. I apologised every time she drew breath long enough to squeeze the words in. Her constant use of the word 'us' alerted me to the fact she was not alone and I needed to find her companions.

Having persuaded Eunice to board the bus I counted heads. Her two companions had crept aboard while she was berating me outside so we were able to leave immediately. I introduced myself and outlined the programme for the rest of the day before walking down the bus to talk to Eunice. Her smart appearance and black rimmed spectacles that matched the black hair framing her face made her look more like a secretary than a holidaymaker. She was still clutching her itinerary and accused me once again of abandoning her at the airport. I was struggling to understand how I could have deserted someone I was never supposed to meet. It was a short transfer and the inquisition did not last long.

The Atalaya Park is a huge golf and tennis complex with several large blocks of hotel rooms. Once we had all checked in our luggage was loaded on to golf buggies and driven to the end of a long corridor and piled up at the bottom of a flight of stairs. There were no lifts in this area. A general reluctance to drag the bags up the stairs had me racing all the way back to reception to find some porters but it seemed they were all busy. While we were dragging bags up the stairs Eunice kept up a monologue about her terrifying experience at the airport. She had waited an hour at a busy airport with two other people. I sympathised and promised to inform my office as soon as possible; meanwhile I was in a rush to confirm all the details of our programme with the hotel management.

As both the bar manager and the maître d' were on a break I had to confirm our Welcome Drink and dinner with reception. It was a ten minute walk to the tennis centre to check which tennis courts we would be using. When I got there the office was empty so I went in search of Antonio, the tennis coach. I imagined an athletic, muscular man in pristine tennis whites. I could not find anyone who fitted this bill so I approached a short, slim man with a hint of a moustache wearing an oversized tracksuit. He was raking one of the courts and I assumed he was a gardener. I asked him where I could find Antonio the tennis coach. He identified himself as that person. It was not a good start.

When we got back to the office Antonio claimed he had no record of our booking. I persisted and after scrabbling through piles of paperwork he found it and offered me the three hard courts. I had a group of twenty-three and needed at least four courts – sixteen playing and a few resting so I needed one of the clay courts as well. Antonio was not keen on this idea as he claimed he did not have the time to police this court to ensure that every player who ventured on to it was wearing the correct footwear. I had no idea what he meant about the shoes as they all looked the same to me but I persuaded him to give us the extra court by promising that I would make sure that it was only used by players with the right shoes. I hoped the players themselves would know who they were.

When I arrived in the bar later that evening the barman was not expecting us. Lines of communication between reception and the bar must have broken down. The barman rose to the occasion and rushed around making jugs of sangria and then putting nibbles in bowls while I poured the sangria into tumblers. After drinking a toast to a good holiday I went through the tennis programme and the optional excursions that would be available. The latter were dismissed on the grounds they were all there to play tennis. I knew already that Arleen was not intending to play tennis and had checked that she could book trips through reception. When Deirdre announced that she was not a tennis player my heart sank. This would complicate my tournament strategy. Both of them had booked the holiday because 'the dates suited them'.

The restaurant manager was not expecting us for dinner. Clearly reception did not communicate with anyone in the hotel. My attempts to speak to him personally had been thwarted by a door that was chained and padlocked between meals. This was more ammunition for Eunice who was keeping me under surveillance. A flustered maître d' led us to three empty round tables in the huge dining area and we were soon tucking into a very impressive buffet. It took me five minutes to walk round the various sections before deciding what to eat. I was particularly impressed by the mountain of seasonal fruits piled up on one of the tables.

I never got a chance to relax and enjoy the food as I was constantly being quizzed by self-proclaimed experts regarding my intentions for the tennis programme. Each of them insisted on explaining how I should organise the tennis. Fortunately I was no novice myself but it was useful to have different opinions to consider. Eunice was not interested in the tennis and kept pestering me for feedback regarding the call I had not yet made to the office. I tried to buy more time by telling her I needed to see the exact wording of her itinerary. It was produced immediately and I promised to make the call as soon as the office opened the next morning. She retorted that the office must have an emergency number and I should make use of it.

I did have Aimee's home number and once the group were settled in the Piano Bar I went to my room and called her. I had studied the itinerary very carefully and it was the same one everyone else had received. It gave my flight time so it was clear that I would be arriving after Eunice. Aimee was sympathetic particularly when I told her that Eunice was gathering support within the group even though she was in the wrong. Aimee was confident that everything would settle down soon.

At breakfast the following morning I reminded everyone that we were meeting at the courts at ten o'clock when I would split them into groups. I went to the courts early to amend my order of play to allow for the two non-players. I was trying to get everyone to play with each other by switching partners after a few games – I wanted to get an idea of the standard. I had the added complication of ensuring that the clay court was only used by players wearing the correct footwear. Eunice was the first to arrive and before she could ask the question I told her that I had reported back to the office and they were looking into the issues she had raised.

The standard of tennis was alarmingly diverse and it was going to be difficult to ensure that everyone enjoyed their games. Partnering a good player with a weak player seemed to work and the morning session went very well. Only a few keen players attended the afternoon session as the golf course proved to be a stronger attraction. I changed the format and organised a singles tournament on the clay court. Once they were knocked out of the tournament they went off to the pool. That meant that I and the last two players had to rake and then roll the clay – under the watchful eye of Antonio. This chore turned my new white socks a delicate shade of pink.

The next morning I started our tennis tournament which would last all week and culminate in semi-finals and then the final on the last day. They were competing as individuals rather than pairs and each match consisted of four games with one partner and then changing partners to play another three games. I kept a record of games won and lost by each individual. Deirdre helped by filling in the scoreboard I had made for this purpose. Arleen was recovering from a late night in the Piano Bar but her accomplices had managed to drag themselves to the tennis courts. As there was a very poor attendance that afternoon I sent them to the hard courts and left them to organise themselves.

That evening when we met for pre-dinner drinks Eunice informed me that some of them were going out for dinner. Her attitude towards me was still frosty and she had not been happy when I told her that the office had sent a message apologising if the instructions on her itinerary had not been clear. I was trying very hard to be friendly but there was a lightness in my step as I raced off to the restaurant, a ten minute walk from the bar, to ask the maître d' to remove the requisite number of covers. It was one of my duties as a Hostess was to make sure no one sat opposite or next to an empty seat. By the time I got back to the bar it was time to return to the restaurant to eat. My after dinner socialising that evening was curtailed by the need to revise my order of play for the following morning. I had to ensure that everyone played exactly the same number of games while equally dispersing the weaker players amongst the stronger ones. My idea had seemed so simple at first.

During breakfast the next morning I was in trouble with the food police when I picked up an apple as I walked from one table to another. The waiter on duty pounced and told me to either put the apple back or sit in my seat and eat it.

Another waiter was stationed by the door searching the bags of suspects and charging any contraband that was found to the room of the person concerned. I noticed some people surreptitiously dipping into their bags and pulling out bananas until there was a large pile of them on our table. There was a lot of whispering and giggling while this was happening and just as I felt the mood was becoming light hearted Eunice thumped down into the empty seat beside me. She cross-examined me yet again regarding my conduct of the tennis tournament including the order of play, the number of games played and the fairness of my system regarding the pairings. Her competitive nature was unnerving – the tournament was supposed to be fun.

Everything went very smoothly the rest of that day but the following morning just as I thought we were all in a routine Eunice scuppered my plans. She had taken some people off to attend the improvers' tennis session and it overlapped with our first hour on the courts. I had to rearrange the pairings and then run back to breakfast to drag some people down to the courts to fill in the remaining gaps. Somehow we managed to complete all the matches scheduled for that session. I was itching to suggest to Eunice that it would have been courteous to inform me of her arrangements in advance. But I had to keep quiet. This worthy adversary was keeping me on my toes and I was in turmoil wondering what her next move would be.

Chapter 5 – November

I did not have to wait long before Eunice struck again. On one of my forays to the breakfast buffet the following morning I heard her denouncing our tipping system. She called me over and asked why I had not started the tips collection because, according to her information, it should have been done. I confirmed the collection would be started towards the end of the holiday. Eunice had raised the issue as a vehicle to announce that she was not going to contribute to a group collection but would do her own tipping. She began to canvas support for her plan of action. Burton was the first to join her. He never tipped because no one ever tipped him. He was a solicitor. I could feel the corners of my mouth twitching. Did he really expect his clients to slap a five pound note on his desk as they left his office?

Plunged into the spotlight by Eunice's public announcement and Burton's loud support I graciously accepted their decisions and acknowledged that tipping was discretionary. It did give me an opportunity to explain the tipping policy of my company. My explanation was peppered with the word discretionary. I used it so many times it began to sound wrong in my head. The amount we suggested was only a guideline. Eunice was welcome to do her own tipping and I was glad that she appreciated that the restaurant staff had been working very hard for us.

We always had the same waiters in the restaurant for all our meals and they were friendly and willing so I hoped people would at least contribute something for them. Personally I would have been very happy if they all did their own tipping but it was company policy to make a collection.

I needed to defend that policy so I went round the other tables and introduced everyone to the idea of making a collection. Most people said they would be happy to contribute. I had to be brief as it was nearly time for our tennis session. I was unaware that Eunice had followed me round the restaurant putting her own views until I met up with Deirdre on my way to the tennis courts and she warned me the debate was still raging. If her outburst resulted in a mutiny amongst the others and no contributions were forthcoming I was in trouble. I had already tipped some people so I hoped some money would be donated as I could not claim it as an expense.

I had to work hard to rescue our morning tennis session thanks to some tardy members of my group and a double booking by the tennis centre. Five minutes after our session started one of our courts was still empty. I was not the only one who noticed this as Antonio had come outside a few times and looked across to our courts. This was unusual as Antonio rarely moved from his office. I left Deirdre on watch and raced back to the restaurant – I had five minutes before we had to forfeit the court and it was a long way between the courts and the restaurant. I chivvied up the players who were still lingering there and set off back to the courts. Deirdre was on our empty court thrashing the air around her with my tennis racket but her rubber flip-flops gave the game away. Antonio was striding towards the empty court with four hotel guests trotting behind him. I intercepted them before they reached the gate and while I was earnestly interceding on their behalf the late arrivals slipped through the gate behind me and I could relax as our tournament continued. As an olive branch I offered Antonio one of our courts that afternoon. It was an empty gesture really as we both knew most of the courts were never used in the heat of the afternoon.

That evening Eunice and her gang went out to eat at a local fish restaurant. I suggested to one of them that they check the hotel dinner menu in case that night was their special fish and seafood evening. It was Fish and Flamenco in the hotel that evening so I was surprised when reception gave me a message from Eunice announcing that she and five others had gone out for dinner. They missed a treat as the abundance and quality of the fish dishes was amazing. Arleen raised a glass to toast 'absent friends'. She and Eunice had not been getting on well and the animated discussion about the tips collection earlier had widened the rift. Arleen herself was generous in every sense. Her plump face was always creased with a smile, her full throated laugh accompanied every conversation and her purse was always open – particularly when it came to good looking waiters. I knew exactly what would happen when Eunice got back and heard the rest of the group raving about the meal that evening. I was ready with my apology – I should have stopped them going out for dinner.

After the tennis session the following morning I had lunch with some of the group in the pool bar and was persuaded to join them on the hotel's short nine-hole golf course. As we walked to the first tee we met Becky who had just finished a lesson with the professional. Her small round face glowed with enthusiasm as she regaled us with tales of her progress to date. She was rewarded with a glare from Dudley when she failed to observe the rule of silence as he was taking a shot. She happily offered advice when balls went astray so to distract her Jade suggested that she pulled her trolley for her. Becky was not really concentrating on her new role and Jade would often find her trolley was not just in the wrong place but sometimes on the wrong hole. Becky's antics were making me laugh as I raced to and fro collecting and delivering clubs. The only serious golfer, Dudley, was not impressed and finally lost his cool when he hit his ball into a bunker. He then whacked his own golf bag really hard and it sailed past his ball. It was the best shot he had played all round.

Before I joined the group in the bar for dinner I called in to the tennis centre to make sure Antonio knew that the next day we would be playing our semi-finals in the morning and our finals in the afternoon so we would be using our courts all day. When I got to the bar Eunice was holding court again and it was her current favourite topic – the collection of tips for the staff. I was having to be very diplomatic and kept insisting that both the giving of tips and the recommended amount were discretionary. I was not sure who was winning the debate but I had not received any contributions at all. Several people suggested that tips should be included in the price of the holiday to avoid the embarrassment of trying to collect money from people. Others felt the only people worth tipping were the chambermaids (left to each individual) and the pianist whose music they had enjoyed every evening. They pointed out that the service in the restaurant was slow, the bar staff were not very efficient, the porter had abandoned their luggage at the end of the corridor and the coach driver was only doing what he was paid to do anyway!

When my phone trilled into life early the following morning my heart leapt into my mouth assuming some disaster had befallen one of my group or, worse, our flights home had been cancelled. It was Burton. When I heard his voice I nearly slammed the phone down in exasperation but I hung on and listened to what he had to say. This was not the first time Burton had rung me in my room. He had called to invite me to join him for a drink one evening but I had gently let him down by saying that the Hostess could not form a relationship with a guest in the group. He had persisted and the following day he had called and suggested we meet up in London. I gave him a mobile number, but not mine. I had not considered this aspect of the job – male guests wanting to date me. It was a fine line to tread – saying no without offending and arousing hostility that could affect other members of the group. I need not have worried as I was his last resort – he had already asked all the other women and they had all turned him down. I was not upset by this news as I had not been attracted to this portly, pompous gentleman who resembled a beached whale when sprawled on his sun bed. He claimed he was urgently required at home for business reasons. I suspected he had realised it was time to quit.

I dragged myself all the way to reception and wished him a safe journey. As I walked back through reception I noticed the timetable for the shuttle bus that operated between the hotel and the fashionable fishing village of Puerto Banus. I had to find some prizes for the winners of our tennis tournament. The prices in the hotel shops were beyond the moderate budget Aimee had given me. Puerto Banus may be the answer. As I had not yet strayed beyond the confines of the hotel complex it was time to indulge in some truancy. But not on my own so I went round our tables at breakfast to see if anyone else was interested. Arleen and a few other people decided to join me so I had a valid reason for going out and could ignore the reproachful glare from Eunice. Before setting off I started the two semi-finals that would be the best of three sets. Eunice had insisted that as we had reached the final stages of the tournament it should be played like a 'proper' tournament. No doubt her involvement at this stage had triggered this suggestion. As it had always been my intention to do this I was happy to comply and skipped off to get the bus.

This was not my first visit to Puerto Banus but I did not recognise it at all. When I was last there it had been a small fishing village clustered round the pretty harbour. Now it sprawled along the main road and the streets were packed with market stalls, traders and shoppers. I was inspired by the local pottery regarding prizes for our tennis tournament. I soon had a bag full of colourful 'cups' and 'plates' to present the following evening. When I finished my shopping I met Arleen for a beer. Arleen was a breath of fresh air and had kept my spirits up in the face of constant criticism from Eunice. Mindful of Aimee's warning "these people are not your friends" it was difficult to apply it to Arleen. I really needed a friend right now. Arleen was my source of gossip regarding the extra mural activities of the group and I had been looking forward to catching up. Arleen assured me she supported my tips collection and gave me a generous amount to start it.

When I got back to the hotel one of the semi-finals was still going on. It lasted over three hours prompting Eunice to proclaim that it should have been the final – probably because she was on the losing side. The final also went to three sets and it was a good match although it was marred by Dudley taking it all too seriously. Dudley was very intense and determined to win. His partner, Jade, was a good player but not obsessed with taking the trophy. Her eye was on the clock as she had an appointment for a full body massage at six. She said she would rather be doing that than playing tennis! This prompted Dudley to waste more time by having a tantrum. They finally emerged the victors and Jade raced off to the spa.

As we drifted away from the tennis courts Eunice told me that she and her gang would be eating out that night. I mentioned that they would be missing the prize presentation and wished them an enjoyable meal. It was a surprise to find them in the bar with the rest of the group for farewell jugs of sangria while I presented the prizes. They followed us into the restaurant for dinner where the maître d' successfully interpreted my frantic signals to restore the table I had cancelled earlier. Eunice and her gang all sat together and I asked if I could take one of the empty seats. Arleen and Deirdre joined us. I wanted to make it clear to both Eunice and everyone else that there were no hard feelings regarding her attitude towards me. I was so anxious to ensure everyone enjoyed that last evening that I failed to notice a mistake with the wines on our table. Eunice had taken charge of the order as it was an opportunity to show off her scant knowledge of wines and a very loose grip on the Spanish language.

The order was one house red and one bottle of the white Marqués de Cáceres. The wine waiter got it the wrong way round but the red wine was poured before the mistake was noticed. The white wine was sent back and three more bottles of red were ordered. We were all unaware that the red Marqués de Cáceres was more expensive that the white version as no one had checked but everyone had assumed that they would both be the same price. When the bill came Eunice miscalculated the amount each individual had to pay as she did not check the number of bottles was correct. Most people had left by the time a second bill arrived. Arleen and Deirdre paid it. As Arleen had drunk at least two of the bottles herself I thought that was fair. But I felt guilty regarding Deirdre as she had drunk very little so I approached the restaurant manager regarding the mistake over the first bottle of wine. They thought I meant all the wine and ultimately halved the whole bill. It was too complicated to try and refund small amounts to everyone on the table so I accepted their suggestion that they cancelled the charge Deirdre had put on her room.

My conscience was clear when I joined the group in the piano bar. The pianist, Araldo Conchi, was superb again that evening. The group asked me if I was tipping him. What an opening! I said I would love to reward him but as Arleen was the only one who had contributed to the tips collection I did not have anything to give him. This resulted in an impromptu collection and I was able to give him something and recoup all my losses. I was so light headed after that I actually stayed up until Araldo abandoned his piano.

Breakfast was a subdued affair the next morning and I had to concentrate very hard to ensure the luggage was loaded in the right vehicles as there were two separate transfers to the airport. It was bedlam when we got to Malaga airport as it was the first day of the winter season and five flights had just arrived so we had to fight our way through to Departures. Once everyone had checked in I crawled into the nearest coffee bar. It would all soon be over.

As I was driving out of the airport car park Deirdre jumped out in front of me. I screeched to a stop. She told me that she was stranded. She had been offered a lift home by Dudley and he had disappeared. As Deirdre had cancelled her taxi she had no means of getting home. I could not abandon her and said I would take her although I did not know where all her luggage would go in my little sports car. When she went off to collect her luggage I spotted Dudley circling the car park looking for her. Somehow they had missed each other. I reunited them and was free to drive home with the top down and music blaring. I enjoyed my trips but sometimes it was a relief to get home.

******

Before I left for my next trip, a beach holiday in Tunisia, Aimee called to say I may have a tricky situation on my hands. It was a small group and there was just one man, travelling on his own. He was unaware of the situation and I would have to break the news to him before he worked it out for himself. It sounded easy and I was full of confidence when I arrived at the airport. I was too early to check-in so I settled down with a book in sight of our check-in desks. I hoped my man would be using our luggage label and I would easily spot him. I was not wearing my badge but I had forgotten about the label on my case and that was how Josephine (don't call me Jo) found me.

Josephine was also travelling independently and as soon as she discovered I was the Hostess she clung to me like a limpet. I could not shake her off and she stayed by my side until the check-in opened. When I suggested she went through to the Departures lounge and I would meet her there later she insisted on waiting for me. It seemed my simple task had now become mission impossible. I decided to abandon my plan to intercept my lone man at the check-in desk and hoped that I could find him at the boarding gate. I went through to the lounge with my new best friend to get a cup of coffee. She said she needed to speak to me. Once we were settled at a table she complained that she was referred to as 'Miss' rather than Dr on our information. I apologised on behalf of my company for this oversight.

Josephine then told me that she had booked this holiday specifically to celebrate her fiftieth birthday in three days' time and she was expecting me to organise something special for her. I said I would do what I could. Normally we organised a birthday card and asked the hotel to provide a cake. I excused myself and put in a quick call to Aimee from a cubicle in the ladies' toilet. As I suspected we did not have a budget for birthday celebrations. I had to deal with this myself.

At Monastir I raced through passport control and was at the luggage reclaim before the bags started coming through. I identified Bert's case and followed it round the conveyor belt until he collected it. I introduced myself and was about to launch myself into my prepared speech regarding his status as the solitary man when Josephine pushed herself between us demanding an introduction. She had been pestering me regarding the members of the group – how many in total, how many women, how many men – and had clearly worked out there was only one man. I had to tell him before she did. I blurted out a combined introduction and explanation. He reacted to both very calmly and said he had booked the holiday in order to visit Carthage. The composition of the group was immaterial.

As we were a small group we were transferred to our hotel in a minibus with the luggage strapped on to the roof above us. It took a while to load the luggage and while I supervised this Josephine went round the group telling everyone that it was her birthday that week and as it was a milestone event she was expecting suitable celebrations. I wondered if she was expecting me to blow up balloons and put squeakers by each setting at dinner. Initially we were all swept along by her enthusiasm and listened to her monologue. Josephine spoke loudly, confidently and quickly and it was difficult to butt in and orchestrate a change of subject which I began to feel was long overdue. I looked out of the window hoping to spot a landscape to which I could draw their attention. But there was nothing, we were travelling along a suburban road that could have been anywhere in the world.

At last we turned off the main road and approached the resort of Port El Kantoui through lush, exotic vegetation beyond which we could see large hotels that resembled white marble palaces. Our surroundings were opulent beyond my wildest dreams. I felt a thrill of excitement as we turned into the drive of our hotel and skirted a fountain before pulling up in front of a two storey white building surrounded by palm trees and colourful flower beds. We were greeted by a member of the reception team and followed him through the palatial entrance. As soon as we were settled on the upholstered, wooden carved chairs each one of us was presented with a bouquet of flowers and a glass of fresh orange juice but no room key. The manager bustled over wringing his hands and apologising profusely as our rooms were not ready. He then indicated that I should accompany him and he whisked me away to his office, firmly closing the door behind us. My first, selfish thought was that he wanted me to move to a bed and breakfast nearby.

He wanted to know if the two women in the group who had booked single rooms, Josephine and Jessica, would share a room for one night (single supplement refunded). Or maybe they would like to go on the two day desert safari on Monday and Tuesday at a fifty per cent discount thus releasing two rooms for the night when the hotel was overbooked. I very much doubted they would accept either of these offers but you never knew. Both ideas were greeted with a resounding no and an impatient request from Josephine to check-in immediately. Fate was not on my side as the only room that was not ready for occupation was Josephine's. I immediately offered her mine but as it did not meet her specifications my offer was brushed aside.

Josephine must have told me twenty times that she would settle for nothing less than a room with a double bed and a balcony that was not on the ground floor. I used her anxiety regarding her room as an excuse to go for a wander round on the pretext of checking her room for her. Our hotel, Hotel Hasdrabul, was amazing. It was huge and the rooms were in blocks like spokes on a wheel – the hub was reception. I was going to love staying there. On my way to check Josephine's room I had a quick peek into my own room. It was fabulous. Situated on the ground floor it looked out on the gardens with the swimming pool beyond. There was a huge double bed scattered with colourful cushions and a spacious, luxurious bathroom with a basket of toiletries. Josephine's room was on the first floor and it did have a balcony but the double bed was two single beds pushed together. When I reported back she decided this would be acceptable.

Two hours later I was locked out of my room wearing nothing but a swimsuit. The pool was just across the lawn outside my patio door so I had slipped out, skipped across the grass and dived in. It was lovely, the water was warm and it was nearly dark so all the hotel lights twinkled around me. When I tried to get back into my room my patio door resisted all my efforts to push it open. The turn down service had locked it. I had to walk all the way round to the front of the hotel and then through reception in a dripping swimsuit with spiky wet hair to ask someone to open my room. The receptionist could barely hide a smile as I traipsed across the marble floor behind the immaculately dressed porter.

It was a race against time to get showered and dressed before joining the group in the bar for our Information Meeting followed by a second drink to welcome us that day. This was served by a uniformed barman who was wearing white gloves – all the bar staff and waiters wore them. They looked very smart but the atmosphere was very formal. We were not allowed to carry unfinished drinks into the restaurant – they were put on a silver tray and carried ahead of us. Our evening meal was a mixture of buffet and service. The service was very precise and although it was impressive it was very difficult to relax. We dared not linger at the table as it was cleared away as soon as we finished eating. We were not allowed to take unfinished bottles of wine and water out of the restaurant to finish them in the bar. We had to leave them on the table to be taken to our bedrooms for us whether we wanted them to go there or not.

After our elegant dining experience of the previous evening breakfast in the Coffee Shop the following morning was a stark contrast. Even though I got there very early there were no empty tables so I had to wait for one to become free. I dared not leave it to join the scramble for food so I sat there until some other people arrived. The waiters were very helpful and as tables became available they extended the small table I was sitting at. During breakfast I suggested we all meet up to walk to the marina. Bert said he was 'busy' and proved to be immune to the pleadings of his female companions all of whom were on the aggressive side of assertive.

We took a short cut through the gardens to the marina beyond. It was like a film set for a Walt Disney production. The entrance resembled an archway into a castle surrounded by walls. Once inside the walls our nostrils were immediately assaulted by a very sweet smell. An extraordinary contraption was clacking away coating almonds with a chocolate mixture. We treated ourselves to a bag of the warm sticky treats and munched them as we explored the narrow shop-lined cobbled streets all leading down to the quayside. In the harbour sleek expensive yachts rubbed bows with pleasure boats including several with glass bottoms. A large wooden pirate's galleon was threading its way through the moored boats setting off for a day at sea with suitably attired tourists on board. It was the ideal setting for a relaxing holiday.

When we stopped for a coffee in one of the bars Josephine re-introduced the topic of her fiftieth birthday celebrations. I did not need reminding as I had been wondering what I was going to do. I had already established that our own hotel was not willing to provide a birthday cake. When Josephine went off to use the facilities we had a hurried discussion and everyone kindly agreed to contribute to the cost of a birthday cake but that was as far as they were prepared to go. They went off to look for a bakery while I waited for Josephine. We strolled back to the hotel together. Now that I had discovered that Josephine did not expect me to punctuate her stream of uninteresting conversation with responses all I had to do was murmur when she paused for breath; I was free to think my own thoughts.

That evening I had to break back into my own room again. I thought I had outsmarted the turn down service but I had not taken into account the porter who delivered my bathrobe. Everyone should have had a bathrobe in their room but most of us did not. I was entrusted with the task of procuring them. This proved more arduous than I had thought possible and involved several trips to reception in order to speak to the right person. The right person, the reception manager, was never available. Finally I decided to deal with the hotel manager who promised to make sure they were all delivered within the next hour. By then I was hot and flustered and decided to cool off with a swim. After pulling on my swimsuit I wrapped a towel round me and put a jacket on before exiting through the patio door. I pulled it shut so that it appeared to be locked and wedged some paper in the crack. When I returned, dripping wet, it really was locked. I could see a bathrobe on the bed which had been delivered in my absence. Every time a member of staff entered a room he checked the patio door. This time I asked reception to give me a spare key card but no, a porter was summoned and he was given custody of the key card.

The nasal tones of the singing pianist in our hotel bar after dinner drove us out on to the streets to seek alternative entertainment. We tried the hotel next door but after one drink in an empty bar we moved on to the harbour and settled down on the terrace of a bar. It was very pretty there with coloured lights decorating the surrounding bars and shops. But after one drink we were informed that the bar was closing even though it was only ten o'clock in the evening. Every shutter was down along our route so we ended our evening where it had begun, in our hotel bar. We were surrounded by large, luxury hotels but there was no night life either in the hotels or round the harbour. Yet both were buzzing during the day. I asked our barman if he could solve this mystery and he said most people went into Sousse, the nearest town, for their evening entertainment.

It was time to explore further afield and the next morning we headed for Sousse and our first taste of the real Tunisia. We travelled there on the 'Noddy' train, a tourist train that made regular journeys between the town and our resort. My 'fare' was a peck on the cheek for the conductor. He was an excitable character but when he threw back his head to laugh at one of his own jokes and banged it hard on the side of the carriage he soon quietened down. When we reached the town everyone wanted to go shopping in the souk. I had never been to a souk so I was happy to go along with my more worldly wise shopping companions. Shopping had never been a hobby of mine but I was captivated by the tiny walk-in shops crammed with colourful jewellery, hand painted ceramics and myriad leather goods. I and my shadow, Josephine, practised our skills at bargaining but only to be polite as we could not find anything we really wanted. We discovered that by offering rock bottom prices and sticking to them the stall holders soon lost interest and turned their attention to more likely prey.

While we were waiting for our companions I was approached by a man offering to take us to a carpet factory where we could view the wares over a free cup of tea. I was a novice when it came to carpet buying and they did not interest me at all but I passed the invitation on to my companions who jumped at the chance. At least it was somewhere cool to sit down and we were offered the choice of a variety of soft drinks while the carpets were rolled out on the floor in front of us. The owner took me to one side and offered me two free carpets for every one carpet my companions bought. I think he expected me to exercise my powers of persuasion but I was not comfortable with the idea of persuading someone to buy something they did not really want. And anyway, how would I get my two free carpets home if I was successful. A more pressing problem was how I was going to get free of Josephine to find a birthday card. I tried to slip away during the carpet demonstration but I was foiled by requests for advice regarding the wisdom of buying a carpet and having it shipped home. Finally, refreshed and empty handed we made our way back to our hotel.

There was no time to shop when we got back as I had arranged to meet Kalifa, our local agent, in reception. Kalifa did not arrive for our appointment and after twenty minutes I gave up waiting for him. I just had time to race to the marina to get a card and find the bakery the group had recommended. Striding along the quayside I ran the gauntlet of boatmen trying to sell me trips in their glass bottomed boat or persuade me to take the group on the pirate ship where the highlight of the trip would be walking the plank. We exchanged some light-hearted banter and when I told them I needed to find a birthday card one of them directed me to a shop that sold them. Once I had purchased a card I set off to find the bakery to order a special cake for Josephine. The owner looked rather surprised when I told him how much I was prepared to pay. I confidently quoted the price my guests had passed on to me but I still had to do a lot of hard bargaining before he came down to my offer.

Mission accomplished I returned to the hotel and sat in the bar waiting for early arrivals for our pre-dinner drinks so that I could get Josephine's card signed before she put in an appearance. I did not have long as we had succumbed to the maître d's request that we eat early. The service was better, as promised, but then the evening stretched ahead of us with very little to do. I suspected we had been asked to eat early because as we strolled down to the marina we were passed by a convoy of our waiters on scooters no doubt heading for the hot spots in Sousse. Of course we could have taken taxis into Sousse but the group turned down this proposal preferring to visit a local bar and then return to the hotel bar for a cocktail.

It was a good opportunity to go and check my emails in the business centre of our hotel. There was one from Aimee to say that one person in my Atalaya group (my previous trip) had commented that I had not played tennis or golf with the group. I responded that naturally I would have played tennis with anyone who did not have partner but the situation never arose. I would have loved to play golf with them even though it was not a golf holiday but I was sure that the company would not have covered my green fee. I received a swift response (Aimee was obviously working late) and subsequently added green fees to my list of non-claimable expenses.

The following day was the big day – Josephine's birthday! I had been dreading it as I knew she would expect me to dance attendance on her all day and make everyone we encountered aware that it was her birthday so she could collect as many birthday greetings as possible. I was at breakfast early to ensure that I got the one large table that could accommodate the whole group. The manager helped me fend off some angry Germans who usually sat there when I explained my reason for purloining 'their' table. He also made a lovely little flower arrangement for Josephine and presented it to her when she arrived. I gave her our card and invited her to join us all for lunch in the beach bar at Hannibal's Hotel. This hotel was our immediate neighbour and we had eaten there several times already so the manager was happy to accommodate us and our birthday cake. Once we had sung several rousing choruses of Happy Birthday I slipped away as I had a lot to do that morning.

My first stop was the bakery to collect the cake. It was beautiful with a special message for Josephine piped across the top. On my way to the beach bar I spotted Bert sitting outside a bar enjoying a coffee and the previous day's copy of *The Times*. I stopped for a chat and invited him to join us for lunch. Bert assured me he was enjoying his holiday and said he would probably join us later. He always joined us for dinner but then vanished into the night as soon as he had finished eating. I took the cake to the beach bar where I decorated it with some candles from my Hostess emergency kit. I got back to our hotel just in time to meet the rest of the group.

Our special lunch was a success as the staff responded enthusiastically to the occasion. When it was time for the cake they wheeled it in on a trolley draped in a white cloth. The head chef joined in the procession of waiters brandishing a large knife with which he ceremoniously sliced the cake. I think Josephine appreciated the effort that had been made on her behalf but she did so silently. When we left she asked the waiters to pack up what was left of the cake so she could take it back to her room. Personally I would have donated the remains to the staff.

When I made my way to the bar early that evening to meet Kalifa I was surprised to find that it was already very crowded. My group had refused to be lured into dinner early that evening as we had eaten a substantial lunch. I was rewarded by a second no show by Kalifa but at least he called to confirm the next excursion. By the time we arrived in the restaurant it was overflowing with people. Our table had been moved from its central position to one side. The maître d' smugly informed me that he had warned me we should dine early. It was early by English standards. Any earlier and dinner would have collided with lunch. We found ourselves in the middle of a huge Gala Dinner in honour of returning guests. All the qualifying guests had a garland of fresh flowers draped round their necks and sat on the long tables that dissected the restaurant.

Each course was a little ceremony and the whole restaurant was served at the same time – apart from our table. The waiters paraded all the way round the restaurant with dishes aloft while a band played Arabic music – loudly. As we were not part of this celebration our food was served when they could fit us in. After an hour all we had eaten was a bowl of soup. It was a set meal but it still took over two hours to serve it. The waiters were very good at avoiding eye contact and it was impossible to attract their attention. When extra items of cutlery or glass ware were required I had to get up and approach a waiter to make my request. We tried to be patient but eventually hunger overcame us and when the restaurant manager appeared I made a personal plea to end our famine. He came over to our table and apologised to the group and thereafter kept the food flowing to our table. After dinner Josephine insisted we join her in her room for drinks and more cake. I was on my own – it was one slice of cake too many for everyone else.

I struggled to wake up the following morning when my alarm went off at 04:15. I was just drifting back to sleep when I remembered why I needed to get up in the middle of the night. I had to knock on Jessica's door to wake her up. She was profoundly deaf so alarm clocks and telephones did not work. Of course her room was as far away from me as it could be – at the end of the opposite spur. I pulled on a tracksuit and set off along the deserted corridors. Reception was empty when I walked through it but a sleepy porter gave me a suspicious glance when I returned. He probably thought I was coming back from a late night assignation. Today four of them, including Josephine, were on the trip to Kairouan (an important Islam pilgrimage site). A Josephine-free day awaited me and I decided to start with an early breakfast. I was greeted by our usual waiter who informed me that the only other person in the restaurant at that hour was the director of the hotel. It was too good an opportunity to miss. I told him that my group was not happy about dinner the previous evening, especially the slow service. He said it was meant to be a special occasion for all the guests and seemed genuinely concerned that we had felt left out. He promised to 'make things right'.

After breakfast I went to reception to wait for Kalifa yet again – I hoped it would be third time lucky and it was. Kalifa did turn up and I was able to give him all the money I had collected. It was not as much as he was expecting due to Jessica confusing ten and twenty notes which were very similar. I had abandoned the idea of pointing this out to Jessica as it would have entailed shouting at the top of my voice or writing it all down. I was going to suggest he take it out of my commission but there was no commission. He let me off. I appreciated this gesture as I was personally responsible for any shortfall. By the time we had completed our business everyone had gone out and I had the rest of the morning to myself – a chance to catch up on some paperwork, a task I found quite time consuming.

When I finally emerged from my room I met some of the group setting off for afternoon tea in the marina so I joined them. We went to the bakery where I had purchased Josephine's cake. When the group told me they had not been therefore before I could feel the pink glow of embarrassment spreading across my face. It was not the bakery they had recommended and therefore had not quoted fifteen dirhams for the birthday cake. No wonder they had looked shocked when I had insisted I would only pay fifteen. Shame-faced I tried to explain what had happened to the manager but he just grinned and waved away my attempt to pay for my tea and cake.

After tea I set off for a solitary walk along the beach towards Sousse. It was beautiful. The golden sand stretched all the way to the town five miles away. I slipped off my shoes and paddled in the warm sea. As I strolled along I noticed a man squatting on the sand puffing away on his Hubble Bubble. As I came alongside him he stood up and started waving enthusiastically at me, beckoning me to go and join him. I was not sure what to do but as all the locals so far had been very friendly I set off across the sand towards him. Maybe he was going to offer me a puff on his Hubble Bubble. He was not. As soon as I got close enough to appreciate it he whipped out his male pride. I turned tail and ran.

Pushing open the door of my room I discovered a letter from the director of the hotel inviting everyone in my group to join him for a cocktail in the bar that evening – an apology for the fiasco at the gala dinner. This time our cocktails included alcohol and it was a very pleasant start to the evening. Several people expressed surprise that the director had known about our struggles at dinner the previous evening. After allowing them to speculate how he could have known – from a discrete closed circuit television system to him posing as a mystery diner – I came clean regarding our chance encounter at breakfast.

Advertised as the 'highlight of the holiday' we had all obediently signed up for the Bedouin Feast the following evening. We had swapped our dinner for lunch at the hotel's barbecue and I made the most of the abundance of grilled meat and salad. I was not really looking forward to our outing that evening as it was bound to be very touristy and accompanied by canteen type food. These assumptions were totally incorrect. When we arrived at the venue we wandered through a large ornamental garden. Working camels and grazing goats were tethered in the centre. Around the edge were small enclosures and each one was being used to demonstrate local skills. Women in traditional dress ground the flour that was used to make dough for the bread that was being baked on an open oven. We were given some to try and it was delicious.

The indoor dining area was decked out to look like a tent and we sat at low tables on plump cushions. Throughout the meal we were entertained by a succession of belly dancers, acrobats and musicians. We tucked into a tasty traditional lamb tagine with couscous. It was the first time I had tried either and I thoroughly enjoyed them. When we finished we went outside again to watch an equestrian display. The horses were splendid and galloped around the paddock their nostrils flaring and hooves thudding on the sandy surface. A variety of horsemen and acrobats demonstrated their skills for us. During this display we were enticed to buy photographs of ourselves arriving earlier that evening. I lingered by the paddock watching the horses, now free of their saddles, rolling in the sand. When I turned back everyone had disappeared and I realised our coach was about to leave. As I set off a man appeared out of the shadows and beckoned me to follow him. Thinking he was going to show me a short cut to the bus park I raced after him. When we rounded a corner I was faced with racks of unsold photographs including mine. Fortunately some of my group had also been diverted there for a third and final attempt at attracting some sales and I walked back to the bus with them.

After an early breakfast the next morning we set off on our trip to Tunis. It was so exciting to be out and about! In Tunis we had a short walking tour through the Medina (old town) and then we were let loose in the souk. I was overwhelmed by the huge, maze of narrow stall lined streets and no directions. Every few steps shopkeepers tried to coerce us into their shops and then blocked the way out. Their sales technique was very aggressive and destined for failure but I bought a pair of leather sandals just to appease them. I returned to our bus early rather than be bullied into spending more money. The guide, French and useless, was already on the bus and he took one look at my sandals and said they would not last more than one day. In an act of bravado I put them on there and then.

The guide was right and one of my new sandals came apart ten minutes after we started our tour of the ruins at Carthage. I had to perch on a wall and wait for everyone to return as I could not hop around on one sandal. From my vantage point I could see remains of the Punic columns that had once stood proud above the most beautiful and richest sea port of ancient times. It had lasted for centuries until the Romans destroyed it. I was spared the long explanations in French that were followed by a brief summary in English. It was a peaceful interlude in the shade of some trees – time to appreciate how lucky I was to experience a history hitherto confined to school textbooks.

Our next stop was Sidi Bou Said, a charming Andalucian style village. We walked up the one main cobbled street with pretty white and blue buildings on either side of us. Josephine decided she wanted to buy a particularly ugly pottery fish and asked me to bargain for it on her behalf. It was hard work but I finally got it down to the price she was prepared to pay. Triumphantly I turned to Josephine to complete the deal but all I could see was her back as she was striding up the hill away from me. I shouted after her that the price had been agreed. She shouted back that she had changed her mind. This was a serious breach of etiquette as it was considered dishonourable to withdraw an offer after it has been accepted. It was a very ugly fish and I could not bring myself to save face by buying it. I mumbled an apology and raced off to join the group. I felt very uneasy the whole time I was there in case I should be pilloried for my lack of honour.

Our last stop was the Bardo Museum. We were all flagging a bit by then but were revived by the splendours of the building that housed this museum, the former Bardo Palace. We had decided to do our own tour as the relationship between my group and the French guide had deteriorated rapidly since he announced that the English were always late or in the toilet. He said this as an aside to the French group but most of us got the gist of it. Before we could start our tour I had to wait for everyone to come back from … the toilets. They would probably be late back to the bus just to prove the guide right. We were late but not deliberately simply because we were enthralled by the wonderful mosaics and impressive ceilings. We were also delayed when Jessica had a dizzy spell on the grand staircase that swept up to the first floor. Her profound deafness sometimes affected her balance and aware of this I had been immediately behind her in case she did topple over.

It was our last dinner that evening after which we promenaded round the marina for one last time. We all agreed it had been a very relaxing week perfectly seasoned with just the right amount of culture. As we had a late departure the next day we had a final cocktail in the hotel bar. Jessica and Josephine were intent on working their way through the list and were soon pleasantly mellow. Jessica had replaced me as Josephine's new best friend so I could look forward to a peaceful journey home the following evening.

It did not work out quite as I had expected as we landed just in time to miss the last bus and I had to sleep at the airport until the first bus left the following morning. Sleep was impossible due to the constant announcements – in six languages – to keep your luggage with you at all times. I would have plenty of time to catch up on my sleep when I got home as there were very few trips in November and early December so my next trip would be a Christmas trip. I had been promised an exotic trip. But exotic in what sense, destination or hotel – I would soon find out.

Chapter 6 – December

Flashing coloured lights around the dance floor revealed faces alight with enjoyment as they cavorted wildly to the loud music. I could only watch in admiration. It was our office Christmas party and the first time I had met any of the other Hosts and Hostesses. Twenty larger than life personalities appeared to be competing to be the liveliest and the funniest in the party. But they were not competing, just letting their hair down and I was invited on to the floor to join them. We were soon chatting like old friends bonded by the vagaries of the British tourist. Petite, vivacious Wilma with her bawdy humour had me in stitches. Ryan, tall and commanding was a great raconteur and mesmerised me with his amusing stories of all the trips that had gone wrong. It was a great opportunity to glean some tips regarding our role. But it was also daunting to discover just how many things could go wrong from clients missing buses to the Host himself being left behind by the local guide.

When there was a lull in the entertainment I told Ryan I was heading for Florida for Christmas. I had been told I had been 'awarded' this trip for good behaviour. His silence spoke volumes. None of the regulars had volunteered for this trip as there had always been problems – possibly due to a local agent who was inclined to hysteria. This did not deter me at all – I was not the hysterical type. Ryan would be passing through Fort Lauderdale on his Caribbean cruise so we arranged to meet up. This would be the third time he had done this cruise and he was hoping for a good one. The first time the weather had been appalling and the cruise had been a disaster. The second time one of his group had taken himself home without telling anyone and Ryan had stopped the ship mid ocean convinced that he had jumped overboard.

On the journey to Florida I had a moment of panic at Gatwick airport when I could not find everyone in the group before we boarded. The queues to check-in had been so long that several people had to go straight from there to the boarding gate. I was able to confirm that everyone was on board but I was not allowed to know where they were sitting. I had just settled in my seat when an announcement was made requesting that a representative from my company should press the call button. Trembling with trepidation I did so. A very cheery stewardess trotted down the aisle to tell me that one of the women in my group had wanted to check that I was on board. Knowledge of my presence was clearly sufficient as she never came to find me during our eight hour flight.

There was plenty of time to speak to all my guests as we shuffled along in the queues to get through immigration. We were all together when we spilled out into the Arrivals hall and found our agent Mary Beth waiting for us. She looked more like a girl guide in her aertex shirt and long tailored shorts. Round spectacles perched on a snub nose in an oval face that was framed by a short, dark bob. She took over immediately confidently bustling around the group offering help with luggage but moving on before it could be accepted. She organised us into a crocodile to walk to the bus. I was placed at the back, the support to her leading role.

It was just fifteen minutes to our hotel, the Riverside Hotel. This lovely, colonial style building was right on the main street of Fort Lauderdale, Las Olas Boulevard which was lined with shops, bars and restaurants. At the back of the hotel was an open-air swimming pool on the bank of the Inter Coastal Waterway. Mary Beth told me that it had been renovated since last year so that was good news as I knew the reports regarding the hotel had been less than favourable. She was quite nervous and clearly anxious that the trip should go without a hitch this time. She told me that last year she and the Hostess had sobbed together in an empty room on New Year's Eve after their guests had stormed off to find some entertainment. She really was a drama queen.

Once everyone had checked in to the hotel and gone to their rooms Mary Beth and I sat in reception to discuss the itinerary for our trip. We were interrupted when Maisie appeared dragging an empty suitcase behind her. She claimed that the case had been damaged in transit. It was so battered I was not surprised she had not noticed the new dent at the airport. Her lank hair and pinched face suggested she had not eaten a good meal for some time and her thin frame was draped with shabby clothes. I suspected she had sacrificed a lot to come on this holiday. Mary Beth immediately took charge. She was not going to be drawn on the possibility that the damage may have been caused during the transfer to our hotel but agreed to call the airline the next day. I doubted that they would be interested as such matters had to be reported before leaving the airport but I said nothing. I would speak to Maisie later. Maisie was clearly disappointed that Mary Beth did not make the call immediately but finally accepted that nothing was going to be done and she left with the offending suitcase. We did not have time to finish our deliberations regarding the itinerary as it was time to meet the group in the bar.

Our Welcome Drink was very informal as everyone had a voucher and could choose one drink. We were all crushed together in a noisy crowded bar and it was impossible to do more than remind everyone that we had the Information Meeting in the morning. Then we went in search of somewhere to have dinner. The bright lights of Las Olas Boulevard twinkled at us from beyond the bar and with one accord we spilled out on to the pavement and set off to explore. Five people had already formed their own group and been christened The Quintet by the others. They were all high flyers, smartly dressed and self-assured and seeking exclusivity so they decided not to join the rest of us for dinner. They did not want to be herded around in a large group. The rest of us dined at the Café Europa which satisfied our need for some food and fast. I had forgotten how large the portions were and when my sandwich arrived I could not resist asking the waiter if it was meant for two people. He was not amused.

The next day, Christmas Eve, did not start well as most of the rooms were without hot water. After reporting this to reception I went to breakfast and was faced with another problem. The Indigo Grill would not accept our breakfast vouchers and when I finally talked them round they would only offer us two choices, a continental or a cooked breakfast. It was a very unhappy group that gathered for the Information Meeting outside by the pool. Even the blue sky and brilliant sunshine did not cheer them up. Mary Beth promised to deal with both problems as soon as the meeting finished. She did not escape the firing line that easily as the group were also unhappy about the high prices for the optional excursions on offer. I could see the hysteria bubbling up inside her as she moved swiftly on to discuss Christmas traditions in Florida. When she asked if everyone had brought something red to wear that evening the hostile silence told her they had not. No one had suggested that we did. There was no mention of this tradition in our information so no one was prepared. Mary Beth stuttered that she had told my company to give us this information. I could see the tears welling up and began hunting through my pockets for a handkerchief.

Realising that her audience was more interested in reclining on their sun beds than discussing optional excursions Mary Beth hastily arranged another meeting that evening when she would give each person a list of all the excursions available and the prices. She warned everyone that this would be their only chance to book the trips and that they should bring their money as well. Her system was very inflexible as people had to make up their minds and pay very early on in the holiday. No refunds would be available if people dropped out, whatever the reason. This was a real deterrent as far as some people were concerned. I tried to soften her approach by offering to take the numbers and collect the money over the following days. I was smartly informed that this was her responsibility and hers alone. I was not even allowed to be the understudy to this leading lady. It did relieve me of the burden and I could relax and enjoy the cruise on the Inter-Coastal Waterways later that morning.

Everyone cheered up as we chugged along the waterways in our little boat. We even spotted some manatees. This extraordinary animal resembles a cross between a furry hippopotamus and a turtle. They swim very close to the surface and are often injured by motor boats speeding along the inter-linked canals. This area was clearly a sanctuary for the rich and famous and most of the commentary related to who lived in which house. Expensive Christmas decorations festooned the immaculate lawns of the rich and famous. It was very strange seeing Christmas trees lit up under a shining sun. My reverie was interrupted when Maisie appeared by my side and diffidently asked me if there was any news about her damaged case. I had no news for her but pointed out that it was the holiday period so it may be difficult to get through to someone. I suggested she waited until we got back to Gatwick and reported it there. I felt very protective towards Maisie as she did not seem to be making any friends in the group. When I asked her if she was enjoying the holiday her eyes lit up – just being there seemed to be sufficient.

We had a second hot water failure that evening and I complained to the girls on reception. As they were students working over the holiday period guests without hot water were a matter of indifference to them. I persisted and eventually they found a manager I could speak to. But he was a temporary manager and waved aside my suggestion that those who had been without water since they arrived should be offered room changes. He gave me a list of empty rooms that did have hot water and suggested I organised a rota for their use. Several people were still rushing around the hotel looking for hot water when the time came for our meeting with Mary Beth so attendance was poor. The Quintet had elected Brenda, a very forceful personality, as their ambassador and she arrived and announced that the trips were too expensive and they could do the same trips more cheaply using public transport. They were probably right but these trips would not include a guide. Very few trips were booked so I negotiated a third meeting the next day for final numbers.

The group were informed of this amnesty when they gathered in reception to go out to dinner that evening. Mary Beth took us to the Sky Café opposite our hotel for our first included dinner. She announced that everything, including the tips had been pre-paid and all we had to pay for were our drinks. She introduced me to the manager and then left. Before we were served our food we ordered our drinks. These orders were taken and the drinks were brought to our table by the same waiters who served our food.

When I was presented with the drinks bill eighteen per cent had been added for tips. Some people had already left and had put their money on the table and others refused to pay any extra for the tip and marched out of the restaurant leaving me to deal with the shortfall. When the manager came to collect the money I queried the inclusion of extra tips. He claimed that different waiters and waitresses had served our drinks. But this was not true and I said so. I stood my ground and the extra charge was removed. But the damage had been done and the incident had left an unpleasant taste.

By the time I had sorted out the bill with the manager everyone had left the restaurant and I was free to make my way back to the hotel. I went up to my room and was soon surrounded by a pile of Christmas presents (provided by my company) and packets of sticky-backed bows that had to be attached to them before dinner the following evening. These presents had filled half my suitcase so I would be glad to be rid of them but it was a nice gesture and I looked forward to giving them out the next day. I called Mary Beth and asked her why a gratuity had been added to our drinks bill. She said she had suggested it as this was what we did in England. She could have run it by me first but I managed not to point this out and even kept my thoughts regarding the tipping system in America to myself. Mary Beth had already made it clear that she would have preferred a more experienced Hostess accompanying the group so it was unlikely she would ever consult me about anything.

I woke the next morning, Christmas morning, feeling very much in the spirit of the occasion. Our hotel was beautifully decorated and the streets were very festive. The breakfast problem had been resolved and we had a lovely waiter, Josh, looking after us. He had arrived early and pushed several small tables together to make one long one. Then he had placed a photocopy of a very varied menu at each setting. As each guest arrived he was immediately by their side with his jugs of juice and coffee. It was a good start to our day.

Our peace was shattered when Brenda rushed in, wild eyed and every hair out of place screaming for help. I leapt from my seat and through her hysterical ramblings worked out that Helena, with whom she shared a room, was seriously ill. I said I would go and see her immediately. Brenda clutched my arm, restraining me and shrieking that she was scared of catching some dreadful disease from Helena. She escorted me to reception to prevent me escaping to deal with Helena who was top of my list of priorities. Brenda was one of The Quintet so there had been no opportunity to get to know her. I had no idea if she was inclined to over react or if she had seen this as an opportunity to get a single room which would isolate her from everyone except her chosen companions.

As Brenda and Helena were paying a reduced price to share a twin I was very surprised when the hotel agreed to give them each a single room. I was also relieved as I was anxious to get to Helena to find out what was wrong with her. Brenda had not given any hint of what the problem might be and as soon as she had procured her own room key she had raced off to have some breakfast. Helena appeared to be suffering from a heavy cold. She did not want to see a doctor. As she did not have any medication with her and I was not allowed to give her any of mine I asked reception where I might find a pharmacy. All the shops were closed that day but I but I managed to find some cold remedy tablets in the hotel gift shop and bought some for Helena.

When I got back to the dining room everyone was still there and we decided to get the local bus to the beach. When we got there some people stretched out on the sand to sunbathe and the rest of us strolled along the front. People whizzed past us on blades and bikes and there were lots of joggers and walkers. Our steps quickened as we soaked up the atmosphere. Some shops and bars were open so we stopped for a drink. I had a gigantic iced tea and after two hours I still had not managed to finish it. During a lull in the conversation I began counting people in my head and I realised that I had not seen Barnaby that morning. He had told me the previous evening that he was recovering from a severe bout of flu, so bad he had even contemplated cancelling his holiday. When I mentioned his absence the others all insisted they had seen him at breakfast and that he was fine. I was not convinced and I decided to return to our hotel to see if he was there.

It was so pleasant strolling along the beach paddling in the sea that I nearly abandoned my mission but some instinct urged me to turn away from the beach and follow the road back to the hotel. I called Barnaby's room and he was there. He had gone back to bed after breakfast and said he would stay there for the rest of the day. All he wanted was some cold beer to soothe his sore throat. I arranged to have some sent to his room. I also checked on Helena who whispered down the telephone that she was okay. It was time to put out the Christmas presents so I collected them from my room and took them to our private dining room. As I stepped through the door it felt as though I had stepped back into my own front room. The flames of an artificial coal fire were reflected in the silver baubles that adorned an old fashioned Christmas tree. I looked forward to our seasonal celebration later.

I changed for dinner and then went back to the restaurant and asked the maître d' to send a light meal up to Helena in her room. I called Barnaby as well to see if he had changed his mind about having some dinner but his telephone was engaged. He was probably calling home to exchange greetings with family and friends. By popular request our meeting time that evening had been brought forward in order to take advantage of Happy Hour when we could consume two drinks for the price of one. None of my guests were there but I was cordially invited to join Christian, a drunken Brit who was propping up the bar. He wished me a Happy Christmas and then insisted on treating me to two very insipid gin and tonics. Christian was hugging an alligator, a carved one, which was probably the only company he had had all day. I was glad when some members of my group arrived and rescued me. The room was buzzing with bonhomie and even The Quintet had been touched by the Christmas spirit. I felt sad that Helena and Barnaby were not able to join us.

As we left the bar I called Barnaby again but his line was still engaged. I could not relax and enjoy the convivial atmosphere and refused some wine when it was offered to me despite the assurances of my companions that I was 'allowed' to drink on Christmas Day. My vision of Barnaby chatting happily to friends on the phone had suddenly become one of a seriously ill Barnaby sprawled in his bed having knocked the phone off the hook. I called once again – the phone was still engaged. I raced up to his room and hammered on the door. When he opened the door and asked what day it was I realised he was seriously ill and needed to see a doctor immediately. For a split second I stood rooted to the spot as myriad thoughts raced through my mind. Would I find a doctor on call on Christmas night?

The girl on reception was very clear – there were no doctors on call that night. Our only option was to go to the Emergency Room (ER) of the local hospital. I nodded in agreement wondering how I was going to get there. But she was already on the telephone ordering a taxi – they, unlike doctors, were available any time any day. I went back to the restaurant to tell the group what was happening and then collected Barnaby from his room and we set off to the hospital.

Although it was Christmas night there was no room in the ER. I felt as though I had walked on to the television set. There were many more relatives and friends than there were patients. Barnaby was seen by the triage nurse as soon as we arrived and given some medication to reduce his fever. We managed to find two empty seats to await our turn. A television blared above us and people were constantly coming and going. One family went out and came back with an enormous tub of Kentucky Fried Chicken which they all tucked into including the 'patient'. This was the final straw for the staff and all the non-patients were escorted down the corridor to a second waiting room. There was no television and it was full of huge comfortable armchairs.

I was woken up by Barnaby who had come to tell me he was fed up with waiting and wanted to go back to the hotel. I could not allow him to leave until he had seen someone and as we had been there for four hours it was time to take action. I chased the triage nurse round the ER until she found a doctor to attend to Barnaby. Antibiotics were prescribed and we hailed a taxi and set off for the nearest pharmacy. I was relieved when we pulled into a huge shopping mall and I could see multi-coloured lights above the pharmacy announcing that it was open twenty-four hours a day for 365 days of the year. But not that day. Our taxi driver was very obliging and we tried two more pharmacies before giving up and going back to the hotel. We arrived there as dawn was breaking.

After just two hours' sleep I had to get up and start working my way through a long list of things to do. First I had to deal with a complaint from The Quintet that we were only scheduled to have four dinners whereas our brochure stated that five dinners were included. Aimee was away for Christmas so I would have to send the fax to the general office and hope that someone would pick it up before next year and deal with the problem. I also had to check on Helena and then find a pharmacy that stocked the drugs that Barnaby needed. I was at our breakfast table very early sipping black coffee and composing my fax when Edgar and Tristan joined me. They were early because they wanted me to sort out a shopping trip that morning. Some of the local shopping malls organised transport between the mall and local hotels but I needed to check that this service was available on Boxing Day. I added this extra item to my growing list. While my fax was being sent the girl on reception booked the shopping mall shuttle. She was surprised when I suggested the shops may be shut. In Florida Christmas only lasts for twenty-four hours and then it is business as usual.

Before anyone else could waylay me I set off down the main boulevard to find a pharmacy to fill Barnaby's prescription. The drugs were going to cost over $100 which I did not have so I returned to the hotel empty handed. I had to go back there anyway to ensure that the shuttle bus arrived on time and the shoppers were there to meet it. Once they were on their way my next stop was the local supermarket to buy some orange juice for Helena and Barnaby and then deliver it to their rooms. Helena said she was no better and she needed to see a doctor. Barnaby was happy to hand over his credit card so that I could pay for his prescription and I went off to collect it straight away.

On my way out of the hotel I asked reception to call the emergency doctor to make an appointment for Helena. On my way back they informed me that the emergency doctor was off-duty for another two days so the only option was the ER. Helena did not want to go there and she decided she would continue to suffer but not in silence. It was an hour before I was able to get away. Finally I had time to ring Mary Beth and alert her to the problem of the 'missing' dinner. She was not interested as her brief was to provide four dinners and she had done that. I also informed her that Barnaby and Helena were ill but I did not expect her to offer any assistance. She did not.

My next task was another hot water patrol and once my statistics were completed I delivered them to the manager. Some people were still without hot water and having to shower in other rooms. It would have been easier if they just changed rooms but the hotel was still resisting this solution. When Maisie was told to shower in the swimming pool changing rooms I insisted that a permanent solution be found. But Maisie was equally insistent that she did not want to make a fuss and as she did not want to change her room I could only hope that the plumbing would soon be fixed.

It was time to check on my patients again. Barnaby was the same and waiting for the antibiotics to kick in. Helena said she would order some fruit to eat. I offered to take her to the ER but she wanted to go somewhere with an appointment system. I did not blame her but I was concerned as she did not seem to be getting any better. Brenda and Sophie were in reception waiting for their cronies when I asked the receptionist if they were sure there were no doctors on call that day. They butted into my conversation to say they thought I should be doing more to find a solution. Short of throwing Helena over my shoulder and dragging her down to the ER I did not see what else I could do.

I turned to Mary Beth in my hour of need. She was already on her way to the hotel for her second attempt to collect the money for the trips. Mary Beth confirmed it was well-nigh impossible to find a doctor during the holiday period. Nevertheless when she arrived she telephoned a friend of hers who knew a doctor. The friend rang the doctor and the doctor rang the hotel. He spoke to both Mary Beth and Helena and an appointment was arranged for Helena at nine o'clock the following morning. Mary Beth then organised some beef broth to be sent to Helena in her room. I was dispatched to the pharmacy to get some extra strength Tylenol to control Helena's temperature.

Once I had delivered the medication to Helena it was a mad rush to get everyone together and ready to leave for the dinner cruise that evening. Our departure time came and went and we were still missing some people so I had to chase them up. Maisie had changed her mind as her feet ached from walking around the shopping mall all day. I persuaded her to join us by pointing out that as she had already paid she would not get a refund. Basil slurred down the phone that he was too tired. I reminded him and the two other no shows that they would still have to pay. But I was only the messenger and whether or not they paid was Mary Beth's problem. Her system did work in my favour after all. Mary Beth also gave me a message to pass on to Maisie regarding the damaged case. She said she had spoken to the airline and Maisie had to contact them at Gatwick and tape it up in the meantime. I thanked her profusely for taking the trouble to make this one phone call. It was important to maintain a friendly relationship with our local agent. Maisie was so overjoyed when I gave her this news I did not have the heart to tell her that it was not a foregone conclusion that the airline would do anything about it.

Our cruise went out to sea and then came back again two hours later but it was a great success. When we boarded the boat there were crowds of people milling around the decks. Soon after we set sail everyone vanished and we were the only people outside apart from a band playing on the deck above us. It was eerie and I went off to explore in case we were missing something. We were not. Our boat was one huge casino and the tables and gaming machines had opened as soon as we were beyond territorial waters. The gaming room was packed with people and the fruit machines, a whole room of them, were busy all evening. People sat there on high stools hunched over the spinning symbols either grabbing handfuls of coins from a plastic bucket on their lap or deducting the stake from a credit card slotted into the machine. We were not there to gamble and we had our dinner in a deserted restaurant before going up to the top deck to drink beer and dance to the live music.

My cheerful mood was slightly dimmed when we got back to the hotel and there was still no response from my company. If my company confirmed that five dinners were included in this trip I would have to organise another meal as Mary Beth was not prepared to do it. No wonder she had reduced my colleague to tears last year.

I was up with the lark the next morning for an early breakfast before waking Helena at seven to take her to the surgery at eight thirty. Josh was already on duty and had anticipated my order, the fruit platter. It was wonderful, orange, strawberries, melon (two kinds), mango, banana, blackberries and raspberries. We were all transferring to the Hollywood Beach later that morning and it was the last time Josh would be waiting on us. As soon as some other guests joined me in the restaurant I said goodbye to Josh and gave him what I considered to be a well-earned tip. While I was waiting for Helena in reception I was given a fax from my office. I did have to arrange an extra meal.

On our way to the medical centre Helena gave me her insurance policy to read as she wanted me to check that she would be covered for this visit. Included in the policy details was a free toll number to call in case of medical emergency! It was a knuckle chewing moment. While I was running around trying to find a doctor all she had needed to do was pick up the phone. I pointed this out and she just shrugged. I was not sure if a cold would count as an emergency although I knew a lot of men who were sure that the common cold could be fatal.

And that was what the doctor diagnosed – a bad case of the common cold. As soon as we got back to our hotel I was counting cases ready to load onto the bus to move on to our next destination. Hollywood Beach had been billed as 'fantastic' by Mary Beth who had promised us that we would love it. But even before our bus had come to a halt I was plunged into a state of shock. Our hotel, a bright pink monstrosity towered above a garish shopping mall. I started checking people in hoping that the rooms looked better from the inside than they did from the outside. They did not. Before everyone had their keys some people were already back in reception claiming that their rooms were 'awful'. The hotel did change some of them immediately.

Throughout this mayhem Brenda was stuck to my side like glue. She was demanding a room on her own insisting that I had no right to expose her to Helena's germs. Her constant badgering presence made it very difficult to deal with all the other problems that were happening around us. Helena had been given her key first and was now resting in her room which was another source of annoyance for Brenda.

I decided it would be better if I spoke to the manageress in private so I asked the receptionist to arrange this for me. She was as anxious to give Brenda the slip as I was and ushered me into an office behind her desk. The manageress was understanding but could only offer me an extra single on payment of a daily supplement of sixty dollars. She explained that we were not staying in a hotel but a large block of condominiums each of which was privately owned. She could not allow one to be used rent free regardless of the circumstances. Once the setup had been explained to me I could understand why there was such a difference in the standards of the rooms. It was a strange choice of venue for our group and I was glad that Brenda had not been a party to our discussion.

Brenda refused to pay the supplement and she refused to share with Helena. I reminded her that she had booked a twin and that the doctor had said that Helena was not infectious. It made no difference. There was only one alternative. I gave her the key to my room. It was accepted with very bad grace.

When I moved in with Helena she complained bitterly because she felt that her malaise entitled her to the single room. She did have a point but I did not think Brenda would appreciate it. I was already in Brenda's bad books as her case had mysteriously been left at the Riverside Hotel. It had been with all the other cases before the bus was loaded but was not with them when they were unloaded from the bus. I had called the hotel and the manager had called back to say they had located it in the ladies' cloakroom where Brenda had no doubt left it after doing some re-packing. It was on its way and I had promised to wait in reception until it was delivered and then take it to her room.

I was a sitting target as I waited in reception. The replacement rooms were worse than the originals. Even our most optimistic guests were visibly upset as they catalogued their complaints. The rooms were small, most of them needed a good clean and several people had to sleep on pull down Murphy beds. I had a look at two of the rooms and they were quite right, they were appalling. It was unacceptable and I needed to contact Mary Beth without delay.

First I had to deliver Brenda's luggage. I steeled myself to enter her room knowing that I would get a hostile reception. I did not know how to deal with the situation so I decided to play the fool. When Brenda invited me to enter I went down on all fours and crawled into the room pushing the case in front of me. This penitential gesture back fired spectacularly as Brenda was not alone. The Quintet sat in a row on a huge white leather sofa. I stumbled to my feet hindered by the deep shag pile carpet. The room was a confectionery of white – carpet, embroidered bedspread and lacy blinds. The blood rushed to my face as I realised that it should have been mine.

I gulped down a great dollop of humble pie in front of all of them. But an apology was not enough. They wanted an inquest about the holiday so far. They aired all their grievances but their main gripe was the dinner cruise they did not go on. This was my fault because I had not insisted that they came with us. They had been adamant that they did not want to go and subsequently regretted this decision. Mary Beth's system came to my rescue again and I reminded them that there had been two opportunities to book the trips when Mary Beth came to the hotel. They were obviously aware that this was happening because they had sent Brenda to represent them. When I pointed this out they claimed that although that was what they said it was not what they meant! I apologised yet again and this time it was accepted graciously and we parted on good terms.

At last I was free to call Mary Beth and informed her that the hotel was totally unsuitable. Mary Beth contacted the manageress who called me and said they would offer some of the group upgrades. Both of them were unaware that this had already been done and the upgraded rooms had been no better than the original rooms. It was not just the rooms – the whole place was unsuitable. Mary Beth was not convinced claiming that it was her favourite hotel. When she realised I was serious she said she thought that maybe we could go back to the Riverside Hotel but they would not be able to accommodate the whole group on New Year's Eve then she hung up on me. I felt very alone but I had to tough it out.

Mary Beth had promised to call me back but she did not and I had to face them all at dinner. Maisie decided not to join us because she had been eating pizza all afternoon. She loved it at the Hollywood Beach. Basil did not appear either. He had been taking full advantage of the cheap beer and was still in the bar. Everyone was subdued. It was not just the rooms but some people had checked out the venue for our New Year's Eve celebrations. O'Malleys Bar was a rather uninteresting shell on the beach where barbecues were held. They were already looking for an alternative venue for their celebrations. We were united in our disappointment regarding our new hotel. Spirits lifted when I had told them we were working on moving back to the Riverside.

After dinner I called Mary Beth but she was not answering on either her home number or her emergency number I called the Riverside Hotel. They said they would be delighted to take us back but there was a problem regarding New Year's Eve. I decided to go ahead and transfer back and worry about New Year's Eve later. I found those who were still up and told them we were moving back to the Riverside the next morning. Joy all round. I sat on the corridor floor under the watchful eye of the closed circuit television camera and wrote out notes to slip under the doors of those I had not seen. I did not get back to my room until nearly one o'clock that night. Helena was in bed and I had to stumble around in the dark trying to undress in the six inch space between the two beds – a Murphy bed and a sofa bed. I had the sofa bed which was very narrow and uncomfortable. It was impossible to sleep.

At five the following morning I faxed my company to inform them we were moving back to the Riverside Hotel. I could not use the phone in my room as Helena was there. The hotel would not let me make an international call from the lobby so faxing was the only option. I hung around waiting for a response until I was distracted by the sunrise and went down to the beach to watch it. It really was a beautiful beach and it stretched for miles. The sea beyond the sand was a massive blue mill pond. The walkway by the beach was already a hive of activity full of people power walking, jogging, cycling, skateboarding and roller blading. I called in at reception on my way to breakfast but there was no response to my fax. It seemed that the decision to move back to the Riverside Hotel was going to rest solely with me.

Breakfast at the Juice Calaboose was such a terrible experience it was comical. All the meals were pre-plated, wrapped in cling film and then zapped in the microwave. They were eaten from plastic plates with plastic knives and forks as we perched on plastic chairs placed around plastic tables. We had to compete for these tables with everyone else having breakfast in the Food Market. When Maisie appeared she announced that she was not moving back to the Riverside Hotel. She had been bored there whereas here she could watch films and eat pizzas all day. She certainly looked more relaxed. I agreed to arrange it. She would not be alone as Basil had also decided this was his preferred venue. I informed Mary Beth who had come out of hiding once the decision to move back to Fort Lauderdale had been made. She seemed to think that we would all be coming back to the Hollywood Beach to celebrate the New Year but I had other ideas. I was going to book a dinner cruise on the waterways.

Our transfer the following morning coincided with a trip to the Everglades and a day out The Quintet had organised in a hire car so I had to deal with their luggage as well as my own. Before we left I told both Maisie and Basil that they were welcome to join us on New Year's Eve but their response was lukewarm. I promised to call them every day before jumping on the bus and setting off for the Riverside Hotel and the next problem – would we have enough rooms for the whole group on New Year's Eve. I had heard that a large snowstorm was brewing over Chicago which could affect travel plans and maybe release a few more rooms.

It was so nice to be back in a decent bedroom and all to myself. Helena and Brenda also had their own rooms so everyone was happy. To celebrate our return we had an impromptu room party organised by Edgar in the room he was sharing with Tristan. The group had moved on and the horrors of Hollywood Beach were becoming a distant memory. No doubt they would be relived in the feedback forms but I had encouraged everyone to forget it for now and get on and enjoy the holiday – it seemed they had taken my advice. After toasting our return we got the Beach Express to the seafront to find somewhere for dinner. In theory the little train was free but in practice the driver expected a dollar from each person every time they used it.

We woke to unsettled weather the following morning and lingered over breakfast discussing our options. Josh was our waiter again and we were taking full advantage of his attentive service and languished in the restaurant until the sun came out and we moved outside to the pool. Everyone was very relaxed. Helena had emerged from her room at last. She said she still felt ill although she did not want to consult the doctor again. Barnaby was fine now but I suspected that Sophie was not very well as she had been unusually quiet at breakfast. The large snowstorm across Central America had become a reality and several rooms had been cancelled. We were now just three rooms short.

When we met later to go out for dinner Helena took a leading role in the discussion about where we should eat. She suggested a Chinese restaurant. No one else was in favour of that option so she formed a group of one and stormed off to find the restaurant of her choice. I had to stay until the final decision was made but I noticed Edgar slipped out shortly after she left and hoped that he had gone to join her. As we could not agree on a particular restaurant we all went to the sea front and split into small groups to suit tastes and pockets. As I was strolling back to our hotel I met Edgar on his way to find the others. He had eaten with Helena but said she had barely spoken to him throughout the meal. I was not surprised as Edgar had gained a reputation for winding people up and most of us chose our words carefully before engaging in conversation with him. I thanked him for trying.

I was excited the next morning when I set off for the shopping mall. It was not the shopping that had aroused this emotion but the thought of meeting up with Ryan, a fellow Host, whose cruise ship had docked in Fort Lauderdale. I was longing to tell him that despite all the problems I had encountered I had not once resorted to tears. I had a list of items required by people who could not drag themselves away from their sun worshipping and I needed to find a card for

Tristan's birthday the following day. After waiting in vain for Ryan at Dunkin' Donuts I returned to the hotel and made my daily call to Maisie and Basil. Maisie answered and said she was fine but Basil was not in his room (he never was) so I left a message to call me in case of need. There was a message on my phone from reception. Ryan had called to say that one of his guests had collapsed in the shopping mall and he had gone to the hospital with him.

Ryan called me later when we were all assembled for our trip to Coconut Grove in Miami. While I was talking to him Mary Beth arrived and escorted everyone to the bus. I was surprised to see her as she was not joining us on this trip. As soon as I finished talking to Ryan I raced to the bus and met Mary Beth coming towards me. She strode past barely acknowledging my presence. On the bus the group were sitting in silence. I asked what had happened and they told me that Mary Beth had boarded the bus and 'apologised' and 'explained' about Hollywood Beach. Some said she had offered one hundred dollars cash refund (to be spent here) and some thought it was one hundred pounds. Whichever it was they were not happy and had not accepted her offer as she had only spoken to the nine people on the coach and they felt everyone should have been approached together. I was so disappointed. I had spent the last few days smoothing ruffled feathers and now Mary Beth had rubbed salt into healing wounds ruining the happy atmosphere I had worked hard to create.

We soon forgot about Mary Beth as we began our evening at Monty's where their Happy Hour was truly happy and featured a raw seafood bar. We queued up and heaped oysters and prawns on our plates for a very reasonable price. We decided to stay there for dinner as well to soak up more of the great atmosphere while enjoying good food accompanied by pitchers of beer. When we finally dragged ourselves away from Monty's we went to Bayside. This complex was quite something; lots of shops and eating places surrounded a small bay that formed part of the Inter Coastal Waterway. The boats on its surface were lit up and cast colourful reflections in the water below. The live music put a spring in our step as we strolled round. Some good news awaited me when we got back to our hotel. We were just one room short for the next night and that was my room. But I had a plan. Austin had to leave very early on New Year's Day so I could have his room after he left. All I had to do was stay awake until five in the morning.

Breakfast the next morning was a double celebration. It was New Year's Eve and Tristan's birthday. Tristan was very popular with the group. When he arrived at breakfast Josh presented him with a Danish pastry with a lighted candle on the top and we all sang Happy Birthday. His gifts included a huge card with a silly badge and some pants with a rude message on the back. Everyone rose to the spirit of the occasion except Helena. I had booked the Galleria free shuttle for her and she had gone shopping on her own. She was not making much effort to mix with the group. If the group decided to go shopping on Tuesday she had to go on Monday. Sophie had not been to breakfast. As her plump figure suggested, she was very fond of her food so this did not bode well.

When I rang Sophie she insisted that she was fine but asked me if I had any aspirin. Legally we were not allowed to dispense any drugs to clients as we were not qualified to do so. I went to her room to explain this. She looked dreadful so I advised her to see a doctor but she said she did not want to. I was so concerned about her that I called her friend on the pretext of asking if she had any aspirin she could give to Sophie. Leila agreed to talk to Sophie and persuaded her that she should see a doctor. I prepared myself for another visit to the ER.

The regular General Manager was back on duty and he found a medical centre that was open. He also arranged for the hotel courtesy bus to take us there and told me to call them when we were ready to come back. We were at the medical centre for over two hours. When I tried to pick up the drugs on the way back they were not ready. However, the driver who collected us said he would go back later to collect them and deliver them to Sophie's room. Now I could relax and get ready for the evening's celebrations.

We started with drinks in Tristan and Edgar's room to celebrate the English New Year and Tristan's birthday. I was also celebrating the news that I could keep my room that night. The evening had started really well and although Maisie and Basil had declined our invitation to join us I was sure they were having just as good a time as we were in their own ways.

I was humming to myself as I skipped along the corridor to reception. My heart sank when I saw Mary Beth waiting there. She had an envelope bursting with hundred dollar notes that she told me she was going to hand out to the group. She was adamant that the group had agreed to accept them as compensation. This was news to me. As far as I knew no agreement had been reached with anyone. I did not want her to spoil our evening so I suggested we deal with it the next day. She told me to back off as it was up to her to deal with the problem as she saw fit and her arrangements with my company were none of my business. This exchange was done very discreetly as we muttered at each other out of the corners of our mouths making sure we maintained smiling countenances. As Mary Beth continued to stand her ground I felt surrender was the best policy and pleading a forgotten item in my room I withdrew.

When I rejoined the group Mary Beth and her compensation had been sent packing and the group were anxious to continue their celebrations. And we did so in style as we steamed along the waterways. People on other boats shouted greetings as they passed by. Every boat was decorated with twinkling lights. The waterside houses and restaurants all looked splendid with their illuminated Christmas decorations. After dinner there was a disco on the deck. The dancing was not just lively but also very silly. I rowed to the rowing song, mimed enthusiastically to YMCA and wriggled and strutted to the chicken song.

At midnight all the boats on the river stopped and sounded their horns while we sang Auld Lang Syne. We danced until we docked at one o'clock. On our way back to our hotel we hijacked the Beach Express and went up and down the Boulevard singing and shouting Happy New Year until the driver announced he was finishing for the night and we had to get off. In our opinion the night was still young so we moved on to a bar. There was only time for one drink as it closed at two. America closed at two so a few of us decided to go back to Edgar's room and finish the drinks left over from our celebrations earlier. The lift stopped at the wrong floor and we all got out and woke up a guest as we searched in vain for the right room. He was wearing his pyjamas when he threw open his door shouting, "Pleeeease, some of us are trying to sleep!" Was it the accent or the striped pyjamas, I don't know but we all got the giggles and scuttled back into the lift. I felt like a joint conspirator and not a responsible holiday rep – but it was fun.

Chapter 7 - January

A persistent ringing from somewhere far away penetrated my mind and woke me up. I tried to go back to sleep but it just went on and on. I rolled over. Through half open eyes I could see that it was still dark. I groaned and renewed my efforts to return to oblivion. But images began rolling through my muzzy head – Edgar and I astride the decorative lion that guarded the hotel entrance; riding up and down in the hotel lift giggling insanely and creeping along the hotel corridors whispering conspiratorially. Had I really behaved like that?

I tried to bury my head in my pillows but the ringing continued. Now it was louder and closer. It was the phone on my bedside table. I answered it and a cheery voice informed me that it was my wake-up call. Was this a joke? Had I really asked someone to call me in the middle of the night? I said thank you and as I replaced the phone I caught sight of a note I had written for myself. Austin 04:30. It was all coming back to me. Austin was leaving very early that morning. I had promised to call him. I dialled his room number and he answered immediately. He was up and ready to go. He did not expect me to get up and go downstairs to say goodbye. That was a relief, as I could not keep my eyes open.

I did go back to sleep but when I woke up I was still haunted by scenes of the celebrations the previous evening. I decided to get up. This was a struggle as my legs were sore after my efforts to follow the actions of the chicken song. The manager wished me a Happy New Year as I went through reception. I stopped to speak to him. Now was a good time to apologise for our behaviour in the early hours of that morning. He had not received any complaints but thanked me for my confession. I had considered lying low but now my conscience was clear and I could enjoy the rest of my day.

It was definitely the last morning we would see our lovely breakfast waiter Josh as he was not working the next day, our last day. We all said goodbye and I gave him another good tip from our collection. His attentive service and cheerful demeanour had certainly enhanced our stay there. When I got back to my room my telephone rang immediately and I had to listen to Mary Beth trilling about the wonderful New Year's Eve celebration she had enjoyed at O'Malley's Bar. She and the twenty guests she no doubt invited as she had our unwanted tickets to give away.

By the time Mary Beth finally hung up I had missed the shuttle bus to the local shopping mall and had to forfeit a few hours inside the bustling, brightly lit, malls buzzing constantly with tinny music. The only option now was to flop on a sun bed by the pool. But there was no peace there as the waiters scurried to and fro setting up tables and chairs for our poolside barbecue that evening. I had doubted that we would actually be eating poolside but now I had ample proof crashing around me. There were always doubts where Mary Beth was involved in the arrangements. I had spent a lot of time double-checking every element of our programme.

That evening we did eat outside but due to regulations the food had to be cooked inside and then carried across the road to the pool area. The group were subdued but seemed happy – I thought this was due to it being our last night and preceded by a succession of late nights. My own enjoyment was slightly marred when one of the waiters awarded himself a one hundred and fifty per cent tip for bringing me a two dollar can of beer. I had given him a five dollar note but I did not get any change. I tracked down the waiter and asked him where my change was and he said he had kept it as his tip. Clearly he did not feel any shame and was not going to return any money. No problem – I had the waiters' tip for the evening in my back pocket so I reduced it by three dollars.

Mary Beth orchestrated another early start for me the following morning thanks to one of her brainwaves. When she had been asked if we could pre-book our seats on the return flight she had told us we could. I had to fax the airline a list of our requests on the morning of our departure and they would allocate seats accordingly. Since this announcement I had been overwhelmed with requests – window seat at the front; aisle seat at the back; five seats together in the same row (The Quintet); extra leg room. I had noted every request and then meticulously transcribed them on to a flight manifest ready to fax to the airline. I also had to book the Galleria shuttle for some last minute shoppers and confirm our courtesy rooms as we had a late departure.

Breakfast was my first priority and I was looking forward to a solitary early meal. But Sophie was there already. She had not been able to sleep due to her cold. She was really excited to have me on my own as she was bursting to tell me how I should have dealt with the different personalities in the group. My first mistake, according to this amateur therapist, was that I did not see myself as other people saw me. She warned me not to take people at face value. I should enquire gently, and often, if they were alright. I should constantly be checking that everyone had things to do with other people, particularly eating in the evening. Finally any problems should have been tackled head on and immediately. I felt inadequate and in need of a course in psychology.

When her monologue of my failings ended I was able to spring to my own defence. I knew her comments were motivated by their failure to join us on the dinner cruise and Brenda's obsession with occupying a single room having paid to share a twin room. I had found all three of the ladies in her little gang very formidable and had been terrified of tackling them about anything. I should have said so but I did not dare. Instead I demurely thanked her for her insight into my skills as a Hostess. Our conversation was peppered by requests for juice and coffee. The service from our new and very reluctant waiter was very disappointing. I had allocated tips for each meal but I could not bring myself to reward someone who made me beg for coffee and juice. As I left I told him I was withholding his tip due to his dreadful service.

During the morning I was pestered constantly regarding the seat allocations. To every enquirer I gave the same answer. I doubted that they would actually respond to me and at best their preferences would be noted and acted upon. Clearly they had forgotten that we were a group booking and no changes had been allowed to our pre-allocated seats when we had checked in for our journey here. As the enquiries continued unabated and the same people asked the same question several times I said I would go and check-in reception again and fled through the back entrance of the hotel.

This entrance, unlike the urban front entrance, took me into another world, the waterside. So far I had only ventured as far as the hotel swimming pool across the road. Now I had time to follow one of the river walks and I set off along the waterway. The water lapped against the retaining banks and the sun sparkled on its surface. I could feel my spirits lifting as I ambled along. There were two river walks and I hoped to do both of them.

I had nearly completed the first walk when I met up with some of the early shoppers on their way back to our hotel. They wanted to know if I had heard about Callan's adventures in the Galleria. I had not. Callan had narrowly escaped being arrested in a record shop. I knew he had been asked by Edgar to return a jacket to the clothes shop he had bought it from as they had forgotten to remove the security tag. Callan had reluctantly agreed and went off with the jacket in his bag. He must have forgotten it was there because his first stop was a record shop. The tag on the jacket set off the alarm and he was detained by the shopkeeper who called the police. Before they arrived Callan explained what had happened and produced the receipt for the jacket and he was released. He went straight to the clothes shop before the jacket got him into any more trouble.

Callan was not back yet and Edgar was sunbathing by the pool blissfully unaware of the events of the morning. This was too good an opportunity to miss and I raced to the pool and told Edgar that I had had a call from the state police checking Callan's identity. I managed to maintain a serious expression while I watched Edgar throwing on his clothes to accompany me to reception to call the police and confirm Callan's story. When I smirked at my own success he twigged immediately. This professional winder up was not amused and scooped me up and held me over the water while I screamed that I was wearing contact lenses. I narrowly escaped a soaking in the swimming pool – fully clothed as well. That would teach me to kid a kidder.

When Maisie and Basil joined us at the hotel they both looked tanned, healthy and happy and assured me that they had enjoyed their holiday. Shortly after they arrived the rest of the group began to gather. Mary Beth, still obstinately pursuing some good will, sidled up to us. The group ignored her. There was a very uneasy silence until a wedding party arrived and distracted everyone. As they began their ceremony in the adjoining room Edgar appeared outside the open doorway on the other side of the wedding group. He was waving a swimming costume and shouting for the owner to come and claim it. We tried to wave him into silence but failed. The wedding guests looked shocked as he began jumping up and down and swirling the swimsuit around his head. I raced round the cluster of guests, grabbed his arm and pulled him away from the open door before explaining that he had just gatecrashed a wedding. He tried to look suitably contrite but failed and I kept him outside until it was time to board our bus.

My complicated list of requests had been ignored and we were all seated together – although some boarding passes surreptitiously changed hands. I survived the flight home despite being next to Sophie and Brenda, members of The Quintet. I was afraid Sophie might reopen the discussion she had started that morning. She had other problems as her rather generous frame would not allow her to pull the table right down to eat her meal and it bounced around on her ample tummy. I curled up against the window and contemplated my next problem – Maisie and her damaged suitcase.

Maisie was told that the damage should have been reported on arrival in Florida. She lacked the guile to suggest that the damage had occurred on the inbound flight. I gave Maisie the address to write to and told her to contact me if there were any problems. I doubted that she would as she would not want to make a fuss. After hugging her warmly we went our separate ways.

* * * * * *

When Aimee called me a few days after I got home and offered me a skiing trip in Les Arcs I was suspicious. I knew that skiing trips and particularly the French trips were much sought after by my colleagues so there must be a problem with this one. Aimee laughed when I suggested that everyone else had turned it down. She conceded that there had been some reluctance to volunteer for this particular trip but only because it was a new trip. This involved writing detailed documentation and I had already impressed her with the reports I had submitted for each trip I had hosted. None of my colleagues had volunteered for the maiden trip but all of them had requested the two subsequent trips. Aimee assured me that even though it was the first time we had been to this resort every detail had been carefully checked.

The only detail that had not been checked was the name of our hotel. We arrived at ten in the evening in the middle of a snowstorm. It was a very small village strung along one road. Our hotel, Hotel Charmettoger, should have been easy to find. But, unknown to us the hotel had changed its name and had not informed prospective guests. I expected the transfer driver would know where he was going but he did not have a clue. He drove down the main street once then he lost his patience and threw our luggage onto the street before driving off.

I stood on the pavement knee deep in snow contemplating my next move. Oscar stepped close to me and murmured that he thought our hotel might now be called Hotel Latitudes. He indicated a sign above us pointing towards a hotel of that name. It was kind of him not to blurt out this information but allow me to voice this thought to our companions. Oscar had been in the group I had hosted at the Sandbanks weekend and I had persuaded him to try one of our skiing trips as he could travel without his non-skiing partner. It was my only option and I told the group to stay where they were while I checked the hotel above us. I sprinted along the path and up several flights of steps which was not easy in court shoes through fresh snow. I rang the bell and finally roused the night porter. By then the whole group was on my heels despite my instructions to wait on the road.

It was the right hotel and they were expecting some late arrivals. Reluctantly the porter began to check us all in. When I asked where we could get dinner the night porter pointed to the exit and said there was a pizzeria in the village. I was stunned as the previous day I had spoken to the manager of the hotel and confirmed that a late dinner would be provided for us. The kitchen had closed and there was nothing, not even a filled roll. Nobody wanted to walk through the snow to the village centre for a pizza at that late hour. There was only one option.

When we congregated in the bar the night porter made no effort to conceal his displeasure because he had to serve us. I pleaded for some crisps and he obliged with two tiny bowlfuls. The bowls were emptied in seconds and he refilled them with the same result. I suggested maybe he could find some larger bowls but instead he plonked a catering bag of crisps on the bar and we helped ourselves. He also rummaged around under the bar and found some packets of nuts and a large basket of wrapped chocolates left over from their New Year celebrations. It was better than nothing. I tried to convince the group that I really had telephoned the hotel and arranged for a late dinner but the majority of them looked sceptical. It was a relief when I could escape to reception as the second lot of arrivals was due. This party was spread over three flights. My first, a party of one, had arrived earlier and was now sleeping soundly in her room.

I waited in the shelter of the hotel entrance until I saw the headlights of a vehicle then rushed down to the main road to escort them up the two hundred metres of paths and steps. Polly and Olga had booked this holiday at the last minute and had paid a hefty supplement for their flight. While checking them in I explained the problem regarding dinner so they joined us for drinks and nibbles. As I had not boasted to them regarding my foresight in organising a late dinner they were not expecting a meal anyway.

Polly and Olga had formed a protest group of two to object about the large supplement they had paid for their flight. They had decided they had suffered an injustice. In their opinion the cost of the flight should have gone down not up. I tried to explain that although this applied to perishable goods approaching their sell by date it did not apply to seats on planes. Anyone who needed to fly on a particular date would pay the enhanced price. This was a logic they could not grasp. They began their campaign by asking each member of the group how much they had paid for their flights. They were not the only ones who had paid extra but none of the others had paid in excess of two hundred pounds. There was nothing more I could do so I left them campaigning in the bar and took my bags up to my room.

Knowing I would have to work hard to make up for a bad start I was up at six the following morning. I walked round a deserted ski resort checking access to the lifts so I could get the group on the slopes as quickly as possible. Ski hire and the ski school office were both in our hotel but I needed to know where to direct them as soon as they were ready to ski. Our hotel was advertised as ski-in, ski-out so I started from the ski and boot room to check the route to the cabin lift. Skiing back to the hotel was easy as it was at the bottom of a ski run. Skiing out was tricky unless you were adept at skiing uphill and then along a narrow path and across a tarmac road. I re-traced my steps in case I had missed something, like a ski run. I had not but I did find a well beaten path through the woods that went straight to the bottom of lifts. Clearly we could only ski out carrying our skis on our shoulders.

It was a real scramble to get everyone kitted out and booked into ski school that first morning as we were competing with all the other guests in our hotel and it was a large hotel. As soon as they were ready I sent them off to the slopes or to the ski school meeting place. I arranged to meet up with them later for lunch. I had to find out what had happened to our dinner the previous night before I could go skiing. I could not find a manager or indeed anyone who seemed to be in authority and everyone denied having spoken to me about the provision of a late dinner. It was time to meet the group for lunch so I left a message for the manager and a request that they arrange lunch for us one day to replace the missing dinner.

I collected my skis and made my way to the meeting point near the ski school. Everyone had been invited to join us for lunch but there were a few absentees. Polly and Olga had formed an elite group of Ski Club of Great Britain members. They had severely warned the rest of the group that they were not allowed to ski with the Ski Club unless they were members. I knew that this was not strictly true as everyone was allowed to join them for one day before deciding whether or not to become a member. Oscar had been asked to tell me that they would not be joining us for lunch that day or any other day as they would be joining the Ski Club group every day. Everyone else was happy with this arrangement and during lunch we dubbed ourselves the 'out' crowd.

We abandoned the slopes quite early that afternoon as it had begun to snow and visibility was very poor. I led the way back down the run that took us to the back door of our hotel. I set off to explore the village but half way there I remembered that the rooming list I had requested several times had not yet materialised. I did a very quick tour of the village and then raced back to reception and said I needed the list, urgently. The receptionist denied any knowledge of my group and if there was no group then there was no list of room numbers. I left a list of names with her and asked her to fill in the room number for each person. Now I was seriously concerned that my non-existent group may not be booked in for dinner that night. I went off to find the maître d'. He was locked in the restaurant but a few rattles on the door encouraged him to come and see what I wanted. He was the only member of staff who was aware of our existence and happy to have us there. He invited me into the restaurant and showed me a long table he had already prepared for us down the centre of the spacious eating area.

That evening I left the group in the restaurant having feasted on a fabulous buffet and enjoyed a glass of the included wine. I was looking forward to a good night's sleep. A plan had formed in my mind and I was anticipating an early start the next morning to bring it to fruition. That first day had been a wake-up call for me regarding my role as a ski Hostess. I had spent most of the time picking up ski equipment and hauling people to their feet. I was going to hire a pair of snow blades, or mini skis. These did not require the use of poles which would leave my hands free to assist my clients. Les Arcs had been the first resort to adopt the concept of short skis that had led to the development of the snow blade. I knew there were several pairs available in the hotel ski hire shop and I needed to get there before the rush started in the morning.

I discovered the hard way that snow blades do not cope very well with patches of ice and I was soon nursing a very sore bottom. I was glad to sit down for lunch even though it was uncomfortable. The morning had followed the same pattern as the previous day and the in-crowd had gone off with the Ski Club with not a backward glance or the slightest hint that any of us were welcome to join them. I had issued a personal invitation to join us for lunch but it was brushed aside. Concerned about this rift in the group I asked Oscar, my mole, what he thought. He said that people would always split into groups to ski so they could find a level that suited them. As everyone was mixing in the evenings it was not a problem.

Soon after lunch I gave up the battle with poor visibility and obstinate snow blades. When I got back to the hotel I found Ben waiting for me in reception. He had lost his wallet somewhere on the slopes and he needed to get the telephone numbers to cancel his debit and credit cards. The contact numbers were on the cards of course. I used the helpline number on my own card and was able to get all the relevant numbers from my bank. As Ben had several calls to make we walked to the village to buy a phone card and use the public telephone. I had already discovered that the telephone charges in the hotel were ridiculously high so it was the cheapest way to deal with the situation.

It took us so long to get everything done and organise funds to be sent to a local bank that by the time we got back to the hotel the others had already started dinner. The In Crowd may be mixing but they did it in their own way by sitting together at one end of the table. Ben and I took the two empty places at the divide. Dinner lasted a long time as the supply of free wine was apparently unlimited. Tongues were loosened but not mine. Polly and Olga served up another course of bitterness regarding the supplement they had paid. I was finding it difficult to deal with these two. It had been their choice whether or not to pay the price quoted and now they were casting a shadow over the whole holiday.

The next day we were blessed with sunshine and all my guests set off in high spirits. The ski and boot room was deserted by the time I got down there. At first I was disappointed that no one had waited for me but then I realized that I was free to explore on my own. We had made arrangements to meet up for lunch so I would catch up with them later. It was such a joy to fly down a slope from top to bottom without having to stop every hundred yards to deal with the incessant requests to stop for a drink or the toilet. I gave them the slip again after lunch by pleading the need to work out some routes for the inexperienced skiers.

The mountain was peppered with delightful restaurants and I soon had a recommendation for lunch on each of the remaining days. I was crossing behind the nursery slope to get back to our hotel when I heard something or someone sobbing and sniffing but I could not see anyone. I stopped and listened and the noise continued. In front of me was a bank of snow and the noise seemed to be coming from there so I moved nearer for a closer inspection. I spotted the top of a small ski helmet. When I brushed the snow away I discovered that the ski helmet contained the head of a small toddler and soon its whole body was revealed. When I tried to speak to it the soft sobbing escalated to full pitch screaming. I took its hand but it pulled it away and left me holding a ski mitten. Just as I was considering taking the child back to my hotel I heard a shout and a ski instructor came running up the nursery slope. He claimed his stray pupil, snatched the mitten from my hand and rushed off again leaving me free to continue on my way.

That night I received a fax from Aimee requesting that, as a matter of urgency, I inspect a hotel for them. Our present hotel was proving difficult regarding confirmations for future groups. I could have added a few more shortcomings myself. Personally I thought our hotel was well below our normal standard. It was built during the tourism boom of the sixties and seventies; its plain grey exterior speckled with small square windows resembled a high rise prison block. Most of the basic rooms had three beds – two bunk beds and a single bed and they were not really suitable for couples or single people.

The other hotel was much nicer. It was situated in the centre of the village, close to all the lifts. The exterior looked like a hotel and the reception rooms were carpeted and nicely furnished with upholstered armchairs and glass coffee tables. Our hotel had bare floors and the occasional plastic covered armchair amongst the basic wooden chairs. I reported back immediately and then it was time to meet the group and take them to the restaurant for lunch. The In Crowd had been enticed to join us by the general enthusiasm for the venue but they sat on a different table with their Ski Club buddies. After lunch I shepherded the beginners back to the safety of some easy runs near our hotel and then retired to my room to soak in the bath. Despite the Spartan rooms we did have the luxury of a bath.

Olga was the first to arrive at breakfast the next morning having been asked by Polly not to smoke on their shared balcony. Her first cigarette had already been smoked outside the main entrance of the hotel. She smoked constantly and her breath smelled of stale cigarettes. I could not help wondering if it was possible to smoke passively from someone's smoke laden breath. Olga served up another helping of the unfair flight supplement. I had not been able to establish any sort of relationship with Olga as we could not get past this barrier. I tried again with a simplified explanation but she was not listening as her eyes kept darting towards the door watching for her colleagues. I suggested that maybe I could ski with her group that morning as all my skiing buddies were having lessons. The idea was greeted with scorn.

Soon after I set off to explore on my own it stopped snowing and the sun broke through. The scenery was stunning – snow laden trees against a background of blue sky. I stopped to take some photographs then made my way back to the meeting point to collect the group. I sent some on ahead to the restaurant while I skied there slowly with the beginners. By the time we got there the others had started eating but they had saved some places for us outside in the sun. The good skiers were keen to profit from the nice weather and left before we had finished eating. We stayed there until the shadows crept across our table and the temperature dropped.

The temperature continued to drop both outside and inside our hotel. That evening the In Crowd went bowling in the village – I was informed but not invited. I was not the only one as only a select few were allowed to join them. This exclusivity sparked some resentment so I suggested that the rest of us walked to Charvet, the next village. It had a true village atmosphere as it was not purpose built like Les Arcs. The bars were not so busy and we could sit together in pleasant surroundings and enjoy a drink and conversation that did not have to be screamed over loud music. The plummeting temperature had frozen the snow and walking back we slid around like novice skaters clinging to each other helpless with laughter.

When morning came it was snowing heavily and visibility was poor but everyone decided to ski. Before I could join them I had to confirm our transfers to the airport. There were three separate transfers all at different times. After several attempts to get through to the transfer company I called Aimee to see if she could help me. Due to the terrible weather I wanted to ask them to bring the times forward. It was a long transfer and the first hour would be spent winding our way down the mountain before we joined the motorway. My command of the French language only extended as far as simple phrases such as "can we have some dinner please?" Aimee spoke French fluently and I knew she would be happy to help me out. Sure that the problem would be resolved by the time I got back that evening I went off to join some of my guests for lunch and then some skiing.

The In Crowd organised a meal out on that night for themselves and a privileged few but they graced us with their presence when we met for pre-dinner drinks. It was not good news for me as they had a new gripe, our tips collection. Polly and Olga had circulated a rumour that I was collecting the money for myself. They were not prepared to contribute as they were not happy because they had paid a supplement for their flights and they also had a very early transfer to the airport. I re-iterated that every penny of the collection would go to the staff. I had reduced the recommended amount everyone should contribute as I felt reception should not be rewarded for their offhand attitude. I had never been given a rooming list and had to compile my own, working through a register of every guest in the hotel. However, the waiters in the restaurant had been friendly and efficient and deserved a reward for their hard work. I was getting street-wise and I had not rewarded anyone for their labours up front. Our transfer driver had forfeited any right to a reward when he dumped our bags on the road. It had never occurred to Polly and Olga to tip their driver.

Thinking about the transfers reminded me that I had not received an answer from Aimee. When I asked in reception I discovered that her response had been sitting on the fax machine all day as they did not know what to do with it. I was still not registered as a guest in their hotel. It was not good news. The transfer company insisted on sticking to the original times which left no margin for delay.

It was snowing again on our last morning and the fresh snow over a layer of ice made it treacherous on and off the slopes. Several people decided not to ski and Valda was one of them. She was a timid lady and this was reflected in her skiing which was competent but cautious. Overjoyed that she had survived five days on the slopes without incident she decided not to risk a sixth day. She mentioned that she had been off work through illness for the past year and would be returning the following Monday. She was determined to ensure she was fit to do so.

Lunch in the hotel that day was a welcome break from the harsh conditions and Oscar's suggestion that they spent the afternoon bowling rather than skiing proved very popular. I was unable to join them as Ben wanted me to take him out to try some more adventurous runs. By then the snow had turned to heavy rain and it was miserable. Ben was a dogged personality and he was determined to squeeze the last run out of his ski pass even though his unkempt hair was plastered to his face and water dripped off his charity shop ski jacket. After an hour he conceded that it was not worth the effort, not because of the weather but because his feet were hurting and he was anxious to get his ski boots off. When we stripped off in the ski and boot room he discovered that he had been wearing his boots on the wrong feet all day.

At last I could slide into a hot bath and luxuriate there until it was time to get ready to meet the group for pre-dinner drinks. I had just plastered my wet hair with conditioner when there was a hammering at my door. I leapt out of the bath, wrapped a towel round me and peered through the crack of my partially open door. A distraught Oscar informed me that Valda had fallen over in the bowling alley and had seriously injured her arm. She was still at the medical centre but was being transferred to the hospital at Bourg St Maurice thirty kilometres down the mountain. The ambulance would be leaving in a few minutes and Oscar doubted they would wait until I got there. He was really upset as he had called the hotel from the medical centre but the receptionist had said I was not staying there. He had run to the hotel as fast as he could. Now I had to move and fast. My hair was still wet and tangled so I stuffed it in a woolly hat and then pulled on some warm clothes. Oscar had gone ahead to make sure the ambulance did not leave without me but even so it was reversing out of the entrance when I got there.

I scrambled into the front and we were immediately on our way. It was a hair raising ride down the mountain as we bumped over potholes and veered round sharp corners. Occasionally Valda would let out a shriek of pain despite having been heavily sedated. I could not do anything; I could not even hold her hand as there was a plastic screen between us. All I could do was shout words of sympathy and get her details for the attendant to fill in his form. I called Aimee to tell her what had happened and she told me to wait until I knew more before calling Valda's insurance company and her daughter.

Once at the hospital I waited while they took some X-rays. The results were not good. Valda had fractured her arm in several places and had to have an operation the following day. It would be several days before she could fly home. I waited until she was taken to the ward and made her as comfortable as I could before calling a taxi to return to the hotel. I had missed dinner by then but I had sent a text to Oscar and asked him to liberate some bread, cheese and wine from the restaurant for me. Oscar was waiting in the lobby when I got back. So was Polly. Oscar was anxious for news about Valda and Polly wanted to know why the packed breakfasts for herself and Olga had not been delivered to reception as promised when I had ordered them earlier. I could do nothing about this problem as the kitchens were now closed. Polly could have asked in the restaurant while it was still open but it was more fun to berate me about the hotel's shortcomings.

I had a long night ahead of me. First I had to call Valda's insurance company and then her daughter Zoe. The insurance company called me back and we went through all the details. They assured me that Valda would be well looked after and that as soon as she was able to leave hospital after surgery they would collect her as they operated a door to door repatriation service. As it was a physical injury there was no necessity for anyone to stay with her. I knew she was sharing a ward with an English speaking lady so at least she had company and when I took her case to the hospital the next morning I would also be delivering a collection of books and magazines donated by the group. I packed my bag in between calls as we were all going home the next day. Next I went to Valda's room and started packing her bags.

It was a rush to get everything done by four thirty the next morning when Polly and Olga were leaving. They were already there when I arrived in reception and scowling. I said I would go outside and watch for the taxi. It had rained during the night and then frozen so every surface was covered with a thin layer of ice. Cautiously I made my way to a vantage point to watch for the taxi. Cars were slithering around on the frozen surface of the road and it occurred to me that they may not get away at all. It was a great relief when I saw their taxi appearing through the gloom and I could finally wave them goodbye.

As soon as they were on the way I collected Valda's luggage to take to the hospital. I had just set off when Polly called me to tell me that their driver was complaining because his fare had not been paid. Unless my company paid the bill for all the transfers they had booked he said all the other vehicles would be cancelled. The bill had been paid and I had confirmation of this payment in the faxes I had received the previous day. I asked Polly to tell the taxi driver I would be faxing him a copy as soon as I got back to the hotel.

The roads were still treacherous and despite the early hour the traffic was already building up. My taxi driver took a short cut down a ski run which was very scary but I retained him to take me back to the hotel. When I arrived at the ward the sister told me they had been waiting for me to wash Valda before her surgery. I did the best I could. When I realised the hospital staff expected me to look after her all day I said I could not as I had twenty people to get back to England.

On my way back to the hotel I rang Zoe to update her regarding her mother's condition. I had hoped that Zoe might already be on her way to look after her mother. She was not. She was more concerned about her birthday celebrations that evening. I explained that the insurance company would not cover my expenses. A volley of calls passed between me, Zoe and Aimee – all on my mobile phone. Zoe must have been very persuasive as Aimee began discussing the possibility of my staying. Our discussion was interrupted by a second call from Polly. They were at the airport and their driver was asking them to pay for their taxi as he had no proof that the bill had already been paid. She put the driver on the phone and I promised to fax the details of payment to him within the next hour.

More problems were gathering on my horizon. I did not have enough cash with me to pay my own taxi fare. I sent Oscar a text asking him to meet me in reception with some money. By now there were queues of traffic everywhere. These had been created by an abundance of tow trucks desperately trying to rescue vehicles that had skidded off the road but they were fighting a losing battle. We were barely moving and the situation deteriorated as drivers began to abandon vehicles on the road and continue their journey on foot. As we crawled along I explained the money predicament to my driver but assured him Oscar would be waiting for me with some cash. When we were one kilometre away from the village the driver pulled over and said that was as far as he was going. I asked if he was going to wait there while I walked to the hotel and then returned with his fare. He gave me an exasperated look and said he would accept what I had in my purse, half his fare.

Both the road and the pavement were so treacherous that the only way I could battle up the hill to the hotel was to cling to garden fences and pull myself along. By the time I stumbled into reception my conscience was nagging at me. I would hate to be in Valda's situation. I did ask reception if they had any rooms available that night but the hotel was full. So, once I had taken the last group to the airport I would be faced with a three hour transfer (at best) back to the area and nowhere to stay. There was a World Cup event in Les Arcs the following week and all the hotels in the area were booked up. I felt that being asked to stay under those circumstances simply to be company for Valda was way beyond the call of duty and said so during my next conversation with Aimee. She agreed with me.

Zoe changed tactics. During a heart-rending call to Aimee she disclosed that her mother had been very ill and had only just recovered. She felt that the strain of being in hospital on her own would make her ill again. I had one ally, the insurance company representative, who said that Zoe was overreacting and should not be putting emotional pressure on me. Valda had not declared her illness on her travel insurance policy which could have invalidated it. The agent called Zoe to clarify this and I thought that was one problem dealt with. Aimee promised to fax details of the transfer payments to the taxi company so that was another worry out of the way.

I just had time for a quick breakfast before the next crisis. Gaye had been due to leave at ten o'clock that morning. I waited with her in reception but her taxi did not arrive. Her flight and transfer had been organised through another tour operator and I had re-confirmed this transfer with the resort representative earlier that week. Numerous calls were exchanged with the representative who had no idea why the taxi had not arrived. He said he would try and find a way to get Gaye to the airport in time for her flight. I set up a mini call centre in my room which I had been allowed to keep after the official check out time. We had a landline, a mobile and internet access on my laptop. Gaye remained calm throughout and even helped me deal with all the calls that were coming in.

Zoe was still working on Aimee despite my telling her the situation and that the insurance company would not cover my costs. Aimee was very soft-hearted and finally promised to foot the bill herself! First I had to get Gaye to the airport. I tried to book a taxi for her but by then no one could get in or out of the village. We had just passed the deadline for getting her to the airport on time when Zoe rang again. I was feeling bad for refusing to stay so I agreed to stay one night until Zoe could get there. When it became clear it would be more than one night as she had an important meeting in London on the Monday I said no. First it was birthday celebrations and now it was an important meeting. What next I wondered. I was not going to be used in this manner and I stood firm in my refusal.

I had just put the telephone down when I realised that there would be an unused ticket on our BA flight as Valda would not be going back with us. I called the representative and asked him to investigate this possibility. Gaye could then come on our transfer to the airport – now was not the time to consider that this one may not arrive either. This suggestion was received enthusiastically and it was not long before the deal had been done and all I had to do was collect a ticket for Gaye at the airport. Now I just had to hope that the roads would have cleared sufficiently for the vehicles to get through to pick us up and get us to the airport in time. They were already late.

Finally three vehicles arrived to transfer us but all at different times so I was filling them up and sending them off as soon as they appeared. I was in the last vehicle and we were soon behind the others on the motorway speeding along through heavy rain. Such was our driver's determination to get us there in time that he seemed oblivious to the traffic around him and the intermittent red lights ahead that indicated that the traffic was coming to a standstill. When he did realise and slammed on the brakes we nearly aquaplaned into the back of the vehicle in front. "Excusez moi," he muttered and then began a series of undertaking and overtaking manoeuvres to try and get through the traffic. He talked constantly with his colleagues on his mobile. When the traffic slowed to a halt they decided to divert across country and we formed a convoy speeding along the narrow lanes. We had a few detours, one into a farmyard and another into a gravel pit but at least we were moving forwards all the time. Thanks to the local knowledge of our drivers we got to the airport in time.

We were on two flights so I sent the groups off to their respective check-in areas and then went with Gaye to get her ticket for our scheduled flight. I had promised the group on the charter flight that I would follow them to their check-in desk to make sure everything was okay and say goodbye. Once Gaye had her ticket I walked to the other terminal building intending to keep my promise but I was not allowed into the building as the whole area was cordoned off. A suspicious bag had been discovered in the check-in area and was being blown up. Before the 'all clear' was given my flight was already boarding. I just hoped they would realise what had happened. At last we were on our way home and I could relax – all I had to worry about was the £79 bill I had run up on my mobile phone. And then there were the calls I had made from the hotel that morning, lots of them.

* * * * * *

When Aimee did call me it was not to berate me regarding the phone bills. She congratulated me on managing to get everybody home in spite of the terrible weather conditions. She also said I had nothing to reproach myself for regarding Valda as it had become clear that Zoe was using me to salve her own conscience. The fact that the hotel had never recognised me as a guest meant they could not credit my phone calls to an account that did not exist.

Aimee had some good news for me. They wanted me to lead a ski trip to Méribel. I had always wanted to ski the Trois Vallées and leapt at the opportunity. I was not deterred when she explained that we would not be staying in Méribel itself but Brides les Bains, in the next valley and a thirty minute cabin lift away. This would have made it difficult for anyone in ski school. But Aimee promised me that there would be no beginners as the trip was advertised as 'not suitable for beginners'. I could definitely rely on this warning – there would be no novices to deal with.

Chapter 8 – February

Damion slipped through the net. He was a complete beginner in a group of good skiers. But Damion did not see this as a problem. In fact his impish face under spiky black hair gave the impression that he thought it attracted some sort of celebrity status. He was supremely confident. I might have found this character endearing if I had not been steeling myself to chaperone him on the ski slopes all week. While Eric was dealing with the non-arrival of his skis at Geneva airport Damion began canvassing for a ski buddy. No one volunteered. Once Eric had established that his skis were still in Edinburgh we were on our way.

There was a rush to sit at the back of the bus leaving Damion at the front with me. This did not deter him and as we made our way slowly through heavy traffic he strolled down the bus talking to everyone. Skiers are a selfish breed and they live for the thrill of speeding down steep slopes. I knew Damion would not find anyone who would ski with him. I tried to enjoy the beautiful scenery as we drove by Lake Annecy. Nature had made ice sculptures in the trees by freezing the water that had splashed over the bank. I lodged the problem of Damion in the back of mind. I knew exactly who would be his ski buddy for the next seven days. Indeed I heard Dirk confirm that and even suggested that I could give him lessons as well.

It was a relief when we got to our hotel, Les Chalets, in Brides les Bains. We received a warm welcome from our hosts Liliane and Jacques both of whom were helpful and efficient. Liliane spoke good English but Jacques did not speak any English at all so I had to dredge up some of my schoolgirl French. The rooms varied a lot in size but they were all comfortable and warm. There was a lift to the second floor and then stairs up to the third and top floor. With no porters and a flight of steps up from the road it took us a while to get our luggage up to our rooms. Hermione was on the top floor and not happy with this arrangement. She claimed that as she would be spending more time in her room than the other guests she wanted a room with a view. Fortunately there were some empty rooms and Jacques was happy to accommodate her request.

My room was a tiny attic room and the only source of light was a glass panel in the roof. It was cosy and cute. I was now alone on the top floor so I knew it would be quiet. As I unpacked I mused over Hermione's statement that she would be spending a lot of time in her room. I did not have to wait long to find out what she had meant. That evening during our Information Meeting Jacques organised all our lift passes and we paid the hotel directly. The price was cheaper than it would have been if we had purchased them from the lift station. Hermione turned down this offer and said she would be making her own arrangements. That was my opportunity to ask if she was intending to ski. She was a smart lady and had discovered that being of a certain age she would be entitled to a discount – a better discount than Jacques was offering. By passing on this information she had side-stepped my question regarding her intention to ski.

When our meeting finished we were invited to buy drinks from the bar to take into dinner with us as there would be no service of drinks during the meal. Several people took the advice of Jacques that it was cheaper and easier to buy wine by the bottle and then keep it for the next evening. This was the theory but in practice there was nothing left to keep. Jacques was definitely on the ball.

It was a happy group that finally made their way into the simple dining room clutching half empty bottles of wine. Sitting around our large, rectangular table at dinner we had a chance to get to know one another and to assess each other's skiing abilities. Dirk was the first to throw down the gauntlet when he announced that he would be at the bottom of the cabin lift waiting for it to open in the morning and anyone who could keep up with him was welcome to come along. Confusion greeted this challenge as no one knew what time the lift would be open so I went off to find out. As I left Damion informed me that he was taking Dirk's advice and he would be skiing with me.

Every day we would have a long ride up the mountain from Brides les Bains to Méribel and then we would have to take another lift to the top of the runs. The lift station was very close to our hotel but at the top of a treacherously icy slope. I slithered up and down it to check the time of the first and last runs. The latter was crucial as it was a long way back by road if we got stranded in Méribel.

After breakfast the next morning we went to the ski hire shop and stepped into absolute chaos. It was tiny and bursting with people who were all grabbing boots, skis and poles seemingly at random. Everyone was tripping over each other and getting very cross. Only one man was serving and he was not being very helpful. He demanded a credit card imprint for every pair of skis hired and payment could be by cash or card when the skis were returned. Some of my guests threatened to go elsewhere but when I pointed out that the other ski hire shops were in the village and a long walk from our hotel they changed their minds. The owner had the monopoly and seemed to take pleasure in making the whole business of hiring skis as difficult as possible. We could have hired skis in Méribel itself at greater expense and not so convenient when we had to return them. I persisted in my efforts to find a compromise and eventually he accepted one card imprint for every five pairs of skis hired.

The whole process took so long that people set off for the slopes in small groups. I had to return to the hotel to look for Hermione who had not been at breakfast. I found her sitting at our table in the hotel dining room. When I asked her if she was skiing today she replied, "not today dear, maybe tomorrow". She was going to explore her immediate surroundings. She was definitely going to ski the next day and would be ready for an early start. I clomped back up to the lift station in my ski boots. I had not had time to hire a locker but that would be my next job. I had seen several people slip over and crash onto the road as they slithered up and down the hill. On my four journeys up and down the hill I had escaped unscathed but I was not going to risk it again.

I found a solitary member of my group there. It was Damion. He had not wanted to wait for me but it was clear the others had managed to give him the slip before he even got on the cabin lift. He was very enthusiastic about having lessons with me and he even pointed out that it would save him a lot of money. I explained that ski instructors guarded their territory ferociously and as I was not a qualified instructor it would be impossible for me to attempt to give anyone a lesson without incurring their wrath. Nevertheless I agreed to ski with him that morning but strongly urged him to book a lesson for the following day.

It was torture. Damion clearly did not like going downhill and traversed a slope and then finally, when he ran out of room, he did a snow plough turn and came back again almost in the same tracks. He descended an inch at a time. I spent all morning waiting for him on the same slope. I felt compelled to give him some instruction if only to get him moving faster. My advice fell on deaf ears so I just had to be patient. My opening came when Damion announced that he intended to ski with the group the next day. I said he would have to improve first so he agreed that he would take a lesson the following afternoon.

We did not meet up with anyone else in the group all day and had lunch together on our own. The others had not wanted to be tied down to a meeting place for lunch. Wistfully I thought of them all enjoying the varied slopes around Méribel. It was not a resort for beginners so Damion and I were confined to a paucity of easy slopes. Dirk had emerged as a natural leader and had gone off with a small, elite group. He had been anxious to include Phoebe, a very experienced skier who had joined us the night before direct from her own chalet in another French ski resort. His face was a picture when she responded that she had hired a ski instructor for the day and would be exploring the resort with him. No one else was invited to join them. She softened the blow by promising to ski with Dirk the following day.

My efforts with Damion did achieve a modicum of success and now he was descending six inches with each turn. I was not only pleased with his progress but amazed at my own patience. My legs ached after snow ploughing all day and I was bored to tears. As we began our descent to Méribel I thought my nightmare was over. It was not. The home run was solid with skiers moving at nerve-wracking speed. We stood at the edge waiting for a gap so that we could get onto the run. A gap never materialised and we were running out of time. I kept urging Damion to slide into the flow – he would have to snow plough straight down as it was impossible to traverse. He could not be persuaded to push out in the surging torrent of humanity. I suggested that I go first and that he followed right behind me and I set off in the hope he would do the same. He did not and I nearly beached myself on the bank trying to check if he was behind me. I stopped and waited in the hope that in sheer desperation he would launch himself down the slope. He did but as soon as he saw me he started to slow down again. I yelled at him to continue and pushed off myself in the hope he would not stop. He did not and somehow we managed to negotiate the human rapids.

We were hailed by some of the group who swished past us and then waited at a junction with a wider piste so that we could all ski down together. This short piste was even more alarming. Near the bottom was a narrow chicane through some orange fencing designed as a safety measure to protect the crowds milling around at the base of the lifts. Most of skiers took this as a challenge racing down twenty abreast and then dropping into single file at the last minute to negotiate the tight turns. Some were unable to control their speed in time and one of them crashed into Conrad who was knocked to the ground. I helped him up and he seemed okay although he had hurt his shoulder. I decided to take him straight back to the hotel. I was pleased to have an excuse to escape the melee. The others did a last run but for me, in those conditions, it was not skiing it was survival.

Conrad went straight to his room convinced that he did not need to seek medical advice. Hermione was in the bar so I joined her and tried to confirm that she would be definitely skiing the following day. She told me she had always wanted to visit the Trois Vallées but she was not so sure that she wanted to ski them. After dinner that evening Annie suggested we have a walk around the village to see if we could find somewhere suitable to have dinner one evening. She had either not believed me or had not heard me when I told the group that there were no suitable restaurants in the vicinity. We scoured every inch of the place and all we could find were three empty bars and a hotel that opened its restaurant to non-residents enticing them in with the menu of the day that did not change all week.

Breakfast was over, well nearly. I leant back and surveyed the scene in front of me. Our long table stretched away from me, the white tablecloth crumpled and littered with crumbs and empty jam sachets. Stained coffee cups were lined up down the centre. Everyone had rushed off to the slopes, eager to get skiing as soon as possible. Their enthusiasm was hampered only by the opening times of the cabin lift up to Méribel. One lonely croissant was left on a large oval platter in front of me and the unused setting beside me. Strange, I reflected, how the spaces filled up from the far end of the table towards me at the head of the table. It reminded me of my lecturing days when the students would all huddle right at the back of the lecture theatre.

I was waiting for my last guest. I stretched my legs under the table and winced involuntarily as my calves twanged, protesting about the surfeit of snow ploughing the previous day. But at least Damion had got to the ski area. Hermione had yet to get that far.

Hermione, when she appeared, was smartly dressed and beautifully made up. She looked just like the air hostess she used to be. Right down to the court shoes on her feet which suggested that skiing was not on her agenda today. Her response to my question was the same as yesterday, "not today dear, maybe tomorrow". Was tomorrow ever going to come I wondered. Hermione came and sat next to me and asked if anyone else had been to breakfast yet. She expressed surprise when I said that everyone had already eaten and gone to ski. She gave the matter a lot of thought and then decided she would come up in the cabin lift with me to assess the situation. Once she had seen the slopes she would make her decision then.

When Hermione joined me later her hair looked as though she had just come out of the hairdressers. Bright red lipstick had been reapplied but at least the court shoes had been replaced by a pair of trainers and the tailored skirt had given way to skin tight black trousers. Hermione purchased her ski pass while I changed into my ski boots. I had advised her that if she was not intending to ski much she may be better buying a day pass but she decided to get one for the week.

The morning rush was over and we had a cabin to ourselves. Hermione chatted happily as we rose above the small village. She had a list of things she wanted to do while she was in the area and none of them involved skiing. Soon the urban landscape gave way to snow clad slopes littered with pine trees. I peered below me looking for a ski run. I had heard a rumour that it was possible to ski down to Brides Les Bains from Méribel but there was no sign of a suitable track. My musings were rudely interrupted when Hermione squealed and grabbed my arm. We were approaching the docking station and some skiers had just gone past the window of our cabin. She announced that the slope they were on was much too steep. I did not have the heart to explain that this was not a proper piste but just a path that led to the entrance to of the cabin lift. It was flat and the skiers were pushing themselves along with their poles.

The next morning when my alarm went off I opened my eyes and discovered that it was pitch dark. It took me a while to work out that it had snowed during the night and the layer of snow on my skylight blocked out every vestige of light. Everyone except Hermione and Damion organised their skiing at breakfast. Hermione opted for yet another 'quiet' morning in Bride les Bains. It could never be anything else. She did promise to come up to Méribel in the cabin lift for lunch so I arranged to meet her later. She wanted to use the ski pass she had bought as she could not get a refund for loss of interest in skiing. Damion and I had company that morning as Joyce wanted an easy morning. I had noticed a long green run down to Mottaret and decided we should take that route. We cruised along until we came to the final descent into Mottaret. This was a very steep slope that had to be negotiated to get to the bottom of the lift. It was chaos. Good skiers slalomed round stranded skiers. Some were frozen to the spot gazing down at the incline below them; some had fallen over and were picking themselves and their belongings up; a few had taken their skis off and were slithering down in their ski boots and two were just sitting on the snow sobbing.

Damion was completely untouched by the drama unfolding in front of him and skied that slope as he did every other slope, a few inches at a time. I hoped his private lesson later that morning would improve matters. After we had delivered him to his instructor I skied with Joyce until it was time to meet Hermione for lunch. We had a late lunch and when Damion joined us he gloomily predicted that his lesson had not resulted in any improvement in his skiing. I was not in the mood to find out if he was any better or not so I suggested he practised what he had been taught while Hermione and I went for a walk around Méribel. Hermione went straight back to the hotel after we had exhausted all the shopping possibilities in the town including the local market.

I waited for Damion. As we were descending in the cabin lift he announced that he felt he was now good enough to join the others on the slopes and did not need any more lessons. As we walked down to the hotel I fulfilled my own prediction about it only being a question of time before I slipped over on the icy path to the hotel. Fortunately I was engrossed in thoughts other than the possibility of falling over so it was a relatively soft landing given my own personal padding and my Michelin man type ski suit (a sale bargain). I was preoccupied with the mystery of my disappearing toothbrush. I had not been able to find it the previous night and after an exhaustive search that morning I was convinced it had been thrown out along with my toothpaste that had also vanished.

Liliane was not on duty so I had to speak to Jacques. First I ran up to my room to look up some relevant words like toothbrush, toothpaste and disappeared. Jacques did not understand my feeble attempt to explain myself so I resorted to mime. He interpreted this as my toothbrush has flown away. Finally he understood that it had gone. He raced upstairs to investigate. He opened my bathroom door and flipped open the small cabinet above the sink. And there they were, neatly placed side by side on the shelf. I had not realised that the mirror concealed a cabinet behind it so I had never looked there.

I was still laughing when I went back downstairs to join the group for dinner that evening. After I had confessed to my stupidity the conversation moved on to organising a meal out in Méribel one evening. I had already done some research and suggested a traditional fondue restaurant. Everyone was in favour so I asked Jacques to book the restaurant and organise a bus to take us all there. This was a lot easier than tracking down a missing toothbrush. Everyone had to choose if they wanted a meat or a cheese fondue.

When I asked the question it gave Dirk, an avid vegetarian, the opening he had been looking for. He had been simmering all week because Hermione also claimed to be a vegetarian even though she ate fish. I had lost count of the number of times he had corrected her statement that she was vegetarian and pointed out that she should call herself either a pescatorian or a non-meat eater. After he had lectured us on the meaning of vegetarian he told everyone that once they had made their choice it was final. He did not want any meat eaters dipping their contaminated forks in his cheese fondue. Although he was technically correct on all the points he made he was not gaining any support within the group.

The next morning I was up early and having breakfast when Jerome limped in and said that the knee he had twisted while skiing the day before and it felt worse that morning and he thought he should see a doctor. I sought Liliane's advice regarding the best place to go and she suggested the medical centre in Méribel – we could get there on the cabin lift. Jerome was happy to wait until everyone had been to breakfast as I wanted to remind them that I needed payment for the bus to take us to Méribel the next evening. We had to wait a long time at the medical centre and finally, after X-rays and consultations we left with a prescription that we were advised to take to the pharmacy in Brides les Baines because it would be cheaper there. I had some lunch with the group before going back down to Brides les Bains to find the pharmacy. Jerome had already limped back to rest in the hotel and I delivered the painkillers to his room.

I walked up the stairs to his room in an attempt to stretch my calf muscles. Skiing at a snail's pace was painful and incredibly tiring. When I got up each morning I spent the first half hour giving a good impression of a cowboy who had just dismounted after being in the saddle for three days. I did not linger after dinner that night as I could hardly keep my eyes open. Dirk was baiting Curtis who was suffering from a serious case of hero worship and their audience was melting away one by one. I did not even have to invent an excuse when I crept away to massage my battered thighs and calves.

I felt more cheerful the following morning when I woke to a clear, sunny day. I always enjoyed our simple breakfast of coffee and croissant with a side helping of fresh bread and a variety of jams. My ski group had increased to four because people were getting tired and wanted a more leisurely pace. I dared not tell them that our pace was slow to hardly moving. Nevertheless the four of us had a very pleasant day. We set off to ski to St Martin de Belle Ville. I was the back marker and I would wait before setting off so that I could ski at least one hundred metres at a time without stopping. I even managed two short runs on my own when the others stopped for a coffee. The only complete runs I had done all week.

We met up with some other people in our group to have lunch in St Martin de Belle Ville. It was a popular place and the tables on the terrace outside the restaurant were all occupied. We had to decide whether to wait for one to become available or move on. We waited. As we stood there patiently other skiers arrived and also hung around hoping for a table to become free. I watched the tables very carefully while my companions chatted behind me. As soon as I saw a large group collecting together gloves and hats in preparation to leave I alerted the others and we circled the table ready to take over when the present occupants moved away. It was never easy seating large groups in busy restaurants but I was learning fast. Our manoeuvre was successful and we were soon seated and perusing the menu.

Ordering was easy. All the restaurants in the area seemed to be staffed with young Australians so there was no problem with the language. Paying was a different matter. Even the simplest meals cost more than my daily expense allowance. I was suffering from a surfeit of hot dogs and coca cola. In the interests of economy and variety I opted for a coffee and a slice of tartine. My request for a glass of tap water was brutally turned down as they were not allowed to serve tap water. I refused their offer to bring me a bottle of over-priced French mineral water. Nevertheless it was very pleasant sitting around the large rustic table with the sun caressing our faces. I was jolted out of my reverie when there was a loud swoosh and a thump followed by screaming. A large pile of snow had descended from the roof above us and landed in the middle of the table next to us. Fortunately no one was hurt and once the occupants had recovered from the shock they joined in the general laughter that accompanied their plight. Their entire meal was under a thick blanket of snow.

Our evening in Méribel was not so amusing. It was memorable for all the wrong reasons. The competitive edge between Dirk and Phoebe spilled over from the slopes onto our bus. Phoebe had brought some champagne which she opened on the bus and shared out in the plastic glasses she had brought with her. Dirk, not to be outdone raced back into the hotel and purchased a bottle of red wine. He made his way to the back of the bus, ignoring the rest of the group who were gathered round the tables in the main body of the bus. He did not offer to share his wine but slumped on the back seat and drank it all himself. This was not a good start. When I set off down the bus to speak to him Jerome put out a restraining arm and suggested I left well alone as Dirk had been drinking all day.

I had done a rough seating plan to keep the meat fondue people and the cheese fondue separate in groups of four in order to avoid any crossing over which could be dangerous. Luckily everyone co-operated and we were soon settled at our tables. The fondue element was excellent but the inclusions, wine and vegetables soon ran out. When I requested extra potatoes we were inundated with chips and additional charges on the bill.

Maybe this was the catalyst to Dirk's outburst although it was more likely due to the fact that Jerome, who had been eating a meat fondue, had speared some bread with his fork and then plunged it in the cheese fondue in front of Dirk. He stormed out and when he had not returned after thirty minutes I went in search of him and found him in the lobby below the restaurant. He was very drunk and refused to come back with me and join the group. I told him where and when we were being picked up and left him to his sulk. I was relieved to find that Dirk was already on the bus when the rest of us boarded. He was hunched into his jacket and did not say a word to anyone all the way back to our hotel.

Dirk was his old self the following morning and when he arrived early for breakfast he invited me to ski with his group that day. I would have loved to spend the day with the best skiers in the group but work had to come first. Jerome required regular anti-clotting injections for his injured knee and as he did not want to get the cabin lift up to Méribel every morning I had to find someone to come to the hotel for the next two days. Next I had to re-confirm our flight and our transfer to the airport. Due to the poor weather conditions and a general lethargy some people decided not to ski but to spend the day exploring Méribel as it was market day. They were all going to meet there for lunch. I had already arranged to meet Dirk for lunch so we all set off together and then I left them at the top of the cabin lift.

This was my first opportunity to explore on my own and I set off for Courcheval. This very French resort was a real contrast to the manic slopes of Méribel. Here the pistes were beautifully groomed and relatively empty. I was very glad that Dirk had decreed we should have a late lunch as it gave me time to cover most of the area before skiing back towards Méribel to join them in a restaurant between the two resorts. I had a quick snack and then left them there. They had skied hard all morning and they were not in a hurry to get going again. As we were leaving the next day it was my last chance for more quality skiing. Not just on that trip but probably that season.

That evening Dirk sent a message to say he was not joining us for dinner but would see us in the bar later. He had been in a strange mood all day. I suspected he had fallen out with Phoebe who had left earlier that evening to drive home. After dinner some people went to the weekly disco in Brides les Bains and were there until the early hours. I did some packing and then joined some of my guests in the bar for a last drink. I arrived downstairs just in time to mediate between Dirk and Curtis. The latter had been blowing his own trumpet as he had somehow managed to ski back to Brides les Bains from Méribel. I suspected he had done it to win Dirk's admiration. He was naïve and desperate to impress the group and in particular Dirk. Curtis had been worshipping his hero all week but with little reward. Dirk refused to be impressed and after telling him he was stupid went on to challenge him on the grounds it was impossible as there was no piste just tree covered slopes. When this gauntlet was thrown down Curtis staggered off to get proof. He reappeared with a pair of battered skis. Fortunately they were his own skis and I would not have to explain their condition to my new best enemy the owner of the ski hire shop. Dirk took one look, grunted and then went off to his room. He was not having a good week. He had been out-skied by a mere woman and now he had been supplanted as the hero of the group by Curtis who had achieved the impossible.

The following day when I looked up through my skylight I could see grey clouds and snowflakes drifting down. I was glad the transfer company had brought the time forward as heavy snowfall was predicted. If we made good time we could spend some time in Annecy. Everyone co-operated regarding our early start with one exception. Curtis was nursing a bad hangover and did not appear at breakfast. When I called his room he said he was on his way. I repeated this process two more times and the third time I told him we would have to leave in five minutes. The bus was already being loaded outside so I told Curtis I would put his skis on board for him. I was standing by the bus about to launch the skis into the boot when Curtis appeared dragging his huge holdall behind him.

Even though it was snowing heavily the roads were clear and we made good time. We reached the pretty town of Annecy in time for a coffee and then a stroll along the canal and a browse through the small boutique shops under the arches in the centre of town. Neither Curtis nor Dirk joined us preferring to go off on their own. For them the holiday was over and their socialising skills had been packed away until the next trip. I knew that this was not an unusual reaction amongst some of our single clients and accepted their verbal brush offs.

At Gatwick I said a lengthy goodbye to Hermione as I did feel slightly guilty that she had spent a week in a ski resort and had not skied once. She was very cheerful about it and grinned as she delivered her parting shot. I was to say hello to Ryan, a colleague, who would remember her as she had been on one of his golfing holidays but had not played golf. I could not leave the airport until everyone had their luggage and Curtis' bag did not appear on the conveyor belt so we both went to luggage enquiries. We discovered that his holdall had split and was being taped up. Curtis was like a cat on hot bricks as he insisted I did not wait. It was a relief to get away but I could not help wondering why he was so anxious I should not be there when his bag was finally delivered. I wondered what he had in it – obviously more than a week's dirty washing.

I did not have long to muse over the contents of Curtis' holdall as my telephone was ringing before I was fully awake the following morning. It was Aimee who wanted to know if I could host a Valentine's weekend in Bideford. It was a small group and they had only just decided to go ahead. I was not a great fan of Valentine's Day and my one and only attempt at a romantic gesture had failed miserably. I had sent a large chocolate heart through the post and it had arrived in tiny pieces. The recipient, a fellow member of my tennis club, had related the story many times in my presence.

* * * * *

It was a long drive to Bideford and I had to get there in time to do some shopping before checking into our hotel. My mission was to find a Valentine gift for each person in the group and on a shoestring budget. As soon as I began my search I knew it was going to be difficult to find something appropriate in the mixture of cheap souvenir outlets with shelves crammed with cheap knick-knacks and the tasteful but expensive merchandise in the upmarket shops. I had some lunch first to consider my options. Somewhere off the main shopping street seemed the best bet and eventually, in a small gifte shoppe, I found some chocolate hearts each in a little silver or gold box. Fortunately the shop had exactly twenty-two left which was just the number I wanted.

When I arrived at our hotel I was greeted by Neville, the son of the owners. He was tall and slim and his gloomy countenance complemented his stooped posture. His handshake and greeting were minimal when I introduced myself. He wanted to know why I had brought such a small group with me. He had been expecting at least one hundred. After making a few critical comments about my predecessor he went on to express disappointment that our Hosts and Hostesses never visited his hotel a second time. I was not surprised to hear this. I was eager to get away from the dark forbidding reception area guarded by suits of armour. This rather strange decor was a symbol of the Maltese heritage of the owners. I maintained a sympathetic expression on my face despite my impatience to get myself, my luggage and my shopping to my room before going through our itinerary with Neville.

My room was cold and damp so I did not linger long and I was soon back downstairs. I had a walk round the hotel but there was not much to see as all the reception rooms were locked. During my meeting with Neville I was assured that the rooms we were using would be open just before we were due to assemble in them. I braved the cold weather to explore outside but there was nothing of interest there. The outdoor pool was empty of water which gave the exterior a rather desolate air. I went back inside and followed the signs to the Reading Room where our itinerary suggested early arrivals should meet. The door had been unlocked to reveal a small lounge with comfy armchairs and illuminated paintings on the walls. Two women in my group were already in there. They were two very jolly women, who introduced themselves as Mavis, "call me Maz" and Jane, "call me Jaz" and then collapsed in giggles. They made a formidable double act, finishing each other's sentences and breaking into peals of laughter at each other's jokes. Their entire conversation seemed to consist of one liners and innuendos.

I was very glad when we were joined by Nicholas. He was tall and good looking and dressed in a sporting jacket with leather elbow patches. Nicholas was very laid back and took Maz and Jaz in his stride. We were chatting happily when the lights went out and plunged us into semi-darkness. There was just enough illumination from the small strip lights under the paintings on the walls to find our way around. This was my first introduction to the hotel's system of timers. I had tried every switch in the room but none of them responded. The heating had also gone off and we were soon driven out of there and back to our rooms to find some light and warmth.

Before meeting the group I put a Valentine gift on each place setting at our table. There was no other indication in the hotel that it was Valentine's Day. Not a single red heart to be seen on the dark, austere furniture. Ours seemed to be the only table in the large, cold dining room. There was no heat in there so I had checked with reception that it would be warm by the time we sat down for our meal. At least the bar was now flooded by light and the old-fashioned radiators were expelling hot air. My guests drifted in for the Welcome Drink at a pace that enabled me to learn all the names and introduce them to each other. Our three course dinner was not the Valentine Gala Dinner we had been promised. We were the only people eating in the restaurant and there was no atmosphere at all. We joked that it was like eating in a museum because we were surrounded by memorabilia of Malta.

After the meal we moved into the Venetian Suite for our disco. This room was enormous and the layout emphasised this. There was a bar by the door and the disco was on the far side of the room. In between the two was a vast expanse of wooden floor. Everyone was overwhelmed by the space and reluctant to dance. The DJ worked really hard to get us all on the floor and I was happy to help by leading a performance of the Macarena. I had thought that Maz and Jaz would be the life and soul of the party but they propped up the bar and did not venture on to the floor once. Maz told me she was not impressed with the group as they were too 'old'. I was surprised by this comment as I thought we had a decent selection of relatively young men but finally it dawned on me that she was referring to the women.

Nicholas surprised me when he announced that the disco had been his whole reason for booking the weekend and he lived to play the air guitar to Status Quo tracks. He would not perform on his own though and insisted I dance with him when everyone else gave up. Nicholas got very grumpy when I left him to go to the toilet and when I returned he announced he would go straight home if I left him alone on the dance floor again. It was a long evening and terminated at midnight on the dot when the timers kicked in and all the lights went out.

The following morning our breakfast slot was precisely one hour, from eight thirty to nine thirty. Everyone was punctual motivated by a general fear of being timed out. The food on the hot breakfast buffet was cold and Neville, who was our waiter, was not impressed when I pointed this out. He collected up all the plates of food on our table and then swept all the platters off the hot plates. Everything was reheated in the kitchen and then plated up and delivered to each person. There was no element of choice. As soon as we finished eating Neville chivvied everyone out of the restaurant ignoring requests for second cups of tea or coffee.

That morning we had an included bus tour. Nicholas brought his own car and with Maz and Jaz as his passengers he followed our bus all day. I wondered if he was ready for flight in case the tour did not come up to his expectations as he gave no reason for doing this. We did not have a local guide to accompany us but our coach driver, Dave, kept up a running commentary. We had plenty of time in Clovelly to watch the video at the Clovelly Centre and then walk through the village and down to the beach where we visited two pubs, one for coffee and one for lunch.

We had very little time at Bude, our next stop, because Dave had to get back in time for the school run. He further reduced our time there by insisting that we could not get off the bus until he had parked in the coach park, a long way from the beach. I had asked him to let us out as we drove along the sea front. We were constantly stopping and starting as other buses disgorged their passengers onto the pavement. Dave insisted he was forbidden to do this. His earlier enthusiasm was waning and he was now focused on his next job. We raced into the town where we split up and either walked along the beach or indulged in a cream tea as there was not time to do both.

That evening I was hosting our traditional Champagne Quiz and I had to cut up lots of strips of paper. It was a race against time to get them done. I dared not delay the start of the quiz in case the lights went out on us again. The Spanish waiter did not understand my system and was not very good at dispensing the bubbly according to instructions. He kept filling up everyone's glass regardless of whether or not they were entitled to a drink. We had just finished the quiz and all the champagne when the lights went out. We stayed there chatting until Neville arrived, clearly impatient because we had not appeared in the dining room at the appointed hour. I felt I was living the Fawlty Towers experience.

Neville escorted us to the disco although some of the group defied both him and the darkness and lingered in the dining room talking. The disco was much better that evening as we were joined by other residents in the hotel and we took up more space in the large room. Nicholas was happy as he did not have to rely on me to keep him company on the dance floor. There were several air guitar enthusiasts around and I was happy to watch them while I chatted to Maz and Jaz at the bar. They were still not tempted on to the dance floor. The previous evening it had been too empty and that night it was too crowded and they did not like the music anyway. When the music finished a small group of us continued to converse until we were driven away by the lack of heating. Neville had not dared switch all the lights off at midnight but he had not felt any guilt at turning off the radiators.

Our plans to end the weekend with a walk were blown away by very strong winds the next morning and everyone had breakfast and left. Just three of us remained – Maz, Jaz and me. Maz and Jaz were getting the train home. We sat and shivered in reception as all the heating had been switched off. As we made small talk under the watchful eye of a knight in shining armour I noticed that Maz and Jaz kept casting glances at each other. Finally Maz asked me if I was also waiting before I went to the station to catch a train. When I said I was driving home they suggested I get going. I was the gooseberry. It was time to move on.

Chapter 9 - March

"Passport, boarding pass and meal voucher." I collected the proffered items and turned away from the check-in desk before the words 'meal voucher' actually sank in. It was only four in the morning and our flight was due to leave at seven so why did I need a meal voucher? I turned back to the girl on the desk and asked her if I needed my meal voucher for breakfast on the plane. "No, madam," she sighed, "we hand out meal vouchers when a flight is delayed for five hours or more." Alarm bells began ringing. "Does that mean...?" "Yes madam. Next please."

I withdrew still clutching my meal voucher. This was really bad news. I was on my way to Lanzarote and two thirds of my group were flying with me from Gatwick. The rest of the group were on a flight from Manchester. As it was clear I was not going to get any more information at the check-in desk I went to the Avro desk as they were the ground handlers for our airline, Translift.

Initially I was told to watch the departures board for more information. The board only stated that there would be an announcement in two hours' time. I needed more information before I met my group so I went back to the Avro desk.

I suspected that my new ally loved to be the bearer of bad news and it was not long before he was stroking his chin and predicting a twenty-four hour delay.

When I arrived at the designated meeting point several of my guests were already there and discussing the delay. Felix was very unhappy about the whole situation and wanted to abandon the holiday and go home immediately. Henry and Gloria were proving to be a very calming influence and backed me up when I suggested we find somewhere to have something to eat together and to wait and see what news the next announcement would bring. As there were still several people I had not seen yet the others went off to find somewhere to sit and I waited in case anyone else turned up. While I waited another announcement was made to the effect that a further announcement would be made in two hours' time. It was time to prepare my guests for the possibility of an overnight stay at Gatwick.

I needed to find the rest of my group to give them the bad news. I went to the Information Desk and gave them a list of names and asked them to put out a message for them to meet me there. They refused on the basis they could only call one or two names but not eight. When I suggested we divide my list into groups of four they agreed to do one announcement with eight names. Six people responded to my message and I took them to join the rest of the group who were gathered round a large table in the eating area. I went back to the Information Desk when the next announcement regarding our flight was due to be made. I also sneaked in another announcement for my two missing persons but they still did not appear. I was sure they must be together and had decided they could manage on their own.

The next announcement referred to a further announcement that would be made in an hour. I decided to take action as it now seemed inevitable we would be put in hotels overnight. I went to see my friend on the Avro desk and explained that we were a group of fourteen people travelling together and we needed rooms in the same hotel. I hoped that by getting my request in early I would succeed in getting us all together in the same hotel. I was right and when the next announcement confirmed that we would be staying overnight at Gatwick I raced back to the desk where my friend had already prepared vouchers for us. I had to tell him that I had failed to find my last two passengers and he kept back their vouchers and said he would try and ensure they were in the same hotel.

We had been allocated rooms in a hotel at the North Terminal and after retrieving our luggage we walked there. While the group were checking in I went into the Brasserie restaurant and booked a table for lunch. It was a really good lunch and lifted our spirits. Our thoughts turned to how we would spend the afternoon. The hotel had a leisure centre but our first priority was to catch up on some sleep to recover from our early start that morning. After the group had left I spoke to the maître d' who promised that he would reserve a large table for dinner. While we had been eating I had been watching a stream of other passengers on our flight arriving and checking in and I knew there would be pressure on bookings in the restaurant that evening. The other passengers had been issued more food vouchers to have lunch in the terminal building so we had been lucky.

I called Aimee to let her know what was happening. I was concerned about the group flying out from Manchester. They should be on their way but I had no way of knowing if they were or not. Aimee had promised to call our hotel to tell them we were delayed. She called me back to confirm that the Manchester group had arrived at our hotel in Lanzarote and that Claudia would be looking after them. I did not know who Claudia was but decided I was very grateful to her. I did ask if my two missing passengers had called the office but they had not. Once I had made all the necessary calls I stretched out on my bed but I could not relax.

Before I met the group for drinks that evening I walked back to the South Terminal to check that our flight was still due to leave at seven the next morning. It was. After enjoying a drink in the plush bar we made our way to the Brasserie where the manager on duty tried to divert us to one of the conference suites where all the other passengers were eating. I stood my ground and insisted that we had a booking in the restaurant. After making a call they decided to honour our booking and we enjoyed an excellent meal together. I was still looking for my missing passengers so I went downstairs to see if they were there. The other two hundred passengers were all eating in one large function room. It reminded me of school dinners as I watched them dipping into the large metal containers full of food that were lined up along one long table. I strolled around looking for likely candidates as my missing passengers but I could not find them. I only knew I was looking for two adults, one male and one female. I wore my badge and my blazer in the hope they may recognise me and make themselves known. No one approached me so I returned to the group upstairs in the bar.

I made one final check before I went to bed. A large notice in reception stated that we would have a wake-up call at five the next morning and our flight would depart at seven. Nevertheless after I said goodnight to the group I went back to the airport to double check the arrangements. I would not settle down until we were on our way the next morning. I hardly slept and I was up before the wake-up call came through. It was Good Friday and instead of preparing for a day of leisure on the beach I was prowling round a deserted reception area wondering why I was the only one there. I checked the boards again and discovered that during the night our flight had collected a further two hour delay and the wake-up call had been postponed until six. I wondered if the others had known before they went to bed.

Gloria nearly had a heart attack because she woke at quarter to six and thought she was late. I was in reception when she appeared five minutes later in a state of panic. I told her there was a further delay and she went back to her room to get ready. As most of us were already up and ready to go we made our way to the South Terminal and checked in early. We had been too early for breakfast in our hotel so I requested breakfast vouchers but was told they were not giving them out. I sent the group off for a coffee and returned to the hotel to find Felix who had enjoyed an extra hour in bed.

While I was waiting for Felix in reception I was approached by a couple who identified themselves as my missing passengers. They immediately began to harangue me for not finding them the previous day. I wondered how they had identified me and they told me they had asked the reception manager. I had left a message with reception when I had checked in the day before so it seemed strange that they had not made enquiries until now. There was no time (and I had no inclination) for an inquest as Felix had arrived and we all set off for the South Terminal. By that time they were giving out breakfast vouchers so I requested one for myself and the other members of my group. Fortunately they remembered us all checking in earlier and we were soon tucking into our meal.

We started boarding the flight at eight that morning and we were all on board and ready to go forty-five minutes later. A further forty-five minutes later the pilot announced that we were missing thirty passengers. Another half hour went by and the pilot announced that the missing passengers had decided not to travel. Meanwhile the cabin crew were running up and down the aisle counting heads. Finally they decided that eighteen people were not travelling and were already accounted for and there had always been twelve empty seats on the flight. It was nearly eleven that morning by the time our Translift flight finally lifted itself off the ground and headed for Arrecife.

It was such a relief to finally arrive at our hotel. The Hotel Antonio was right on the beach, the Playa de los Pocillos, and it looked really attractive from the outside. I did not anticipate any problems regarding the rooms as I was sure they would reflect the light and space of the reception rooms. Nevertheless I settled down in a comfortable seat to while away thirty minutes before going to my room. My optimism proved unfounded and within minutes a stream of people came back to reception with complaints about their rooms. Two rooms did not have balconies and the hotel promised to change them the next morning. Gloria complained that her room was dark due to a large palm tree right outside the window, she was shouting and stamping her foot and resolute that she would not spend even one night in that particular room. I had no idea if my room would be any better but I just handed over my key and suggested she have a look. She was back soon after and grinning like a Cheshire cat. Yes she would take it. I wondered what I had given away.

It was not long before I found out. I was fumbling around in my ground floor room that was deprived of any natural light by the palm trees in the courtyard outside when my phone rang. It was the manager of the hotel requesting that we meet immediately. The manager was annoyed because I had given my nice room away even though I had done it unwittingly. I thanked him for having given me such a lovely room. I explained that I had not given it away deliberately but a quick resolution had been imperative as one of my guests was complaining about her room and the hotel were not able to find an alternative. The manager said that everyone would now want one of the newly renovated rooms and they did not have any more rooms of the same standard. I had to hope that Gloria would keep her mouth shut but I doubted that she would. The manager was obviously upset because his gesture had gone wrong and promised that he would find me a better room the next day. I would be glad to move away from the sombre courtyard.

My next task was to find the Manchester group. First I decided to introduce myself to Claudia but was told, "Claudia no here". I hoped she had been there yesterday when needed. When I found four of the Manchester contingent sunbathing by the pool I discovered that Claudia had also been absent the previous day and they had all been left on their own. Once that complaint had been aired we moved on to discuss their rooms. Matilda was very annoyed because she did not have a room like the one in the hotel's brochure. She had brought a copy of this leaflet with her and kept stabbing her finger at a picture of one of the rooms. It was one of the nicest rooms of course and in the wing that had recently been refurbished. She had already requested a room change and had been told that it was not possible as the hotel was full. I said I would see what I could do. Already my vision of a room on the third floor with a sea view was slipping away.

That evening when the whole group finally gathered together for our Welcome Drink I met the other members of the Manchester group. None of them were happy with their rooms which they claimed were shabby. It was obvious that Gloria had been boasting about her refurbished room. They confirmed that no effort had been made to welcome them and get them together the previous evening but, with one exception, they had all found each other. That exception, Bess, was still missing and no one had seen her all day. I rang her room and as there was no answer I pushed a note under her door to say we would be at dinner. Rather than wait any longer I suggested we all went into dinner. Bess was already there, sitting at one of our tables. She was an independent person and not worried about being on her own. The previous evening she had eaten early and then gone to bed. We lingered over our meal and I was relieved to see that despite a shaky start the two groups did seem to be mixing well.

As we had already missed a whole day I anticipated problems organising all the trips that everyone wanted to do. I was at breakfast early the following morning in the hope of assessing which trips would run prior to our Information Meeting. But not everyone got to breakfast and those that did were more interested in discussing Cyril's antics in the nightclub the previous evening. Most of them had been to Amadeus just across the road. Cyril had been presented with two bottles of wine to persuade him to stop singing with the resident female vocalist.

As the local agent was not sending anyone to take our Information Meeting I had to lead the discussion myself. Several people wanted to hire cars and do the whole island in one day so the meeting was inconclusive and short as people began to drift away to sunbathe by the pool. I went to reception to organise the room changes. All the requests could not be met. I was offered another recently renovated room and four people were moved. I could not persuade them to give my new room to someone else. In fact I got another reprimand for giving the first one away to a client. The manager promised that the other requests would be dealt with later that day.

I had suggested that we all walk along the coast to the old harbour at Puerto del Carmen. Our hotel was at the end of a four kilometre promenade that connected our beach to the old town. Only one person turned up and that was Felix, a keen photographer. Our walk was punctuated by frequent stops to take photographs and it was mid-afternoon by the time we reached the old harbour. It was very pretty. White buildings ringed the stone-wall enclosed waters on which bobbed lots of colourful boats. We had a fresh fish lunch in a café there overlooking the harbour. It was very pleasant sitting there chatting and I learnt a lot about photography, hitherto a closed book to me. We did not leave until five that afternoon and I ran all the way back to the hotel as I had completely forgotten that I should be organising the remaining room changes at five thirty. Felix followed behind at his own pace.

When I rushed into reception I was met by an irate Matilda. She had rejected the room the hotel had offered her as it did not look like the one in the brochure. I managed to swap everything round so she got my 'better' room and I moved into her room. As the room had to be cleaned before I could take up residence, I was hanging around in the corridor with my luggage when Gloria found me in limbo. I was getting anxious as I needed to shower and change for dinner. Gloria offered me the use of her shower and after opening the door went off to the bar for a drink. It was a lovely room, spacious and sunny with a magnificent view across the bay. I bitterly regretted the impulse that had made me give it up.

After dinner that night everyone strolled along the front to Ned Kelly's bar. I promised to join them later but first I had to deal with two room changes that should have taken place that day until the manager had changed his mind. He clearly thought that the occupants would have given up by then and was surprised when I asked him to make sure they were organised the following day. It did not take me long to find my companions. I could hear them almost as soon as I left the hotel. Ned Kelly's was run by a Glaswegian couple. The husband served behind the bar and his wife was the entertainment. She sang and did some 'chat'. The wife drank a lot and as the evening got later so her chat got coarser and her audience became louder as they voiced their encouragement. I could not bring myself to enthuse about the whole experience and when put on the spot I screamed back that it was an 'interesting' venue.

Most of us were up early the following morning as we were going to the market in Teguise. I had quickly solved my problem regarding the organisation of excursions as there was an agency and car hire just across the road from our hotel. I even persuaded them to collect us from our hotel so that we did not have to walk to the pick-up point on the seafront. Our early start meant that we got to the market before it became crowded and hot so we were able to wander around in comfort. It was a large multicultural market and the stall holders ranged from local gypsies selling tablecloths to Africans peddling carvings and beads. Some of these stall holders would bargain but the locals had a fixed price system for their leather goods and ceramics and stuck to it rigidly. On the fringes of the market were several shops offering tastings of cheeses, wines and liqueurs. It was a great experience but we were happy to clamber into the cool interior of our bus when it left at midday.

Driving back was a chance to appreciate the interesting volcanic landscape and at last, I could find out from our local guide the significance of the striking sculpture on the roundabout near our hotel. This was one of many sculptures by César Manrique and we were told we would see similar works of his all over the island. But Manrique was not just a sculptor, he painted, he designed, he planned, he built and he advised. His fabulous wind sculpture had whetted my appetite to see more.

I had a lot to do when we got back to the hotel. First I had to check that the hotel had found new rooms for Matilda and Hilda. I checked the rooms they were being offered. I was pretty sure they would not want them so I persuaded the manager to come up with some better alternatives. My next task was to discuss possible trips with each individual and to get everyone to sign the card for Matilda's birthday. I found everyone except Felix who had gone off on his own on the local bus as no one else was interested in exploring on public transport. Everyone else spent the morning sunbathing and I joined them after checking once more that the room changes really would happen that day. The 'new' rooms would be ready at twelve and I passed this message on to Matilda and Hilda who were lounging by the pool.

Despite the hot sunny weather there was a chill in the air around the pool. After a promising start a rift had appeared in the group and had now widened into a chasm. The Gatwick group were on one side of the pool and the Manchester group were on the other side. Whichever group I joined I felt that the other one was watching me. Finally I sat between them and tried to read a book. I saw Matilda and Hilda leave the poolside just after midday but they returned soon after. There had not been enough time to change rooms so I went across to them to see if everything was okay. They told me that the receptionist had said that the rooms were not yet ready. I went off to reception to check and discovered that the rooms were ready but that the girl on reception (a temp from Arrecife) had been annoyed because she thought that one of the women had been very rude. She had retaliated by saying that the rooms were not ready. Hilda did have an abrupt manner but I doubted that she had been rude. I thought the girl was out of order and I was getting the backlash of her action. I confirmed that the rooms were ready and then went and gave the good news to the two women.

Finally I was free to join some of the others for lunch and we went to the hotel bar and restaurant on the beach. It was very pleasant sitting there watching the sea lapping on the sand as we enjoyed the cooling breeze. When the bill came Cyril told the waitress to give it to him. He felt that as he was an accountant he should deal with it. After announcing that the bill would be split equally between all of us he did a quick calculation and told us how much we all owed. As we delved in our purses for the money Cyril produced a small wooden box and told us to put our money in there. He said he needed some cash so he would charge all our meals to his room and settle the bill at the end of the week. This was my first introduction to his 'magic' box. I had requested a separate bill so I was not party to the trick I was sure he was playing but I could not put my finger on exactly what was going on. We all left together and although I had heard people telling

Cyril they had put in extra for a tip or that they did not want any change as that was intended for the waiter he did not leave any money on the table. It was all stuffed into his magic box and he went off to sign his bill.

I went back to my room to confirm a trip the next day. Just three people had booked it as several people had hired cars to go exploring and the rest of the group were only interested in getting a tan. When I arrived in the bar for pre-dinner drinks that evening I was informed that the Manchester group would be dining in the town. That left the Gatwick group eating in the hotel. I was very sad when I heard the news. I had worked really hard to keep the group together but there was an air of hostility when everyone was in the same place at the same time. I did not know what had happened to create this division. I really felt I had failed. Henry, a sensitive person, had noticed that I was upset and offered to tell me what had caused the great divide provided I promised to keep the information to myself. I promised. He told me that Cyril, after he had been imbibing all day, had announced to everyone around him that he thought that the women in the Gatwick group were a lot prettier than those in the Manchester group. Despite the fact this was just one drunken opinion the women concerned, egged on by Matilda and Hilda, had taken his words to heart and were now refusing to cross the divide between the two groups.

I had to put my own disappointment behind me and concentrate on my dinner companions. After dinner we chatted in the bar against a background of hotel entertainment, Spanish dancing but not flamenco. When the hotel entertainment finished we all went out on the town. I left my dinner companions in Ned Kelly's bar and went to join the Manchester group in the Hard Rock Café where they had eaten that evening. They were clearly pleased that I had made the effort to find them and I realised the importance of not taking sides and spreading my time evenly between the two warring factions.

There was a brief entente cordiale at breakfast the following morning when everyone united to sing Happy Birthday to Matilda when I presented her with her card. The truce did not last long and when I went out to the pool they had split into two 'camps' again. Bess was blissfully unaware of the conflict and continued to plough her own furrow flitting between the two groups. I was being careful to spend the same amount of time with each group as I sensed that when I was sitting with one group the other one was not just watching me but timing me. If I suggested an outing I had to make sure that everyone was invited – not just as a group but personally. That evening it was the Manchester group who invited me to join them for a Chinese meal in Arrecife. As my brief was to eat in the hotel every night unless the whole group was eating out I had to turn down their invitation but I did offer to try and swap their hotel dinner for lunch that day. I joined the small group that was dining in that night and they persuaded me to stay and to watch the hotel flamenco show after we had eaten. It was not the flamboyant affair we had anticipated. Two mature women danced around an elderly gentleman who tottered about in trousers that were too long and a waistcoat that was too small. They performed to recorded, modern music and all three frantically clicked their castanets but otherwise there was not much movement. After the display I walked into town to join the others at Ned Kelly's for a drink. Keeping the peace was wearing me out.

We had another early start the following day when most of the group set off on the north island tour. We were transported on an English speaking only double decker bus. Our first stop was Teguise slumbering peacefully after the bustle of the market the previous morning. Teguise was the ancient capital of Lanzarote until the title was handed to Arrecife. After a short walking tour of the town we set off again and wound our way up through a mountain pass to Mirador de Haria. From this, the highest point of the island we looked down on the Valley of the Palms, the town of Haria and the volcanoes for which the island is famous. It was also an opportune moment for a coffee break.

We spent some time at Cueva de Los Verdes (green caves). The name has nothing to do with the colour of the caves but is the name of the family that inherited them. Once used by the locals as a refuge from pirates and slave traders they have now been developed as a tourist attraction with paths meandering through the lava tunnels. These tunnels link large chambers where the roofs have collapsed creating an open space. Our walk through the caves was carefully timed so that when we arrived at the underground lake we all experienced the optical illusion created by reflections that we were standing on the edge of a precipice. The guide was excellent and built up the drama, telling us not to stand too close to the edge, until he flicked a small stone into the water creating ripples that spread across the shallow lake. We all laughed at our gullibility before moving on to the next chamber that is now used as a venue for concerts.

After the caves we went to Mirador del Rio, a viewing point at the northern most point of the island. From the high cliffs of this shore we looked down on the five islands just off the coastline. The largest, Gracios, is only just over one kilometre across the water and offers a true retreat for those wanting to get away from it all. Designed and built by César Manrique the viewpoint is discretely positioned among the rocks and enclosed by lava stones harmonising with its natural surroundings. It is another fitting tribute to his vision which was the enhancement of tourist attractions as tasteful sites through the fusion of natural elements and modern amenities. Before the island was overwhelmed and transfigured by increasing numbers of tourists he had prevailed upon the authorities to introduce planning regulations to control development. He also weaved his own particular magic as he fashioned sites of interest from the natural features around the island. His works have become famous landmarks that are enjoyed by both tourists and locals.

Although Manrique died in a car accident in 1992 his achievements are honoured and his work is continued by the 'Foundation César Manrique', an organisation established to conserve his creations. The foundation occupies the house that César Manrique built for himself in his own personal style and decorated with pieces of his own art work. This building incorporates big bubbles in the black lava that form some of the rooms and a gallery of his paintings and sculptures.

After lunch, a tasty buffet of Canary food, we visited Jameos del Aqua, a collection of natural caves in the lava that Manrique had developed as a complex of interesting sights. Shortly after entering a volcanic tunnel we came to a beautifully landscaped lagoon of salt water. As we peered into the dark water we could see the little white Jameito crabs. Continuing through the tunnel we came to a lovely garden with a swimming pool, all decorated in the style of César Manrique. At the end of the garden there is a large cave with great acoustic qualities that has been converted into a theatre. We also had time to stroll round the museum while we were there. This was the second site developed by Manrique that we had visited and I could appreciate that he had brought an innovative and refreshing approach to tourism. Inspired by Felix's enthusiasm I had bought a camera and my day had been enhanced by my efforts to capture some stunning images.

I was so hot by the time we got back to the hotel I decided to have a swim in the sea to cool off. I changed and went down to the beach. The weather was undergoing a dramatic change. The sun had hidden behind dark clouds and a frisky wind whipped up grains of sand that swirled around me. The sea still looked calm and inviting so I carried on and after dropping my towel on a sun bed I waded out into the water. I had only swum a few strokes when I felt the current begin to tug at my legs trying to pull me out to sea. I splashed back towards the shore and scrambled to my feet, stumbling towards dry land. I was nearly there when I was captured by a wave that rolled me over time and again in the foaming froth. I was a good swimmer but I felt helpless against the strengthening undertow. I redoubled my efforts and the sea finally spat me onto the beach. I had been swept a long way along the beach from my entry point so I walked back and collected my towel. I met Henry who was intending to swim and I warned him that the sea was getting very rough. I knew he would not attempt to succeed where I had failed and he turned back towards the hotel with me.

After showering I went out for a walk. It was still very overcast and a restless wind tugged at my shorts as I strolled past eerily deserted beaches. A short way along the promenade where the sea was smashing down onto the rocks that ringed a small cove I spotted some scuba divers who were clearly searching for something. I stopped and watched for a while then moved on to explore the shops along the parade nearby. Browsing the wares on sale was impossible as everyone had retreated from the beach into the shops and I soon got tired of trying to push through the crowds. I returned to the hotel and switched on my television to watch the local news. To my horror I discovered that the frogmen had been looking for a missing swimmer and that three people had drowned off the beach where I had tried to swim earlier. It was such a shock I felt very subdued. I decided not to mention it to anyone in the group when we met later for pre-dinner drinks in Felix's room before we all went out for dinner.

It was a matter of pride to me that I had actually managed to get everyone to agree to having dinner together in a local restaurant. I was not surprised when the Manchester group did not join us for pre-dinner drinks. I was relieved when we arrived at the restaurant, La Canada, and found them sitting at one end of the long table that had been set up for us. It soon became clear that the restaurant had overstretched itself trying to serve twenty people at once. My romantic notion of a grand reunion had overridden my practical nature as I knew that I should have organised two tables for such a large number. The food was very good but it took so long to get through the meal that by the time we had finished everyone was in a rush to pay and head off for another night on the town.

Cyril was quick to seize his opportunity and whipped out his magic box. My earlier suspicions regarding some sort of scam had been voiced by other members of the group and several people had requested that I organise separate bills so they could pay the restaurant directly. I was working down the table with the waiters when I noticed that Cyril had ensnared his own waiter and cash was changing hands at his end of the table. I could not intervene publicly so I just had to hope there would be no problems.

My hopes were dashed when Henry and Felix approached me the following morning to say that Cyril had taken their money for the meal the previous evening and had promised to give them their change but so far they had not received it. I had to take action. Cyril was on his own drinking a beer in the poolside bar when I found him. I asked him for the change he owed Henry and Felix and he told me that he had given both lots of change to Henry. As I had spoken to both Henry and Felix together I knew this was not true but I could not denounce him as a confidence trickster. I asked Cyril to make sure they were given the money due to them and hoped he had a better nature that would prevail. As I heard no more about this incident it seemed that he did.

The following morning I enjoyed a long solitary breakfast and started writing my report while I waited for my guests to appear. I did not have much company during the meal but I spoke to everyone later that morning round the pool. First I sat with Them and then I joined Us for a while before we all had lunch in the hotel snack bar but on two separate tables. Felix had decided to hire a car to do a quick tour of the north of the island as he had not done the bus trip. He invited me to join him and I accepted. Henry invited himself along because he thought it would be improper for me to go off with one male member of the group. He was probably right but my thirst to go exploring had overridden reason.

Felix really was only interested in taking photographs and while looking for opportunities to do so he lost concentration and veered off the road. He hit some small rocks and punctured two tyres. We had one spare tyre but we needed two. We flagged down a car and the driver took Henry to the nearest phone box to call the car hire company. He also brought Henry back to join us by our stricken car. Henry changed one wheel while we waited to be rescued. I said, jokingly, that we should flag down a car from the same hire company and ask them to give us their spare wheel. No sooner said than Henry had done it and it was not long before we were on our way again. We stopped to call the hire car company to tell them what we had done. Felix was in no rush to get back and he was still stopping to take photographs, oblivious to my growing concern. We had a farewell drink with canapés scheduled for seven thirty that evening and I had to be back in time.

When we pulled up outside the hotel at seven twenty I raced up to my room and managed to shower and change in the five minutes available to me before I was due downstairs. Our little soiree had been arranged by the hotel as an apology for the problems with the rooms. Everyone ate in the hotel that night but again we had Them and Us tables. I sat with the breakaways as I had not spent much time with them. After dinner I also went out with them for the same reason. First we went to the Bristol pub for karaoke but there was none. Then we went to the Castle where we endured the worst hypnotist in the world. Our last port of call was Ned Kelly's bar but it was not as lively as usual because the wife was on the wagon.

The Manchester group was the first departure the following morning. Henry came to say goodbye but he was the only one in the Gatwick group who dared to cross the divide. Their taxis had arrived early and we started loading up in the hope the missing passenger, Matilda, would join us soon. She did not so I sent two taxis on their way while the manager called her room. Matilda told him it was not ten o'clock yet and as they were not due to leave until ten she would be there at ten. Eyebrows uplifted he gave me the gist of the conversation and passed the phone to me. I told her that the taxi was already there and the others were waiting for her. She reiterated that she would be there at ten and put the phone down.

We settled down to wait. She took her time and then when she did appear she breezed past me, dropped her suitcase by the door and went outside to take photographs of the hotel. I chased round after her suggesting it was time to get in the car. Her travelling companions glowered at her though the windows. Matilda may be sticking to her guns that she was not leaving before the appointed time but her stand misfired as according to everyone else's watch it was already past the hour. Hilda finally lost her patience and got out of the taxi. That was enough to persuade Matilda that it was time to gather her belongings together and jump in the car.

An hour later I left with the second group. I had sat in reception reading for that last hour and when Cyril arrived to check out I moved a little closer to the desk as I was curious to know how large a bill he had to pay. In theory he had signed around fifty lunches to his bill. There was nothing to pay. My attempts to work out what was clearly a scam were interrupted by the arrival of other guests. When I casually asked Felix and Henry if they ever got their change from Cyril they replied 'sort of' but did not elaborate. I would never know the secret of that magic box.

Thankfully our flight left on time and as we rose into the sky my thoughts turned to my next trip. Sometime ago Aimee had called me and said she had allocated the Inca Trail to me. My response had been non-committal. I really wanted to see Machu Picchu but I did not want to spend four days walking there. Nor did I want to camp en route – I liked my home comforts too much. If I said nothing maybe she would forget and find someone else. Nothing more had been said after that initial discussion and I assumed the trip had been given to Ryan who usually led it. I was very relieved as I was sure anyone who had booked the trip was expecting a six foot, athletic male Host and would feel very let down if he was replaced by a five foot nothing blonde. But just before I left for Lanzarote I received a package from Aimee. It was the information for the Inca Trail and my name was on all the literature that had been sent out to the clients. It was official, I was off to Peru.

Chapter 10 – April

Tents do not have sockets. When I realised that I would have nowhere to recharge my laptop I was in despair and called Aimee. As expected, she had no practical experience of camping but she did lend a sympathetic ear. After some banter about my habit of keeping a diary when I was away she suggested that I submit my handwritten record of events in place of a formal typed report – subject to the contents being 'suitable' for the purpose. I could not wait to put pen to paper.

Monday 16 April
I set off for Heathrow at four in the morning and empty roads and check-in desks with no queues meant that within an hour I was on my way to the Executive Lounge where I was meeting my group. Some of them had already gathered there and three of them, Ringo, Dora and Ramsay, had been to Borneo with Ryan, a colleague of mine. They had expected he would be leading this trip and cross-examined me about my presence rather than his. They did not understand that we all worked freelance so the company decided who would take each trip and we had no control over this decision. I struggled to move them on to another subject and finally succeeded. My confidence had ebbed away as they sang Ryan's praises. This was my first really big trip and already I felt that I did not have the

experience to cope. The three of them raised their glasses to each other. Clearly they were going to be a lively bunch and two ring leaders were already emerging – Ringo and Dora. I was not so cordially invited to join them.

The next person to join us, Myra, brushed aside my greeting as she wanted to complain that a vegetarian meal had not been ordered for her on our flight to Madrid. No one was getting a meal on that flight but there was the option to buy snacks and drinks from a trolley. I happily blamed the airline for not putting this on our flight manifest. Myra insisted I confirm her meal on the flight from Madrid to Lima as soon as we got to Madrid. I made a note to do so and turned my attention to some more new arrivals.

As soon as we arrived in Madrid we headed for our boarding gate and when I had made sure they were all there I left them on the pretext of checking the vegetarian meal. Long haul flights always offered a vegetarian choice and when I rejoined the group I told Myra that this was the case. Then she wanted to know if there would be more than one choice for vegetarians. Her attitude was very aggressive and it was not the first time I had met this attitude from a vegetarian. I wondered if this was a by-product of not eating meat.

When our meal was served I was told it was pasta or nothing! I said nothing and asked for extra bread, which I got but not extra butter as it was restricted to one pat per person. One steward took pity on me and put together a nice meal that included some fresh fruit. My neighbour was not so considerate. He moved around a lot except when he put in ear plugs, eye mask and got out his own pillow to go to sleep. This was when I had an irresistible urge to go to the toilet. The film choice was terrible and as we did not have individual screens I had to keep craning my neck to try and follow a film that was often completely blocked from my view by people doing gymnastics in the aisle to avoid exposure to deep vein thrombosis.

At last we arrived in Lima where we were met by Nieves who organized the loading of our luggage onto the roof of our bus. The surplus bags had to be packed around the passengers. I asked Nieves to request a larger vehicle for the remainder of our trip but when she shrugged her shoulders in response I suspected my request would go no further. I decided to contact our local agent directly. On arrival at our hotel, Hotel Jose Antonio, I helped with the check-in and arranged to meet everyone in the bar an hour later for our Welcome Drink. That just gave me time to buy some water from the shop across the road and to send an email to the agent from the Business Centre of the hotel.

After the Welcome Drink I suggested that we went across the road to Café Amore for dinner. No one wanted to move from the bar and Ringo decided to organise a kitty. Everyone contributed but I did not as I did not want another drink. I went up to my room, which smelt like old socks and did some unpacking. When I dropped my key on the floor and I was scrabbling around under the bed I discovered a pair of smelly socks so that was one problem solved. Now I had to prise my group out of the bar.

When I went back to the bar they were on their way to Café Amore and I joined them. It was a reasonable menu for reasonable prices. When the bill came

Andrew grabbed it and decided to put the rest of the kitty towards the total and divide the balance between us. He asked me to contribute twenty sols but I refused as I had not had a drink and my meal only cost ten sols. Some had already put their money in so effectively they paid twice. Ringo and his pals had also had second beers so it all seemed very unfair but those affected said they did not mind. I left them to it.

Tuesday 17 April

I was up very early to explore the area and find the local bank and supermarket. I could not find the latter before it was time for breakfast. Some of the group were already there and the rest arrived soon afterwards with the exception of Ivy who was last, enjoyed a leisurely breakfast and then kept us all waiting. Despite our late start we only drove as far as the bank two hundred yards down the road so that two people could change travellers' cheques. Bella and Ivy had chosen to ignore my advice to do this at the airport even though everyone else had seized the opportunity. Nieves should have refused to stop but instead she smiled sweetly and said, "of course". Her graciousness was no doubt oiled by the expectation of a good tip. I had already pointed out to the group that there was a bank just a few minutes' walk from our hotel so the culprits could have changed their money after the tour.

We waited in the bus for thirty minutes and as there was still no sign of them I went to see what was happening. The bank had to ring the issuing bank because Bella was cashing more than $100. All she had to do was reduce the amount and I told her so. She refused even though she was making the whole bus wait. I asked Nieves to try and speed things up while I went back to the bus to tell the group what was happening. Murmurs of discontent floated around me as I sat resolutely looking straight ahead of me until everyone was back on the bus.

At last our tour was underway and started with a circuit of the city on our bus. We alighted at the Church of San Francisco to visit the crypt which was the first public burial ground in Lima, bones and all. Next we walked to the Plaza Mayor where we watched the changing of the guard at the Government Palace (House of Pizarro) which was very colourful. Our last stop was the cathedral and after wandering around this impressive building we had lunch in Miraflores. Our hotel was located in the same district and I was relieved to hear that this district was one of the few areas where it is safe to walk around. After lunch we had a stroll by the Pacific Ocean before visiting a privately owned textile museum. The Amano museum was not a big hit with the group. We were there for an hour and it was very repetitive as the exhibits were all kept in cabinets and there was a lot of opening and closing of drawers.

On our way back to our hotel I asked Nieves to point out the elusive local supermarket. She offered to take me there and some of the others joined us to do some shopping. It could hardly be described as a local supermarket as it took us an hour to walk back to our hotel. The truly local supermarket had burned down in January but Nieves had not thought to mention that. I was hot and cross after that experience and on returning to the hotel I set off with Myra, Bella and Ivy to explore the hotel's outdoor swimming pool on the top floor. Myra managed to shut me in the lift door by pressing the close door button prematurely which she thought was terribly funny. I did not and retired, hurt, to my room. My day was not going well and now I had to memorise our itinerary. Ringo and his fan club expected me to be word perfect regarding every minute of the time we would spend on tour.

That evening I managed to find Nieves before we all met up to go out to dinner. I needed to go through the itinerary with her as Ivy wanted the precise length of all the journey times. I was still scribbling frantically as everyone gathered in reception before setting off to the Rosa Nautica restaurant. It was in a stunning location, on a pier stretching out to sea. It was quite 'posh' and the food was very good. We had a set menu with choices for each course. The drinkers had several bottles of wine at vastly inflated prices but they had a good, if somewhat noisy time. Myra was particularly inebriated and chatting up the waiters. She was shrieking and laughing on the bus all the way back to the hotel. As we had an early start the next morning most people went straight to bed but the drinkers headed for the bar. I booked the wake-up calls and porters for everyone and then went to my room to pack.

Wednesday 18 April
I threw down some breakfast at six and then checked that all the bags had been collected from outside the rooms where the group had been asked to put them at six thirty. Three bags were missing but I caught up with their owners in breakfast and the bus was still loaded and ready to go by seven. We drove for forty minutes to the archaeological site of Pachacamac outside Lima. It was a four kilometre walk around the site on gravelly tracks. Myra complained as she was wearing flimsy sandals and she had to keep stopping to remove the small stones. I had advised everyone to wear trainers and the evidence was irrefutable as she was the only one not wearing suitable shoes. Clearly Myra did not respond to general announcements and tartly informed me of this fact.

Our next destination was Chincha for lunch. As it was a three hour drive there was a rush for the toilets when we arrived. I joined it but stayed at the back of the queue until all the other women had used the facilities. I was unaware that Toby had fallen when he put his foot into a wide crack in the paving stones as he got off the bus. He had injured his ankle and the pain was so bad he had passed out. When I came out of the toilets I was surprised to see that very few people were sitting at our table. I was on my way outside to find everyone when Myra came rushing in and shouted, "What are you doing in here when Toby is ill outside?" No one had thought to come and tell me. I supposed they were relying on my mind reading skills. I rushed outside and found Toby slumped on the ground looking very grey.

The local doctor was summoned and he examined the injured ankle and said it was definitely not broken. I insisted on an X-ray so he drove Toby and me into the town where it was X-rayed at a small private clinic. It was fractured. Toby hopped back to the car and we went to another private clinic where a plaster was put on. Money exchanged hands at both clinics. When we got back to the lunch venue everyone had finished eating and they were all sunbathing by the pool. I settled Toby on the bus and then rounded everyone else up and we set off to Paracas in the Pisco district. Our journey took us across some wasteland where we experienced some horrible smells – rotting fish from the fish market and fishmeal factories. We were staying at the Hotel Paracus on the Paracus Peninsula and after checking in there we were off again to visit the Paracas National Reserve. Toby stayed in the hotel. He had a lot to think about. He was desperate to continue the tour with us but it was impractical, especially when we started the trek.

After leaving the hotel we drove through a wilderness towards the sea and then walked along a cliff top in a nature reserve to watch the birds. When we got back on the bus we set off to find some flamingos but darkness was falling and the flamingos had flown. It was time to return to the hotel where I immediately started working on the documentation to repatriate Toby. Having spent a few hours on his own he had realised it would be pointless to try and continue his holiday. Once I had collected all the information I needed I wheeled Toby into the hotel restaurant where the others had already gathered for dinner. Our hotel was in the middle of a wilderness so we had no choice but to eat there as we had no transport available. The setting was beautiful as the hotel was on the sea shore and there were lovely views through the restaurant window.

I left the group having dinner while I dealt with Toby's insurance company. I called them and they called me back. We went through all the details and then I faxed them all the documentation including details of our itinerary so they could contact me when they had decided how they would deal with the situation. I did not mind missing dinner. It was a relief to get away from Myra's sharp tongue. She had joined the 'we want Ryan as Host' bandwagon and was giving me a harder time than the other three. I struggled to understand their attitude as the fact Ryan was not their Host had nothing to do with me. I had not even requested this trip. Having done all the paperwork I had no option but to join the group in the dining room if I wanted to eat that evening. Ringo (I was warming to him now) gave me some of their lovely red wine and would not take any money. I did not stay long as I was expecting a call from Toby's insurance company and it was likely to be in the early hours of the next morning.

Thursday 19 April

I did not get any telephone calls during the night and was woken by our wake-up call at six thirty. My bags were already packed so I put them outside my room and went to breakfast. This was already laid out and was very sparse: just coffee, tea, juices, bread rolls and jam. I asked for some cheese and was presented with four slices of processed cheese and a bill for eight sols. When our bus arrived I was glad to see that my pleas for a better bus had succeeded. We travelled in comfort in a larger, modern bus that had effective air conditioning and a spacious boot that took all our luggage.

The first activity that morning was a boat trip but we had to hang around waiting for the mist to disperse before we could start boarding. The trip lasted two hours and we were all crammed into a small speed boat with no toilets. First we circled a rock formation known as the Candelabra and then we chugged around the Ballestos Islands to see the birds and the sea lions but we could not go ashore. Toby had come with us rather than sitting alone on the bus. The boatmen made a big fuss helping him on to the boat and then the guide trod on his injured foot three times. Toby was very independent and refused any help and would not use crutches preferring to hobble by himself on his plastered leg.

We had lunch at Huacachina Oasis our next destination. After the meal I organised some sand buggies and sand boarding on the huge sand dunes around the oasis. Everybody joined in and we spent nearly two hours racing up and down the dunes – it was fantastic. Justine, Amber and I were put in a small jeep while the others were in larger buggies. I was able to relax and really enjoy the experience. We stopped to take photos and to have a go at sand boarding – descending lying face down on a board that had been smeared with oil. Everyone had fun and I felt that finally I was being accepted by the whole group.

The final leg of our journey was to Nazca where we were staying overnight. The following morning we would have a very early start to fly over the Nazca Lines. However, during the journey Nieves suddenly announced that the group could do the flight over the Lines that evening if we got there by five. Agreement to this suggestion was unanimous. A little later she interrupted our excited chatter to inform us that only half the group could do the flight. Minutes later that figure was reduced to just five of us. As it happened we were fifteen minutes late arriving and after some discussion the pilot decided it was too late to go flying.

Nieves then decided that we should revert to our original programme and visit a cotton ginnery where we could watch how they made cotton. It was getting dark and the ginnery was outside so there did not seem to be much point in going there. As I could sense that the group were getting impatient with the constantly changing plans I said we should ask the group to decide. Everyone voted to go straight to the hotel. We also had to decide whether or not to take the first flight at six the next morning. Some people were very much against such an early start but as the majority said yes we booked the first flights and I arranged a late breakfast in the hotel when we got back after we had flown.

Our hotel in Nazca, Hotel Majoro, was an old hacienda. It was simple but charming. All the rooms were on the ground floor and spread around a lovely garden. As we checked in I changed rooms to get Toby near the reception area as Nieves had forgotten to ask. There were no telephones in the rooms and I had a long walk to reception to receive and make calls. Before going to my room I rang Toby's insurance company who said they would call back in thirty minutes. I had to move fast to unpack and shower before racing back to reception. I had just finished when someone knocked on my door to say the call had come through. It was a courtesy call to tell me that no decision had been made yet regarding repatriation and they would call me the next morning at nine – three in the morning Peru time.

When I joined the group in the bar they were very rowdy and some plotting was going on regarding seating arrangements at dinner. Some of them even rushed into the restaurant while I was still going through the programme for the next day. When I tried to talk to them again after dinner I had competition from a large group of Italians in the restaurant and they got so noisy I could not continue. As I sat down I muttered to myself that I would try again when it was quieter. Myra, who never normally listened to anything I said, heard me. She leapt to her feet and started yelling at me that she had paid a lot for the holiday and that I was her rep and she demanded that I give them the information immediately. Without drawing breath she forbade me to get the 'hump' with her again. This was a dig regarding an incident that morning when I was taking a picture of some pelicans and she had deliberately run towards them screaming and making them fly away. I think anyone would have been annoyed by such childish behaviour.

I repeated that I had said it was too noisy to talk to everyone right now but I had been intending to say that if we could not fly for any reason the wake-up call would be cancelled. As everyone else had melted away at the beginning of her confrontation I took the opportunity to ask her not to keep telling me I was taking the 'hump'. I said this quietly and politely but this did not suit Myra who got even madder, louder and ruder. She set off towards the bar but then came back and had another go at me. I immediately said I was sorry if I had upset her. That calmed her down and she hugged me and went off to the bar happy as Larry. She kept saying how much the holiday meant to her but in a loud and insensitive manner. It did not seem to occur to her that she may be ruining the holiday for other people. I was too upset to join the group in the bar.

Friday 20 April
Toby's insurance company did call me at three the next morning. They were going to repatriate Toby and would look for a flight from Lima the next day and call me later. I went back to my room after the call but I could not sleep and lay awake until our wake-up call, a knock on the door, arrived. Myra overslept as she had dozed off after responding to her wake-up call but she still made it by the time everyone had gathered ready to leave at six for our flight over the Nazca Lines.

Nieves had only just arrived herself by then but showed no sign of urgency as our departure time came and went. She was not her usual cheerful self and after hanging around saying nothing she took me to one side and told me that the ginnery was angry because we did not go there. Yet she had suggested the programme change. If we had done the flights the previous afternoon we would not have gone anyway. Nieves said that would have been okay but it being too dark to see anything apparently was not a valid excuse. It was a pointless discussion so I suggested we set off.

When we arrived at the airfield ten minutes later I could tell by the way Nieves was talking to the pilots that there may be a problem. There was, we had arrived too late to go on the first flight and now we had to wait as another airline had been given clearance to go first. When I joined in the discussion I told Nieves that she should have told me exactly what time we should have been there to ensure we were on the first flight. She should have told us to hurry when she arrived at the hotel but she said she did not like to rush people. She had also been pre-occupied regarding the ginnery. I was struggling to keep my cool in the face of such inefficiency. As we talked I nodded and smiled in order to give my guests the impression that all was well between us.

We had no other option but to sit and wait. We were entertained with an interesting video about the creation of the Nazca Lines while we did the flights in small groups. I was in the last group to fly and I was glad breakfast came after rather than before the flight. There was some quite sharp banking to show the designs to the passengers on each side if the plane.

After breakfast we packed our bags ready to be collected and loaded on the bus for our long drive back to Lima. We could fit in a visit to the ginnery so I tried to make amends by suggesting to Nieves that we visited the ginnery that morning. She pursed her lips petulantly and said no as it had been booked for yesterday and today was too late. That was news to me. She should have told me that the previous lunchtime and then we could have planned our journey around it. Although we discussed the itinerary every day she obviously reserved the right to make last minute changes. Before we left we walked round the back of the hotel into a cotton field where Nieves told us about cotton production.

After driving all morning we stopped for lunch at a vineyard, El Catador, where they made a sweet wine and Pisco, a strong alcoholic drink distilled from grapes. It is the national Peruvian drink. We were offered a choice for lunch and most of us opted for fish and chips. They were so good they were memorable. Before leaving we had a tour of the vineyard and distillery and a chance to try and buy some Pisco. I loved the tart, tangy taste of this liquor and appreciated its sleep inducing properties.

We drove for another two hours before having a break at a service station. I called the insurance company from there and they told me that Toby needed a fit to fly certificate. Nieves called our hotel and arranged an appointment with the hotel doctor. We were late getting there but he was waiting for us and I went straight to Toby's room with him. He tapped the plaster, took Toby's blood pressure, wrote a short note and then presented Toby with a large bill.

Before I could meet the group in the bar I had to confirm Toby's transfer to the airport. Nieves had given me a number she said her boss had given her. I called it several times and each time I got an ansaphone message and asked them to call us back, which of course they never did. Finally I called our agent directly and I discovered that I had been wasting my time as the agent was collecting Toby at four thirty but I had to promise that Toby would pay for this transfer. I also had to promise that he would pay for any phone calls they made on his behalf. It was a strange culture.

At last I could go to my room and discovered I had a whirlpool bath. Just what I needed – I made use of it before meeting the group in the Café Amore over the road for dinner. We were too tired and it was too late to go further afield. I went straight to bed after eating as I had to be up at four the next morning.

Saturday 21 April

I really struggled to be downstairs in reception at four thirty. I was not sure if I would have to accompany Toby to the airport. Fortunately the agent had sent Marvin to accompany him and as he seemed to know what he was doing I did not feel obliged to go with him. The rest of the group had a wake-up call at six and we departed for the airport at seven. On arrival at the airport we stayed on the bus while our bags were unloaded. As we waited I went through the rules regarding sharp objects and liquids in hand luggage and stressed that these rules did apply to internal flights. I was repeating what I had said the previous evening but there was always someone who was not listening.

A Swiss Army knife was found in Ivy's hand luggage. She was sent back to the desk to check it in separately. On her second attempt to get through the security check some nail scissors were discovered. These were confiscated. Ivy never listened to anyone properly which resulted in some funny exchanges but it also meant she never knew where she was supposed to be and what she should be doing.

Our flight to Cusco was on time and we were met at Cusco by Christian who accompanied us to our hotel, the Hotel Picoago. I had to collect all our boarding passes on the transfer as our agent wanted proof that the departure tax had been paid using the money that Nieves had given me when we checked in. I did this while we waited to check-in to our hotel. The building was originally a Spanish nobleman's palace and it had been built around a very attractive courtyard. We were told to help ourselves to coca tea which is good for altitude sickness. Some people were already feeling the effects. I had certainly noticed the difference – when I got off the plane and walked towards the terminal building it had felt as though someone had thumped me on the chest.

Before he left Christian informed me that our trekking guide would meet us at midday for a briefing in the restaurant on the fourth floor. I dumped my luggage in my room and went upstairs in the hope of meeting our guide before our briefing. Faustina was already there and I helped her get our kitbags (duffles) upstairs. Several people in the group had hired sleeping bags and were concerned because they had not yet received them. Faustina assured me that the clients would get them at Urubamba where we started the trek. (I had to repeat this to Ivy at least three times.) Faustina was a very bright and attractive girl but I soon discovered that she did not like being asked questions. During our briefing she brushed off any questions with a brief 'I tell you later' and then forgot to do so.

After the briefing we walked the short distance to the main plaza to find somewhere for lunch. We had been advised not to eat a large meal on arrival in a town at altitude and also not to drink alcohol. Cusco is 3,800m above sea level and as none of were used to being so high we were happy to follow this advice. We only had a short time to eat anyway as we were due to start our city and sites tour with Faustina at two that afternoon.

Our tour concentrated on Inca ruins beginning with the archaeological site of Sacsayhuaman. We had to walk up and down steps while exploring this site which was good practice for walking at altitude. The ruins were dotted with locals all trying to sell us remedies to prevent or treat altitude sickness. At the second archaeological site, Q'enqo, Myra succumbed to the condition. Fortunately she was walking with me at the time and I was able to support her before she crashed to the ground. We were at the back of the group so I asked Amber to get Faustina. Meanwhile some locals helped me with Myra. We made her comfortable against some rocks then one of them smothered his hands with some oil which he rubbed on her face and then he held the bottle under her nose.

Myra was in a bad way and when Faustina arrived (with Ringo and Dora of course) she had to call the bus driver to bring us the oxygen cylinder. As soon as her breathing was regulated Ringo and Ramsay carried her back to the bus. On the bus Dora and Ringo just took over – they could not help themselves. But on this occasion I was happy to let them get on with it as Dora used to be a nurse so she knew what she was doing. I was very grateful and said so. When Myra came round on the bus she asked for ice to put on her face as it was burning up. That was one local remedy that was never destined to work.

We all went straight back to the hotel where Myra was lain on a couch in reception and the doctor was called. Myra had neglected to inform anyone that she had a lung defect which made her very susceptible to altitude sickness. Nevertheless the doctor predicted a full recovery. It was some time before we could take her to her room in a wheelchair – she was still using the oxygen cylinder and a doctor had been called. Ringo and Dora were still purporting to be in charge but when it came to dinner arrangements they were happy to step down and let me stay with Myra while they went out to eat. It was bizarre – Myra being left with the person she had been taking the piss out of for the last few days. Ringo and Dora organised dinner that evening at a restaurant I had already booked. They also hired walking poles for those of us who wanted the retractable kind. Once they had left I just lay on the other twin bed while Myra slept on hers.

Myra slept until eight that evening and then she woke up, talking. She told me all about her husband leaving her (I wondered why). But she did kind of apologise for having been horrible to me earlier in the holiday. I had thought I would have to sleep in Myra's room that night but due to her amazingly quick recovery there was no need. I collected some coca tea and went to my room and got straight into bed. I had a terrible headache, right behind my eyes which was either altitude sickness or stress. For my dinner I ate one of the free chocolates in my room and some peanuts I had acquired on the flight to Lima.

Sunday 22 April

We were on the move again today and we had to pack everything we needed for the trek into our kit bag subject to a weight limit of ten kilos. Portable scales had been provided to ensure compliance. Our own bags and excess belongings would be left in Cusco awaiting our return. As soon as I had completed this task I sought out Lucas. Several people had noticed him videoing Myra's collapse the previous day and considered his actions distasteful. I had been requested to ensure he erased it. Lucas claimed he had done nothing wrong and he actually wanted to show the video to Myra and ask her what she wanted him to do. I said it was better that Myra did not know what he had done and that it should be deleted. Reluctantly he agreed.

We were off to the Sacred Valley to visit some of its archaeological sites. It would be good practice for the trek as there was a lot of walking on ascending mountain paths. First we visited Awana Kancha to look at various types of llamas and watch the locals weaving. Every time someone raised a camera to take a picture a demanding hand was put out for money which tainted the authenticity for me. We drove on to the ruins above Pisaq where we spent two hours exploring them. Myra was still quite weak and stayed in the bus although she did get out and walk to meet us when she saw us coming back towards the bus. She seemed fine if a little subdued today. Everyone else was coping well with the altitude.

Our next stop was in Pisaq itself. As it was a Sunday the local market was at its best and bursting with souvenirs and alpaca sweaters. We were encouraged to buy anything we wanted as our shopping would go back to Cusco with our bus the next day. I did buy an alpaca sweater but it was coming with me as we had been warned that one of our nights under canvas would be really cold. We had lunch in a makeshift café in the market squashed round small wooden tables on little stools. A variety of tasty local dishes were brought to the tables and we enjoyed dipping into them.

Our next Inca ruin at Ollantaytambo involved clambering up several steep flights of steps. Myra came with us this time and coped very well. Below the ruins was a very small town but we did not linger there this time as we would be returning the next day when the porters stocked up there for the trek. We continued to our hotel for that night – Hotel San Augustin Monasterio de la Recoleta at Urubamba. This lovely hotel used to be a monastery and had some very unusual rooms – some were split level. They were all set in a beautiful garden. While checking in we also had to choose our meal from the a la carte menu as we were too far away from the nearest town to go out for dinner. Faustina had been more relaxed during the day and when I had mentioned that I was looking for a small towel she took me to the local market in a local three-wheeler taxi. It was a pretty little town with a very Spanish main square. We got to the market as it was closing down but I quickly found what I needed and we went straight back to the hotel.

During our evening meal we were entertained by a Peruvian steel band but they played English songs which did not really work. When we had finished eating, but not drinking for a second night everyone went straight to bed. We would be starting our trek and we all wanted to be fresh and ready to start our trek the next morning. I was so excited about the adventure ahead of us I was finding it difficult to wind down. I listened to music on my MP3. I had never understood the need for an MP3 until I started travelling and certainly on this trip it had been a godsend.

Monday 23 April
I was up very early and walked around the hotel to take some pictures as it was so attractive. I was delighted to discover they had unlocked the little church for us so that we could see inside. This church was rarely used now. It was beautifully decorated with a large marble altar that looked like a chapel within the church. The first time I looked inside Myra was in there praying so I withdrew and waited until she came out. Myra had told me she was very religious and prayed every day for her husband to come back to her. Sadly the way she spoke to people and the way she behaved did not reflect this devotion to God or her wayward husband.

I organised the collection of the kit bags and then weighed each one to check that none of them were over the limit. Next I had to collect together everything that was going back to the hotel in Cusco where it would be stored. When I went back to chase up the last two people I met Peggy scurrying through the cloisters clutching her stomach and heading for the toilet. As I waited outside for her Justine drifted by and told me she was coming down with the flu and felt really ill. Both women said they were determined to do the trek and we all set off on schedule.

Our first stop was Ollantaytambo. Lots of trekking groups had stopped in this tiny town which bristled with an air of anticipation as trekkers queued for the toilet and congregated outside the small shops discussing the merits of coca candy and mūnar which are both good for the effects of altitude. It was also a last chance to buy a walking stick for those who had not already hired one. They were very cheap wooden ones in different lengths but the length could not be altered for steep downhill sections.

Before actually starting the trek we had to drive for another hour along a road and then a rough track to an open area where our porters and assistant guides, Reynardo and Jeraldo, were waiting for us. We hung around watching them pack everything up and after a really final visit to the toilets we set off. Despite my initial misgivings I was raring to go but I had to curb my natural instinct to stride out quickly as I was walking at the back with Peggy. Almost immediately she announced that she needed to find a 'bush'. This was not easy as we were in the middle of a small settlement and had just crossed a railway line. When we found somewhere suitable she said she could not 'go'. Reynardo had been walking at the back with us but at the first stop he swapped with Jeraldo who plodded along behind us for the rest of the day.

Peggy got very bloated and moaned continually that she was in a lot of pain. She was not the only one as my legs were aching from walking so slowly. Jeraldo just plodded along and did not offer any assistance. When we finally caught up with the others for a snack break I arranged with Faustina that Jeraldo should carry Peggy's rucksack for her. Justine had been walking with the main group and seemed to be coping. Myra had fully recovered after her collapse in Cusco but was wearing a strappy sun top. I was concerned that she would get sunburnt and managed to persuade her to cover her shoulders with a tee shirt to protect them from the sun and the straps of her rucksack.

We all met up again for lunch. We ate al fresco at a large table but with the luxury of our own toilet tents. We were really enjoying a simple meal of chicken, bread, vegetables and salad when Peggy suddenly threw up on the ground right by the table. I followed her to the toilet tent with some wet wipes.

After lunch we continued as before except that Justine joined us at the back as she was feeling worse. Reynardo took her rucksack and walked ahead of us while Jeraldo plodded along behind us. The last part of the walk was uphill to the campsite at Pacaymayo and they both struggled. When we arrived our tents had already been set up and pre-allocated but we were expected to blow up our own mattresses. Justine wanted to go straight to bed so I asked Reynardo to blow up her mattress (and Peggy's) and I rolled out her sleeping bag. While I was dealing with the invalids Ramsay inflated my mattress for me. I was touched by this act of kindness. I took Justine a cup of tea and that was all she had, she did not join us for afternoon tea and she did not have any dinner.

Peggy did not join us for supper either. Karen just had some rice soup and then went straight to bed as she was not feeling well. Linette rushed out after the soup and was sick outside so she went off to bed as well. Everyone else went to bed as soon as we finished eating. We were all exhausted and there was nothing else to do anyway except have long discussions about whether or not to have a ladies' loo tent and a men's loo tent and then which should be which. There were two tents and each one contained two toilets – a pink one for number one and a second, without a lid, for number two. Chemicals had to be sprinkled on top of the latter after use and all used toilet paper had to be put in the plastic bag on the ground. It was certainly a new experience sitting on one toilet looking at other people's offerings and working out when to switch to the other one.

As I walked back to my tent I looked up. The sky was just amazing, so clear and sprinkled with stars including the Southern Cross. I scrambled inside and fought my way into my sleeping bag. It was very difficult to sleep as the tents were pitched on sloping ground so the mattress slowly made its way down the tent aided by the slippery plastic ground sheet. My sleeping bag also slid down the mattress so it was a continual process of hitching back up the tent. There was nothing else to do but listen to music until I dozed off.

Tuesday 24 April

I actually slept and was woken at six with a cup of black tea and a bowl of warm water to wash in. We had forty-five minutes to pack our 'duffles' before breakfast. We had to wash our hands before every meal, a good rule that was strictly enforced and there were always water, soap and paper towels outside the dining tent. One of the guides would be on guard to check we obeyed this rule. That first morning it was porridge followed by toast and jam. Hot water was always available to make tea, generally coca tea for altitude. Our dining tent was quite small and very full when everyone was in there. The small campstools round the table were neither very comfortable nor very stable. Peggy was feeling better but tired but Justine now had an upset stomach as well as the flu

Today was the hardest day as we began a five hour uphill trek to the top of Dead Woman's Pass at 4,200m so altitude was likely to be an issue. I walked at the back with Peggy and Justine, Karen and Linette. Our two new companions had decided to join us as they felt the pace they had walked at the previous day had contributed to their feeling ill that evening. It was a really nice group and we walked well together. Initially Reynardo took the lead with regular stops and Jeraldo plodded along behind. When we stopped for a snack break Reynardo left us and I took the lead. Justine really struggled but she was determined to finish the trek. En route we saw some lovely flowers and giant humming birds. When Reynardo was with us he told us all about them but Jeraldo was not so knowledgeable and barely spoke anyway.

We all had lunch together but we ate inside the dining tent today as it was threatening to rain. The views were amazing and I was glad I had been at the back and had time to enjoy them. Dead Women's Pass still towered above us and after lunch we had to contend with a long steep uphill section. Faustina started walking with us but soon got bored and skipped off up the hill and left me to pace them again. We did forty paces, had a break, forty paces and then a break all the way. It seemed as though we would never make it but finally we could see the rest of the group waiting at the top of the pass. When we came into view they started singing and shouting – some of the comments from Myra were not too helpful – she had clearly forgotten the support she had received from the group when she collapsed. We made it to the top an hour after the others. By then it was raining steadily but that was better than relentless hot sun.

Once we had taken group pictures we were off again following a steep descent on slippery stones. Linette struggled at the back and I often had to give her a helping hand. When we finally arrived at our campsite at Phuyopatamarka our tents were pitched on the hillside. There was a very steep descent to the dining room and a long walk down a path and over a bridge to the toilet and shower block. The showers were fed by water from a waterfall above us and I had it on good authority that they were freezing cold. Justine went straight to bed with a cup of tea and I organised some toast for her later. I also got her water bottle refilled and as the water was still hot she used it as a hot water bottle. Ramsay had already blown up our mattresses for us.

I was really impressed with the quality of food considering that we were camping and that night we had vegetable soup, spaghetti and chicken followed by pancakes as dessert. Lucas asked if there was an alternative to pancakes, Faustina just said no. Lucas looked chastened. He seemed to have developed a crush on Faustina and rushed to sit next to her at every meal.

We all had an early night. It had been a really long tough day and even the good walkers admitted that. I was heading for the toilet block with Peggy and Karen when Peggy soiled her pants – twice. I got her to the toilet block and waited while she cleaned herself up and then she walked back in her knickers (fortunately she had taken a clean pair with her) as the floor was too dirty to contemplate putting her trousers on again in the cubicle. Back in my tent I was soon relaxing to the soothing rush of the stream nearby.

I was settling down to sleep, and had just removed one contact lens, when Peggy called out that she needed to go to the toilet again but could not remember where it was. I told her to cross the bridge and then dragged on some clothes and followed her up there. I fell through my tent flap and broke the zip in my hurry. This was not good news as it was a freezing cold night and it meant one side of my 'door' was open to the elements. There were two layers to this door, a mosquito net that was completely closed while the outer layer was left partially open at the top to prevent condensation. I waited for Peggy to finish and then we walked back together and settled down again. By then it was raining steadily and during dinner Faustina had calmly announced that the tents were not waterproof. She told us not to touch the inside walls as this would make the water soak into the fabric. If only I could control my mattress to that extent. I stuffed everything inside my duffle and put it at the end of the mattress. It stopped me sliding right down the tent and I fell asleep to the steady drumming of rain on canvas.

Wednesday 25 April
When my cup of tea arrived at six the opening in my tent flap revealed a beautiful sunny morning. I crawled outside to use my washing bowl which was easier than sliding around the plastic groundsheet on my knees. Before going to breakfast I checked on the invalids. Justine seemed a bit better but Peggy was still weak and tired. They both tried to eat some breakfast – scrambled egg and bacon. While we were eating Myra scolded me for using the gents' toilet rather than the ladies'. I bit my tongue, smiled sweetly and said I was not going to wait for the ladies' which was occupied when the other toilet was free.

That morning we were ascending again. The same 'team' of five brought up the rear with me pacing them from the front and Jeraldo plodding along at the back. Although the sun was shining it was not too hot but we were ready for a rest in the shade when we stopped for lunch. Peggy lay down on the ground beside our table causing several people to voice their concern. I suspected she was beginning to enjoy all the attention she was getting. As usual, being the last to sit down, I got the campstool that was in permanent danger of tipping over.

During a lovely lunch of guacamole and avocado with onions, cheese, bread and salad Justine whispered to me that another disaster was pending. Her period had started but she had nothing with her. I asked all the ladies in the group but none of them had anything with them – or were not saying. I had met this attitude before when we were in the desert and I had been rushing around so much I had forgotten to put on any sun cream. I had asked my companions for some. Myra said Ivy would lend me hers, Ivy ignored me and Toby finally gave me some at the third time of asking. Later, when Myra realised that I had sun cream combined with insect repellent she was always asking if she could have some of my sun cream. Everything that was mine was theirs but not vice versa. My failure to find any suitable towels (she was very particular) plunged Justine into a state of depression and she began talking about quitting. I said I would not let her give up at this point and even asked all the young women we passed on the trail if they had any sanitary towels with them. None of them did.

Despite my concerns about Justine I really enjoyed the afternoon walk. We were walking along the original Inca trail overlooking stunning views and lined with beautiful flowers. Reynardo was a keen photographer and he was using a serious camera. He showed us some good places for taking photographs. When we got to our camp, a fabulous place right on a peak, Peggy dug deep in her duffle and found some sanitary towels for Justine. I walked down to the camp below ours and an American lady there gave me some. Faustina sent two porters off to get some more. Justine was still depressed as she said she needed lots of supplies but cheered up slightly when the porters returned with two large packets for her. But it cost us because Faustina said I had to give the porters a large tip and the specified amount made quite a hole in our collection. I did mention this to Justine but she clearly did not feel obliged to contribute towards this extra expense. At least she was happy to continue the trek and I was happy too as I suspected that had she quit I would have had to leave with her and I doubted I would ever have the chance to do the trek again.

That night our camping area was very small and I was in the back row of tents. My tent was pitched next to Myra's and her guy ropes were precariously near the edge so it was rather tricky going to the toilet in the dark. Neither Peggy nor Justine joined us for tea or supper so I took some food to their tents on my way to bed. Most people were anxious for an early night but Dora, Ringo, Jacky, Ivy, and Lionel stayed outside talking loudly. The porters were listening to a football match on a radio so it was very noisy. I was finding it hard to concentrate as I struggled to divide the tips according to Faustina's suggested amounts.

Faustina had given me a list of the tips that each member of her team should be given and some brown paper bags to put them in. She had not realised that the amounts were beyond my control as our information recommended a particular sum for the tips. It was my responsibility to collect the money and then distribute it. I was rather shocked at her attitude as we consider tips to be discretionary and awarded for a job well done – it seemed that in Peru they were seen as an expectation and treated as a wage.

I had heard that Faustina had been canvassing the group regarding tips but they had referred her to me. I could only promise to do my best. It would have been easier to give the whole collection to Faustina and let her deal with it but I had organised several people to do separate presentations so I wanted to do it myself. After an hour of squinting in torchlight as I tried to read her writing and then reduce the amounts proportionally I gave up. Despite all my concerns I slept quite well that night but it was so cold I was wearing all the clothes I had with me including my new alpaca sweater, a hat and gloves.

Thursday 26 April

Our wake-up call the next morning was very early as we were walking up to the top of the peak above our campsite to watch the sun rise. It was amazing. Our porters carried our early morning tea up there for us. After breakfast, before setting off on the final stage of our trek, we said our goodbyes to the porters and the assistant guides and gave them our tips. I had finally sorted them out that morning but I had missed breakfast. It was quite a ceremony. First the porters sang us a song and we responded with a very dodgy version of 'When you walk through a storm'. Then I took the floor to say a few words of thanks of my own before asking different people to make the actual presentations.

This did not go down well with Faustina who pushed me out of the way and took over, completely ignoring me. I felt totally humiliated and very angry as it was our money she was giving away. While I was side-lined I took the opportunity to do some creative re-divisions of our tips at her expense. I wanted to reward Reynardo and Jeraldo for their patience with the slow walkers.

When we set off I was at the back again with the 'usual' five but Peggy was very much slower today as she had suffered a relapse and we were soon on our own. I ambled along ahead of her stopping regularly to wait for her to catch up. Jeraldo plodded along behind her – it was unbelievably slow and almost unbearable. Peggy complained constantly that she felt dizzy but that was hardly surprising as she kept looking up at the mountains behind her. I told her to look forward all the time and, eventually, so did Jeraldo. We finally joined the others for a snack and toilet stop – au naturel in an Inca ruin.

On the next stage we lagged behind again. It was excruciating. Peggy was very game but also very self-centred and her conversation was all about Peggy. We finally joined the others at the lunch stop, which this time was in a restaurant as our porters and cooks had gone straight to Machu Picchu and some would be going home immediately. It was a chance for me to remind Faustina that it was Lucas's birthday the next day and to ask if she had arranged a cake for him. She said she would do it later. The local guides did not like using their mobile phones if they could possibly avoid it. I also told her that Peggy and Justine had decided they would like to stay in a hotel that night so I asked Faustina to arrange it. She said we would do it when we arrived in Machu Picchu Village but she would not ring ahead to book one. She would not give me the numbers so I could call them on my mobile. It was very frustrating being unable to help.

When we set off again Peggy walked so slowly we were barely moving. The others had been at the Sun Gate for more than an hour when we finally joined them. The sight of Machu Picchu bathed in brilliant sunshine way below us brought tears to my eyes. It was the most magnificent sight I had ever seen. After a photo stop we walked down to the ruins themselves. This time I had some company as Ramsay and Bella dropped back to walk with us. After a short time exploring the ruins we boarded the tourist bus to Machu Picchu Village.

We got off in the centre of town and the group split up. Several people went to the thermal baths on the hill at the top of the main street and the rest went shopping. I went with Faustina, Peggy, Justine and Bella to find a hotel. Bella was going to pay a third of the price just to use their shower. They took the first room they were offered and I left them there after freshening up in the hotel toilets. It was time to meet the others at Pueblo Viejo where we were having supper. The restaurant had a nice atmosphere and I had a satisfying meal and two beers to help me sleep. Thankfully it was our last night under canvas.

Faustina said it was a mile to walk back to our campsite but it was much more than that. Then we had to play 'find your tent' as, like last night, they had changed the order again. I took Peggy's tent which was the first empty tent I came to. The campsite had a shower and toilet block but it was disgusting as large moths fluttered around piles of rubble and dirty water dripped out of the taps. My tent was next to the one that Dora and Ringo were sharing and I could hear them talking in stage whispers. They really seemed to believe that it was up to them to organise everything and they were making plans for the next few days. I could not wait to get away from them.

Friday 27 April
Dawn was breaking when my cup of tea arrived and I crawled out of my tent to drink it outside. At the same time Dora crawled out of her tent. When she saw me her jaw dropped open – she must have realized I had been there all night and would have heard them talking and plotting. I have never seen an adult reverse so quickly on all fours as she shot back inside her tent to tell Ringo I was their neighbour.

At breakfast we celebrated Lucas's birthday. Our remaining cook had made a cake with a stack of pancakes and stuck a candle on the top. It went down like a lead balloon. Apparently Lucas had stopped celebrating his birthday fifteen years ago and he hated pancakes. He was very grumpy and complaining of a cold. He could not even manage a smile when I gave him the card we had all signed and he did not open it. Faustina had signed it which would have cheered him up.

When we caught the tourist bus to Machu Picchu Faustina was already on board with Peggy and Justine both of whom looked rested after their night in a hotel. Peggy was complaining that she had a lung infection but still dragged herself round the guided tour of Machu Picchu. It was a glorious sunny day so we saw the ruins at their best. When our tour finished I got the bus back down to the town and walked up to the thermal baths to see if I could find Lionel's hat, which he had left there last night. It was a leather hat that had been round the world with him three times and was very precious. I searched everywhere, even the male changing rooms, but it was not there.

I was sent off to enquire at the Municipal Office in the main square. The hat was not there but I was told to return an hour later. On my second visit I was told to go back thirty minutes later. On my third visit I was just greeted with a shrug of the shoulders. I gave up and went to the restaurant where we having lunch. Some of the others were already there including Lionel so I gave him the sad news about his hat.

After lunch we walked to the station to catch the train to Cusco. It was only just across the street but we had to walk up several flights of steps to get our tickets checked and then walk through a market before going down some more steps to the platform. Our kit bags had been delivered to the restaurant while we were eating. The lack of porters meant most of us had to carry them ourselves. I noticed that Faustina organised the few porters available to carry her kit bag and those of a few favoured guests. I was not one of them. Pay back for the tips maybe. Mine was so heavy I resorted to dragging it along which soon wore a hole in it but I was beyond caring by then.

The train journey was great and included a snack and a fashion show. The models were the young steward and stewardess who coped very well with the lively banter from our group. We left the train at Poroy and continued our journey to Cusco on a private bus as it was quicker. Before meeting for dinner we had to return our walking poles and find somewhere to eat. Ringo and Ramsay took care of the poles while I found a restaurant.

The Inka Grill was popular with everyone. I tried the local delicacy – guinea pig. I could not eat a whole one but opted for the starter version, the crispy guinea pig pancakes. The atmosphere was very relaxed. We were all glowing, clean and triumphant at having completed the Inca Trail. When the bills came several people tried to pay with the 100 sols notes Ringo had given us as our refunded deposit money. The restaurant rejected them but gave no reason. I thought that maybe they were suspicious as the notes were all brand new. I suggested we try them in other shops before we took the matter any further and then left them to mull it over as I had a lot to do before I could think of going to bed.

Saturday 28 April
As I walked through reception on my way to breakfast I tripped over Ivy's bag. I found its owner in breakfast, bewildered because she was the only one there. She had confused the times and thought her bag should be outside her room at six. When it was still there at six thirty she had brought it downstairs with her. Despite being the first in breakfast she was still the last on the bus and kept us waiting while she dithered over a selection of paintings offered to her by Joseph one of the street sellers who was outside our hotel day and night. Finally, after fifteen minutes, she selected two paintings to add to the six she had already

bought. Despite the delay we arrived at the airport in good time for our flight to Lima. We were all looking forward to meeting up with Nieves again.

It was Marco who met us in Arrivals and he seemed surprised when we enquired about Nieves as he was to be our local guide during our stay. Marco soon impressed me with his efficient manner. His short slim frame was encased in a smart suit including a tie and his feet were clad in shiny leather shoes. He was one of the smartest local guides I had worked with. He was not only smart in appearance but he did not have a phobia about using his mobile either. Within minutes of my making the request he had booked us tables for lunch at Rosa Nautica. He also persuaded our bus driver to take us there for one dollar per person.

After checking into our hotel we set off for the Rosa Nautica. Lucas did not join us preferring to stay in the hotel to nurse a cold he had suddenly acquired. Our hopes of sitting outside were thwarted by rough seas but the waiters found us a large table in a bay window so we could watch the surfers below us. We had plenty of time to appreciate the excellent food as our next appointment was mid-afternoon at the Gold Museum. When Marco collected us he coped well with the hilarity and singing in the bus on the way to the museum. Some people were not too keen on visiting a museum but he assured us there would be something for everyone. He was right as the museum was in a complex with shops and a café so there was plenty to do for those not interested in the museum.

Lucas was in a bad mood when he joined us for dinner that evening and I had to bear the brunt of it. By then I had started a contact list and I asked people to write down their email addresses. Lucas had to point out that maybe not everyone had an email address. He even asked Ramsay if he had an email address and informed me that he did not. When I pointed out that I had actually said email address or other contact he told me to 'chill out'. I was still simmering when we arrived at our dinner venue. Mango's was in a lively oceanfront shopping mall with shops, restaurants and amusement arcades on two levels. News of Lucas's bad humour had spread and I had to take the empty seat opposite him. I was soon on my feet again to deal with a menu crisis. We had to choose from five set menus but they were all in Spanish. I got a rough translation from the manager but as I went through them I realised there was no vegetarian option. I was beside Myra with a vegetarian menu seconds before she opened her mouth in protest.

When I sat down again Lucas had decided he wanted to substitute a beer for the included cocktail in the set menu. The restaurant manager would not allow this. Lucas asked me what I thought and I said that I could not really do anything if the restaurant had said no. He clearly expected I should override their decision and mentioned that when things were going wrong he had supported me. I was not aware that things had ever gone wrong and was very grateful to Bella who came to my rescue and between us we moved the conversation on. Lucas was gracious in defeat and offered me his unwanted Pisco sour. I was happy to accept.

My third Pisco sour was complimentary from the management to atone for the starters which were too salty to eat so I had sent them back. After much negotiation and another round of cocktails we were served large platters with a selection of starters. The main course was cold when it arrived and that had to go back as well. It was a disappointing last dinner but my spirits were lifted when Myra of all people presented me with a beautiful llama shawl as a gift from the group to thank me for my efforts on their behalf.

Sunday 27 April
Home sweet home! Our final journey together went smoothly. I thwarted an attempt by Iberia to transfer two people to a later flight from Madrid to Heathrow and dragged Lionel and Ivy out of a bar just in time to board the flight. Even a flat battery in my car was swiftly dealt with in my race to get home and relax with a decent cup of tea.

* * * * * *

I had survived my toughest test so far and I was delighted when Aimee called to congratulate me a few days later. She had good news for me too. When I had begun to work as a Hostess I had told her, several times, that I was a keen golfer and had also served on my golf club committee so I was competent regarding the organisation of golf competitions. In fact that was the only area in which I did have experience. Despite this it seemed I would have to shadow the regular golf Hostess so they could assess my ability in this area. After nearly a year I had given up hope and now my time had come. The regular golf Hostess was unable to take the next trip, golfing in Andalucia, and it was being offered to me. I said I would be delighted. But there was a drawback. The trip left the following day. All the documents would be faxed through to me.

Chapter 11 - May

It had all looked so simple on paper. Due to an overbooking situation in The Royal Andalus Golf Hotel, half the group had to spend the first night in a different hotel, Tryp. In reality it was fraught with problems. Several people were not happy with the arrangement but instead of contacting the office before travelling they raised their objections in the Arrivals hall at Jerez airport. Kay was the first to protest. Due to a family crisis there had been some doubt whether she would travel at all. She had therefore been given a room in Tryp.

I had been assigned a room in the Royal Andalus. I was not expected at either hotel as our Operations Department had forgotten to book a room for me. They were working on the theory that once I was in the hotel they would not throw me out. But if I spent the first night in Tryp I may never get into the Royal Andalus. Kay had decided to come on the holiday but was anxious that her family would be able to contact her at any time so she had given them the contact details for the Royal Andalus. I felt obliged to change with her.

Percy had also been put in Tryp for one night. He tackled me on the transfer bus demanding immediate compensation of £100 for the inconvenience. Guy came to my rescue as he was travelling with a friend and they had been split up so he agreed to swap with Percy to be with his friend. Once that problem was resolved I had to distribute the lists of starting times for our golf competition the next morning. First I had to alter them to reflect the hotel changes that had just taken place. This was not easy in the dimly lit, jolting bus. The group had insisted that the lights were turned down for our journey to the hotels.

Finally I had to scramble over large suitcases and several golf bags to give everyone a copy of my list and answer any queries. Our transfer bus was too small for forty-one sets of luggage and golf clubs to be stowed in the boot. I was working hard to make this trip as smooth as possible despite the obstacles in my way. Finally I battled my way back to my seat and sat down. I hoped that I had managed to load the luggage in the right order so that the luggage for our first stop, The Royal Andalus, would be easily accessible.

We did not arrive at the Royal Andalus until nine thirty that evening and the maître d' wanted the people staying there to go straight into dinner. I told the manager that I would settle that group and then walk to Tryp to join the others. He looked astonished. My company had been told that the two hotels were within walking distance of each other and anyway a shuttle service would be at my disposal. Neither statement was true – I was not surprised as I had already learnt that there was no honour amongst hotels and travel agents. There was no time to sort anything out as I had to get straight back on the bus and go to the Tryp. Fortunately Kay had lingered in the lobby while I was talking to the manager and volunteered to get everyone to the golf course the next morning. We arrived at Tryp fifteen minutes later and went straight into dinner. Tryp was not a hotel but a block of apartments and we each had our own. As we were all a long way from reception I arranged to store all our golf clubs overnight in a room by reception ready for an early getaway the next morning.

When the coach arrived the next morning to take us straight to the golf course Melvin was missing. He had lost his way back to his room after breakfast. We had to take all our belongings even though the original agreement had been we would just take our golf gear. The coach was supposed to go back and collect the cases later. This arrangement did not suit the hotel. I had been informed the previous evening that everything had to go at the same time. I persuaded two receptionists to help us with our luggage as there were no porters on duty when we left.

We were late arriving at the golf club, Club de Golf Novo Sancti Petri, and the first group had already begun their round. Kay had been true to her word, not only had she got the whole group there she had also started to send them out. Fortunately the golf club had been expecting us. The green fee tickets had already been processed for everyone and golf trolleys had been provided. All I had to do was pay for them as soon as everyone had teed off.

An hour later everyone, except me, was out on the course playing. As we had to play in fours I was always going to be the odd one out in a group of forty-one. I went back to the golf club to introduce myself and pay for the golf trolleys for the week. Some people had requested electric buggies for the rest of the week so I dealt with that as well. Everyone at the club was very friendly and helpful and my spirits, dampened by our difficult start, were rising. I walked round the course to check the progress of my group. They were all competent golfers and were enjoying the course. I was envious, I longed to get out my clubs and join them but I had to go to the last hole to collect the cards as people finished their rounds. We all had lunch in the clubhouse and then I walked to the Andalus hotel to check-in.

The first thing I saw when I entered the hotel was our luggage piled up in a corner of reception. Another broken promise as the manager had assured me all the luggage would be delivered to our rooms by the time we arrived there. I went to the desk and tried to point this out but was constantly interrupted by the arrival of German guests who just talked over me. And worse, the receptionist snapped to attention and abandoned me to deal with them first. It was too much and during the third interruption I experienced a total meltdown.

I ordered the receptionist to come back and deal with my problem. Amazingly she responded positively, rounded up some porters and the luggage was soon being transferred to our rooms. Just two cases remained. In my haste the previous evening I had forgotten to inform the manager of the two name changes. Well, one name change and an additional guest. It took a lot of explaining and pleading but finally they booked us both in. I was given a suite but in a manner that suggested this was a punishment rather than a treat.

The hotel was right on the beach and had excellent facilities. Most people had some sort of a sea view and there were no complaints about the rooms. The only drawback was the slow service at reception as they always gave their German guests priority and there were also some complications created by one man on reception who said yes to everything but it subsequently transpired that that was the only English word he knew. By early evening everyone was settled and all the minor problems such as no towels, locked safety deposit boxes and missing toiletries had been resolved and we gathered for our Welcome Drink. We used a small meeting room for this and toasted a successful week with champagne while nibbling crisps and olives.

We also had our own small dining room for our evening meal. This was marred by an unpleasant argument because Percy refused to pay the full price for the wine he and three others had drunk. He claimed that he had ordered the house wine at €14 and had been served a bottle that cost €18. He and his companions flatly refused to pay more than €14. Rather than prolong the argument I made up the shortfall of €4. Percy, who looked as though he could easily afford expensive wine, was clearly going to be a thorn in my flesh. I tried to forget about him while I watched the Flamenco show after dinner and then joined some of the group for a last drink.

That was a mistake as Aubrey was one of them. He was drunk and objectionable and he upset a few people, including me, with his offensive remarks. I excused myself as I needed to finish doing the cards for the next day. I went back to my room which I hated already. I was on the ground floor overlooking the beach with a path going past the huge picture windows, of which there were several. There was a constant trail of people going to and fro and as everyone walked by they glanced into my room so I had to keep the curtains drawn all the time. The manager was unsympathetic and assured me it was the best suite in the hotel – for a goldfish.

Everything ran smoothly the following morning and once all my guests were on the golf course I walked back to the hotel and sat on the patio to do a chart of who had played with whom. As soon as I had finished it was time to return to the club to collect the cards and have some lunch. We gathered outside the bar by the smaller clubhouse near the first tee of the second eighteen holes. After lunch I went out by myself and played the nine holes that wove their way through the pine trees. I finished just in time to get back and change for pre-dinner drinks. Each of us who had stayed at Tryp the previous evening had been given a bottle of champagne to compensate for the inconvenience and we were meeting together to enjoy this bounty. Fortunately we had our own room again as corks were flying around and it got very noisy. I had to wait until we had finished dinner before I could read out the draw for the following morning and tell them about the excursion to Seville on our free day. Then it was back to my room to write out the cards.

As we had later tee-off times the next morning we were able to take our time over breakfast. After I had sent them all off the first tee I played nine holes on my own. It was a beautiful course with several different sections and I played nine holes by the sea. There was no rush as I had plenty of time before I had to check them at their ninth hole as the competition today was a four ball betterball stableford and it would take them several hours to get round. As soon as the last group was through I moved on to the last hole to collect the cards. During lunch in the clubhouse I confirmed numbers for our trip to Seville and then went back to the hotel to make the booking. I had requested payment before dinner when we met in the bar but several people side-stepped this arrangement so I had to run round the tables at dinner collecting the money. I had not had time to do the draw for the next competition in two days' time but I did not think it would be a problem.

It was a problem. Tee times were an issue for some people and my meal was punctuated by continuous requests to know what time they would be playing the day after next. I promised to do it immediately and pin it on our notice board (recently acquired from reception) in the lobby. I had only just settled down to do the draw when my phone rang and it was Kay to say she had to leave in the morning as the condition of her father had worsened. I went straight to her room and we organised her flight for the next morning. I could not help commenting on her lovely room and she suggested that I move into it and then inform reception after the deed was done. I moved most of my things that evening and then completed the move early the next morning. Reception was informed once the move was completed.

That morning was our free day and some people played golf and some of us went on the trip to Seville. I had organised this trip through a German company as we did not have the twenty-five people necessary to organise our own trip. It was a very good trip and our German guide, Thomas, lived locally in Chiclana. He spoke excellent English so he was able to give a lot of information about the area as we made our way to Seville. In Seville we had our own local guide, Pablo, who again spoke excellent English and entertained us with humorous stories as we explored the Pavilion, the Alcazar and the Cathedral. Unfortunately it rained on and off all day and after one serious drenching we stood under the wave of hot air coming from the overhang of a shop to dry off.

I had some free time wandering around the city on my own while the others went on a boat trip. I really enjoyed this interlude in my busy schedule. As I sat on the river bank waiting for the boat to return I focused once again on the task in hand. The following morning I was organising a singles competition. This had generated a lot of enthusiasm and friendly rivalry had crept in. I had intended to join in but due to Kay's departure this was no longer possible so I had to make some quick changes. I would have the new order of play ready to post on the board before dinner that evening.

By the time we met for dinner that evening tension was mounting and nerves were fraying. Some strategic changes were requested in the order of play. I had to stand firm as the draw had been done to ensure that the better players went out first so that play would progress without any hold ups. As experienced golfers they understood my reasoning but were resisting as they wanted to play with their friends. Finally we found a compromise and the good players moved down the order to join their less experienced friends. I lost count of the number of times I rewrote the draw and it was after midnight before the final version was posted on the notice board.

I was on the tee very early the following morning. The air was fresh and I could smell the newly cut grass and hear the hum of distant mowing machines as they finished preparing the course. How I longed to go out on the course and forget everything but the challenge of steering a small white ball through the avenue of trees that stretched ahead of me. My thoughts were interrupted by the arrival of the first players. Once they were half way down the fairway the next group set off. It was a steady stream until everyone was out playing. By then it was time to walk to the ninth green to watch the first group go through and ensure there were no hold ups in the field. This sometimes involved telling a player that they should abandon their attempt to finish playing a hole as the number of shots they had taken had strayed into double figures. Most conceded the point but Percy would snap that he had paid to complete every hole on the course.

As soon as the last group had finished playing the ninth hole the first group were walking down the fairway of their final hole and I had to hurry to get there before they left the green. When everyone had finished playing I set off along the beach to find a venue for lunch on our last day. There was just enough time before beginning the task of checking the cards and finalising the draw for the following morning. I walked for forty minutes before turning back. It was glorious as there was nothing there but sea, sand, and one restaurant which I booked. I was refreshed and ready to complete my tasks before enjoying another splendid buffet in the hotel restaurant.

The following morning was my first, and last, chance to play golf with the group and I played in the last four with Melvin, Anthony and Erika. Melvin was using a buggy but he was on his own as the rest of us preferred to pull our own manual trolleys. He was a real pain being totally unaware of anyone else on the course and veering across our path as we tried to play a shot. It took us a long time to get round and when we walked into the golf club for a late lunch it was deserted. The only sign the others had been there was a stack of completed cards on an empty table. I picked these up and settled down to calculate all the results for the week. These would be revealed at our prize giving that evening. This took place in a small meeting room before we went into dinner. There were some mutterings about the quality of the prizes (supplied by my company) which were rather strange choices for golf players and in particular the ladies' silk scarves decorated with horses' heads. Otherwise the occasion went well. Percy was furious when I told him he could not exchange his leather passport holder for something else from the hotel shop as the prizes had not been bought there.

On departure day as we did not leave until the afternoon most of us took our time packing before meeting up for lunch. A few people did get up early for a final round of golf. I walked to the clubhouse with them as I had to arrange for our clubs to be collected and delivered to the hotel in time to load them on to the transfer bus. The hotel minibus was not operating that morning as it was being serviced. I arranged for all the clubs to be left outside the caddie master's room to be picked up later. I was not convinced this would happen. And it did not. When I walked back to the hotel after lunch I discovered that three sets of clubs had not been collected. The hotel manager sent the driver back to look for the missing clubs and he returned with three sets of clubs but none of them were ours. I had attached a company label to every set of clubs so the driver would know which clubs were to be collected. There was no time to organise another trip to the clubhouse. As soon as our transfer bus was ready to leave we set off for the clubhouse where we located the missing clubs, loaded them and set off for the airport.

I had only been home for one day when Aimee called me regarding my next trip to Bangkok and Bali. It was no longer Bali due to problems in Indonesia so we were going to Hua Hin in Thailand instead. All the documentation would be faxed through to me and I would have to collect my revised airline ticket at the airport on the day of departure.

* * * * * *

I had so much paperwork to plough through before the trip that I did not pay much attention to the clients' lists. Therefore when I met the group at Heathrow I was surprised to see a familiar face. It was Barnaby. He had been a guest on my Christmas trip. Barnaby hugged me warmly and then turned to our companions and announced that we were old friends and had spent a night together in Florida. I was taken aback and very embarrassed. I stuttered an explanation of the circumstances. I was already seeing another side of Barnaby – the joker in the pack. Fortunately the others had more important issues on their minds. Each person had received a telephone call from my company explaining that our Foreign Office had advised against tourists visiting Indonesia. They had been offered either a full refund or an amended trip to Thailand. They had all agreed to come on the alternative holiday and now they wanted an inquest. I knew as much as they did and said so. Their main issue was that Bali would have been all-inclusive whereas Hua Hin was bed and breakfast. The fact it was a superior hotel did not seem sufficient recompense for 'free' food and drink.

We arrived in Bangkok at 04:30 the following morning and then we had to queue for two hours to get through immigration and collect our luggage. It would have been easy to miss our escort as she was four foot nothing but our driver, who towered above her was gallantly holding her sign above his head and was easy to spot. During our transfer Tata introduced herself and gave us some information about Thailand and Bangkok. She was inundated with questions regarding activities that guests wished to pursue while in the capital. Thai courtesy demands that negative answers are never given and to the fifteen questions she received she gave ten positive responses and five maybes. I hoped my guests did not think she actually meant what she had said.

They did and were eagerly making plans when we all met later to walk to the local shopping mall for lunch. This was our first experience of Bangkok traffic and after some bravado about crossing the busy roads we conceded defeat and used the pedestrian overpass that added at least fifteen minutes to our walk. It was very hot and humid and we were relieved when we entered the air-conditioned atmosphere of the huge shopping mall. As we gathered round several small tables in a snack bar and discussed the activities in store for us their excitement was tangible. I tried to introduce the idea of cultural constraints that we should be aware of.

I realised I had to span the cultural differences as tactfully as I could and my opportunity came when I met with Tata to discuss our itinerary before we had our Information Meeting with the group. Tata was very well organised, she had a sunny disposition and we gelled immediately and had soon agreed our programme. Fortunately I had made a note of all the requests that had received a positive answer and managed to weave them into the programme. I would have to deal with the maybes if they were mentioned again. Soon after we had finished planning the programme the group began drifting into the lobby. The meeting went really well mainly due to Tata's enthusiasm and her desire to please everyone. It seemed she was succeeding.

I was looking forward to our traditional Thai dinner accompanied by classical Thai dancing that evening. But my heart sank when my shoes were taken hostage as we entered the restaurant. I knew what was coming as we padded along behind our waitress. We threaded our way around large knee high tables surrounded by cushions scattered on the highly polished wooden floor. We were going to have to sit cross-legged on the floor for our meal. I had not been able to sit cross-legged on a floor since my unfortunate accident in Spain. I watched my companions arrange themselves around the table and planned my strategy. There were some proper tables and chairs in a far corner of the restaurant – maybe I could sit over there. As that would no doubt be misconstrued I decided I would have to adopt my own version of sitting cross-legged. It was a huge relief when I lifted the tablecloth to push my legs under the table and it revealed a large pit in which I could dangle my legs. I celebrated with a glass of Thai whisky with soda which I had discovered was a very pleasant combination.

We set off early the following morning to visit the Floating Market, Damnoen Saduak. Sadly we could not get into a boat and paddle around the market inspecting the wares on sale. We had to do our shopping from a wooden platform and a series of walkways but it was fun. The whole area seemed to be festooned with hand painted T-shirts. They were very pretty and so cheap it would have been churlish to refuse this invitation to treat. We also visited a local village to tour a salt farm and watch a demonstration of coconut sugar making so it was a busy morning. We returned to Bangkok for lunch, a delicious Thai food buffet. I was really enjoying the food on this trip unlike my companions some of whom were already craving fried food English style.

After lunch we went to the Royal Lapidary Factory. It was my first experience of a hard sell. On arrival we were offered a drink and then ushered into a room to watch a video about the manufacture of jewellery in Thailand. As our route was lined with uniformed staff it was clear we had no option. When we were finally released into the huge showroom we each had a sales person shadowing us. When I stopped to look at a very attractive wallet my minder was by my side immediately proffering similar products. I moved on and was somehow manoeuvred into the jewellery section where my minder tried to interest me in some earrings. I said I did not need any as I preferred rings. Trying to be clever I specified silver rings as I could not see any on display. That was not a problem and a shop assistant reached under the counter and produced two silver rings. One was a sapphire ring, my favourite stone and in a beautiful setting. Apparently these were in the sale so I could afford it. It was such a bargain I could also afford the wallet that my escort was still holding for me.

We had to make our own arrangements for dinner that evening and there was a majority vote not to eat Thai food and to eat in a restaurant close to our hotel. I booked tables in the Rio Grill in our hotel as that satisfied both demands. This restaurant was a Brazilian Churrascaria featuring lots of different grills including sausage, chicken, lamb, beef, pork, spare ribs and all accompanied by soup and salad with deep fried banana to finish. It was not a venue for vegetarians but fortunately there were none in this group. After an early dinner we visited the Pat Pong all night market.

I had booked the hotel minibus even though it only seated eleven people. I was sure some people would drop out but no one did. It was quite a challenge to pack fifteen people into the bus but we managed by starting with a layer of men and then fitting the women on top of them. I was very glad it was not too far as I clung on to the back of the front seat as we lurched through the city traffic. But it was worth the effort. As we spilled out of the bus we were immediately a target for stall holders wanting to show us their goods. We perused huge displays of fake watches and sunglasses and pondered over hundreds of cheap T-shirts as we strolled around. Despite the heat and the crowds it was an interesting and rewarding experience. I bought a 'Calvin Klein' T-shirt for fifty pence.

Pat Pong road was lined with numerous dubious clubs with men and girls loitering outside them trying to lure people in and then zap them with one hundred pound cover charges. Some of the men explored this option but were not enticed inside. We eventually emerged from the crush and I organised tut tuks to take us back to the hotel. We broke one of Tata's golden rules regarding survival in Bangkok. Once we were all aboard our respective three-wheeled vehicles we challenged our drivers to get us back to the hotel first. Challenge accepted nothing got in their way, red lights, cyclists and pedestrians were shrugged aside as we raced through the night. It was exhilarating but scary and I was glad that it was night and there was not so much traffic about.

The following morning we visited the Royal Palace. Although it was crowded and humid it was a memorable experience for two reasons. The first was the stunning architecture and exquisite statuary. The second was being abandoned by Tata. She was only four foot six and even with her lacy umbrella it was sometimes impossible to pick her out in the crowds. We were pushing through a really dense patch of visitors when we got caught up with a family posing for pictures. By the time we had extricated ourselves Tata and the other half of the group had vanished. We had no idea where they had gone and it seemed Tata was unaware she had left some of us behind. I called her even though I knew she had switched her mobile off when she had started our tour that morning. My call went straight to voicemail but I left a message – just in case.

After looking anxiously round for several minutes I decided to rely on a rule of my childhood. If you get lost go back to the last place you remember being together. We re-traced our steps and waited. Just as it seemed we would have to make our own way back to our hotel Tata appeared. She had not realised we had become separated from the group and had led all the others out of the palace just after we got tangled up. She kept apologising as we made our way to the exit. I was just relieved to see her and said so – but I did remind her to switch her mobile back on in future.

That afternoon we were free to explore on our own so after a snack lunch together we split up and went our separate ways. My objective was the Hard Rock Café to book tables for dinner that evening. This would be a new experience for me as I had never eaten in one of these establishments before. I liked the look of the very distinctive interior. When I returned later with the group I was taken aback by the number of people purporting to eat there. Despite having booked tables we still had to wait for one to become free. We were crammed along one side of the bar and we had to synchronise our eating as we could not to lift our American fare to our mouths simultaneously. Conversation was impossible it was so noisy so we ate and left. It had rained very heavily while we had been inside and there were huge puddles on the roads. We hailed tuk tuks to take us back to the hotel. Due to the rain there were not many around so some people decided to walk. They were the wise ones. I was dripping wet by the time we got back to our hotel thanks to the tidal waves that washed over our vehicle as we raced through the surface water.

When I went to breakfast the following morning Pansy told me that Ralph had heard late last night that his father had died. Several of them had been drinking in the hotel bar when the call came through. The news was not unexpected as Ralph's father had been ill for a long time. They had not called me as nothing could be done until the next morning. I called Ralph and asked him if he needed to go home immediately. His preference was to continue his holiday for a few more days as the last year had been tough for him. Before I called his insurance company I spoke to Thai International Airlines as they had an office in our hotel. They were very sympathetic and promised they would see if they could change his flight for the date he had requested. I suggested that in the circumstances they might do it free of charge. I explained that there may be problems claiming compensation from his insurance company as his father had been ill when he came away on holiday. They promised they would do their best. Next I had to arrange a transfer back to Bangkok.

Our agent was very understanding when I called him to discuss it. He immediately offered to organise the transfer free of charge. Finally I called Ralph's insurance company and gave them all the details and updated them on my efforts to organise his journey home. I agreed to let them know as soon as I had any news. Meanwhile they would also check flights and the validity of his insurance in the circumstances. They promised to call me back. By the time I had made all these arrangements Tata had arrived to accompany us to Hua Hin. After a quick explanation for my state of unreadiness I raced upstairs and stuffed all my belongings into my suitcase. I was back downstairs just as our bus drew up outside the hotel. We had to splash through steady rain to get on board.

It was still raining when we arrived in Hua Hin three hours later and the resort did not look very attractive through the grey veil of moisture. I was struggling to raise my guests' flagging spirits. I pointed out that the hotel we were staying in was a luxury resort with excellent facilities and several restaurants. In Bali we would have been staying in a typical beach-side all-inclusive venue catering for large numbers and no hint of the exclusivity we were about to enjoy. I had already discovered that many of our guests researched their accommodation very thoroughly but strangely not when last minute changes were involved. Thanks to some untimely reminders that we should have been in Bali an air of discontent was spreading through the bus. After checking in and unpacking most of us met up in the lobby and went to the hotel's snack bar for some lunch. When the bills arrived some of the group became very hostile as it would have been 'free' on Bali. Owen was particularly bitter and his attitude was infecting the others. As soon as I left them they got in a huddle which made me suspect they were plotting something.

They were and they could not wait to tell me their plan when we met later for our Information Meeting. They told me not to include them in any arrangements for dinner as they were going to eat in the hotel every night. They would keep the receipts from each meal and send them to my company requesting a refund on the grounds the holiday should have been all-inclusive. They wanted my advice regarding this ploy. Fortunately my input was delayed by the arrival of our local guide, Wan Pen, who had come to talk to us about optional excursions. Wan Pen was charming. His slight frame and floppy dark hair that thatched his boyish face suggested he was much younger than his twenty-three years. He was also a very experienced guide and quickly surmounted the awkwardness in the room while he spoke to us. The meeting ended with a discussion regarding where we should have dinner. Wan Pen was happy to suggest a local restaurant but the group were divided. Four were eating in the hotel, six wanted to make their own arrangements and the others were happy to walk into town with me for dinner at the recommended restaurant.

We had a really good meal at a very reasonable price. Initially subdued my companions soon cheered up and we raised a glass to our intention to enjoy our Thailand experience. We were all excited to be there and fascinated by the night time activity in the streets as we walked through the town. From the open fronted workshops we could hear the clattering of old-fashioned Singer sewing machines; both electric and hand driven. In the light that spilled out of the shops and workshops we could see the shiny backs of cockroaches that looked like a stream of water in the gutter as there were so many of them. At the end of one of the narrow, dimly lit streets we were drawn towards the colourful illuminations on the stalls of the night market. Some of the group were drinking in the bar when we finally got back to the hotel. I was still full of enthusiasm about the sights we had seen but their conspiratorial air soon drove me to my room. A message pushed under my door stated that everything was in place for Ralph's repatriation.

At breakfast the next morning I discovered that the six who had eaten independently had patronised a really cheap local café and three of them were now ill and confined to their rooms. I spent the morning collecting the money for the trips and visiting the sick. As soon as everyone had given me their money I called Wan Pen and he arrived soon after to collect it. I was now free to have lunch with Barnaby in the hotel snack bar. I had discovered that Barnaby had a mischievous streak and was enjoying all the intrigue that was going on. He had a foot firmly planted in each camp and took great delight in acting as my mole. His light-hearted banter soon cheered me up. Particularly when he told me that he had found some dog dirt on the beach that morning and Owen had made a note of this to include in his letter of his complaint. When we were joined by other members of the group the conversation moved on to the subject of tailor-made clothes. I had mentioned that I was intending to get some clothes made and several people in the group had decided to follow suit so I arranged an outing to the tailor.

Nick, a local tailor, had been recommended by Wan Pen and I had already been to look at his premises in town. He operated from a large air-conditioned shop whose walls were lined with bales of fabric and shelves of pattern books. His operation looked much more professional than the shacks in the town centre with handwritten signs pinned to shabby curtains draped around the front. I had seen people having their measurements taken in the street and I had decided I wanted something more discrete.

Nick was charming. When he took our measurements he told us he would keep them for two years. I responded that I wished I could too. All of us ordered items of clothing and he gave us the prices. I then started bargaining which surprised him but we did get some money off. While the others were busy with materials and patterns Nick took me to one side and said he had not expected us to bargain. He gauged his prices according to the nationality. The Americans would pay anything; the British expected a fair price and the Germans would bargain hard. He felt he had offered us a fair price but was willing to reward my audacity with a small discount across the board.

Only half the group had booked the Hua Hin by night tour that evening. The dissidents were not only boycotting local restaurants but excursions as well. They missed a real treat. Wan Pen arrived with a fleet of trishaws and we set off for the station where we visited the Royal Waiting Room and inspected the golf course there. We pedalled on to the Sofitel Hotel where we walked around its fabulous garden. The air was cool and fresh thanks to the fine spray from the sprinklers. As we paused to admire this oasis of green we suddenly realised that the 'hedge' we had just walked through was an elephant and around us various other animals pranced on the top of small, round shrubs and a flock of flamingos grazed on the lawn. It was the most stunning example of topiary I had ever seen.

Next we went to the harbour and watched the deep sea fishing boats come in and unload. After strolling along the jetty we arrived at the restaurant where we were having dinner. Our meal was very good and everyone was relaxed and finally warming to the small town of Hua Hin. After our meal Wan Pen led us through the streets to the night market. Throughout the tour Wan Pen was very interesting and informative. After the market visit the trishaws took us back to the hotel where I joined the four dissidents in the bar for a cocktail. I did not want them to add my indifference to their growing list of complaints. I had a Slow Motion cocktail which arrived in a large ceramic snail which I was allowed to keep.

When I got back to my room there was a message to call Aimee. I returned the call and discovered that Aimee was curious to know how the group were reacting to the last minute change of destination. She was sympathetic when I told her about the four dissidents. There had been some unrest in Indonesia that day and Aimee suggested I pass this information on to the group as it justified the decision to keep us in Thailand. I said I would but I doubted it would help as they were so entrenched in their belief that they had suffered a great injustice.

At breakfast the next morning we discussed the eating arrangements for that evening. As there was a consensus to eat in the hotel's Italian restaurant the dissidents decided to join us. I agreed to book tables and to try and get a meal deal. I also mentioned that I was going to visit Nick the tailor again. I was taking him an outfit I wanted him to copy for me. It was too good an opportunity to miss. I asked if anyone wanted to come along and said I would book the courtesy shuttle from the hotel. No one was interested and Kirsten took the opportunity to inform us that she had found a contact through the hotel. Her tailor would come to the hotel to take her order thus avoiding any contact with the local community.

I wondered if that receipt would be added to the pile she was collecting for a rebate. After I had negotiated a discount with the Italian restaurant for their all-inclusive buffet that evening I set off for the town on my own.

That afternoon I walked along the beach that fronted our hotel. It was a fabulous sandy beach and went on for miles walking away from the town. Polo ponies from the local club were being exercised on the firm sand at the water's edge and locals tried to tempt me with fresh fruit and a variety of souvenirs. I bought some bananas and they tasted exquisite. When I turned back to walk towards the town I discovered this was a matter of timing as there was a stream that ran down through the town, across the beach and into the sea. At high tide it was not possible to wade through this. At low tide it was probably not a good idea to try.

When we met in the bar that evening I gave them the details of the deal I had made with the Italian restaurant and made it clear that no drinks were included. I also reminded them that it was much cheaper to drink the local drinks as imported drinks were really expensive. Barnaby was missing so I called him in his room. He arrived nearly an hour later and then insisted on having a drink in the bar. Some people decided to join him but the others wanted to go and eat straightaway. Two tables had been set for us and this first group filled all the places on one of them which was a happy coincidence. I sat on the other table on my own and waited for the rest of the group. Owen joined me soon afterwards. He had failed to persuade the others to quit the bar and took the opportunity to air all his grievances yet again. He was not a patient person and after ten minutes he stormed off in a huff. When the others finally joined me for dinner Owen was not with them.

Most people said they enjoyed the meal but Kirsten got cross because it cost more than she had anticipated. She had forgotten my warning that the imported wine was very expensive and that the price on the menu did not included tax and service which were added later. As she left she spat at me, "It's okay as long as I get it all back", and then she went off to bed. It was getting harder and harder to remain cheerful when faced with people so determined not to enjoy a holiday they had chosen to come on. As she had been putting all her food and drink on her room bill she was going to have another big shock when all the extras were added.

The following morning Owen delayed our departure on the trip to Samroi Yod Park. Several people had been late meeting us in reception and then, just as we were about to leave, Owen disappeared. We waited for him on the minibuses. When he finally arrived and climbed into my vehicle I noticed that he did not have his rucksack with him. I pointed this out and asked him where it was. He told me that someone was looking after it for him so we set off.

At the first stop, a pineapple plantation, Owen discovered that he did not have his rucksack after all. He blamed me for not picking it up for him when he left it in reception. I did not know he had left it in reception because I had been outside getting people aboard our vehicles. I told him that if I had seen it I would have picked it up. But I did not see it. He then claimed that I had told him that someone had taken it for him. This was simply not true and he had driven me to the point where I was not prepared to be 'nice' any more. I stood my ground. I told him this was not true. Other people aboard our minibus had heard his accusations and came to my rescue confirming that I had asked him where his rucksack was before we left our hotel. Now it was more important to retrieve the rucksack than to establish fault so I told the guide what had happened. She organised one of the minibuses to take Owen back to the hotel to get his rucksack.

Our next stop was a coconut plantation where the locals trained monkeys to climb the trees to pick coconuts for them. We watched a demonstration during which the monkey threw coconuts down on us indiscriminately. We drank the fresh coconut milk and ate some of the flesh before moving on to our next stop, a small fishing village. Here we swapped our minibuses for two small shallow boats and chugged off down the river to the sea where we disembarked on a beach. After some refreshments we set off to explore a cave. Our local guide bounded from rock to rock in his flip-flops while we struggled behind him in stout trainers. Wan Pen had described the walk as rugged but had underestimated the steepness of the gradient. It was also incredibly hot underground and some people gave up and walked back to the beach. The rest of us continued to the temple in the cave and then scrambled up the rocks above it and emerged on the cliff where we could enjoy views of the coastline.

After rejoining our companions on the beach we had some lunch and then swam in the rock pools fringing the sea. As we lounged in these pools we joked that the water was hotter than the bath water in our hotel. No doubt this would have been added to the growing lists of complaints but as the compilers of this list had shunned this day out it was treated as the joke it was meant to be. We lay back and relaxed in the warmth of the water and sense of companionship. All too soon it was time to walk back to our boats and then board the minibuses to return to our hotel.

Ralph left early that evening and several people joined me in reception to say goodbye to him. He gave me some money to buy some drinks for everyone and after he had gone we went into the bar to toast his safe journey home. I did not wait until everyone was together as I felt it was more fitting to buy drinks for those who had made the effort to see him off. While we were in the bar Kirsten, one of the dissidents, appeared wearing one of two blouses that had been made for her and carrying the other. The one she was wearing resembled a patterned sack with an opening at the front. She assured me the second one was just as bad. She wanted to know what she could do about it. She had already bought three other blouses from the same tailor and she was also having five pairs of shoes made. Clearly she was not as short of money as she had been claiming.

Whatever her attitude had been to the holiday she was one of my guests and I agreed to try and help out. First stop reception to find the girl who had recommended the tailor. She could not help as she had no means of contacting him. He was a friend of a friend who had asked her to recommend his business. I spoke to the manager who was apologetic but said that there were no controls regarding these small businesses that sprang up overnight. Kirsten had been lucky the first time as her tailor had found a good machinist. The second time it had been a different machinist and the quality was much poorer. Kirsten did not have any contact details as the man had just called at the hotel at appointed times. I could do nothing more to help and could only suggest that if Kirsten saw him in the hotel to let me know. I doubted he would come back while we were there.

Kirsten's experience fuelled her aggression and her determination to drag everyone down with her. As people gathered in the bar they were regaled with details of her latest disappointment. She was spoiling the holiday for other people and it was time to intervene. On the pretext of calling them to order to discuss plans for dinner that night I once again apologised for the change in destination for their holiday. I then moved on to suggest they put their complaints aside and we make the best of it. They were in a place they would not visit again and they were wasting time they would not have again. We might as well concentrate on the positives of the resort we were in and enjoy exploring it. I suggested we walked into town to eat at a local restaurant but once again the dissidents excused themselves and went off to the hotel's restaurant.

Everyone else walked into town where we had a lovely Thai meal in a bright, modern restaurant. I loved Thai food and indulged as often as possible. Even for breakfast. I was feeling really healthy. Back at the hotel the dissidents were waiting in the bar. I did not join them as usual as their conversation had not moved on. The weather was too hot, the food was too expensive and there was nothing to do. I was glad they had not come into town with us then they could have added sewing sweatshops and cockroaches in the gutters to their list.

It was another hot and humid day and my plans to wallow in the warm sea were foiled by the arrival of a massive shoal of jellyfish. Both large and small varieties were scattered on the surface of the water. I retreated to the pool and sat reading in the shade, occasionally venturing in to the water to cool down. It was a fabulous hotel. The pool was surrounded by luxuriant vegetation and I could hear the soft murmur of voices from the pool bar at the far end. I had just read the same page three times when some of my guests approached and reminded me that we were due to go for a fitting at the tailor's that afternoon. It was a welcome diversion and we collected an audience as we left. At the tailor's we had an impromptu fashion show. Afterwards we treated ourselves to an ice cream in the only ice cream parlour in town.

Most of us ate in town that evening and after dinner we went to the Melia Hotel and took the lift up to the seventeenth floor to see the view across Hua Hin. It was fabulous. Barnaby, who was relishing his self-appointed role as devil's advocate, was comparing the hotel with ours and making mental notes to pass on to the dissidents. He highlighted the fact that this hotel had a doorman and ours did not but then our hotel did not have a door. I left them enjoying a drink in the Melia and got a trishaw back to the hotel. It would be a very early start the next morning for the River Kwai trip.

The day started with a three hour minibus journey to Kanchanaburi with Owen moaning for the entire journey. Why he had come I had no idea but we all wished he had not. At Kanchanaburi we went round the Jeath War Museum which was set out like a replica of the camp where the prisoners had been kept while working on the railway and the bridge over the River Kwai. Pictures and newspaper cuttings were displayed above the elevated bamboo bunks where hundreds of prisoners would have slept together. We all found it very moving and wandered around on our own reading the articles displayed on the walls and trying to imagine the unimaginable.

It was a subdued group that boarded a speedboat and raced down the river eventually arriving at the bridge itself. Pierre Boulle who wrote the book of the same name was also responsible for changing the geography of Thailand. He had never visited the bridge but knew that the 'death railway' ran parallel to the River Kwai for several miles so he assumed that when it crossed a river it was the River Kwai. He was wrong as it crossed the River Mae Khlung. When David Lean produced a film of the same name and tourists arrived in their thousands to see the bridge there was only one solution and the river was renamed Kwai. We slowed down to pass under the bridge and then moored up, got off, and walked to the train station. We would be crossing the bridge by train. It was not the original bridge but the steel bridge that had been built to replace the wooden one that had been completed a few months earlier. Some of the original tracks of the 'death' railway had also been lifted but we could still see disused sections of the original railway that had been laid along a route hacked manually through the rugged countryside by the prisoners of war.

As we waited for our train, a local train that runs from Bangkok to Kanchanaburi, and then over the River Kwai to Nam Tok our local guide, Pom, warned the women in the group not to touch the Buddhists monks that would also be travelling on the train. There were so many of them it was difficult to avoid brushing their flowing orange robes as we made our way down the narrow corridor to our wooden bench seats. These seats were hard and uncomfortable and the train was very crowded. There was a continual stream of purveyors of soft drinks, beer, pre-packed food and fresh fruit. Persistent sellers of T-shirts followed in their footsteps. I sought some relief and fresh air by leaning out of an open window. The Buddhists monks shrank back into their seats as I approached them and our guide screamed at me to take care not to touch them. I felt like a leper.

At Namtok Station we had lunch and then we were picked up by the minibuses and taken to the Sacred Cave inhabited by a statue of Buddha and a monk who was sleeping there as part of his training. After the cave we went back to the cemetery in Nanchanabura where the Allied soldiers who died while building the bridge were buried. Row upon row of headstones recorded unit, rank and age. As far as I could see they were all Sherwood Foresters and all between the ages of eighteen and twenty-one. Everyone was quiet during the three hour drive back to our hotel, no doubt reflecting on the sights we had seen that day.

When I arrived in the bar that evening most of the group were already there, sitting in a tight circle, leaning inwards and whispering. I pulled up a chair but nobody made room for me. Rather than force myself into the ring I suggested we add another table but there was no movement on the comment that we did not know how many more people were coming. They clearly did not want anyone else to join them so I moved to another table on my own and started to make notes for my report. Then I saw Barnaby going into another part of the bar and I joined him and Owen followed me in there. When the others went off to eat in the hotel restaurant Kirsten did come and tell us where they were going but I was not sure if this was an invite or a statement. Neither of my companions showed any interest in joining them so I stayed in the bar with them.

When the question of what to do for dinner was discussed Owen sheepishly asked if we could go and eat in town. This was a real turn around. He had joined us on two excursions and now he had decided to break out of the hotel and sample the local cuisine. I was delighted. We walked in to town and ate in one of the seafood restaurants built on stilts on the beach and stretching out into the sea. We could hear the sea crashing below us and shortly after we sat down the fishing fleet arrived and we watched them unloading their catch on the jetty across the bay. We shared four different Thai dishes accompanied by steamed rice and these, with two rounds of drinks, cost a grand total of £8. After the meal we had a stroll around the red light district and then moved on to an open air bar for a drink. Some of the others were in the same bar and expressed envy regarding our eating experience that evening. I think they regretted being swayed by the dissidents to join them in the hotel.

I had hoped that the whole group would eat together on our last night and at breakfast that morning I introduced the idea. Kristen refused to be parted from her principles and her remaining two supporters declared their intention to join her in the hotel restaurant. Barnaby and Owen had made their own plans for the evening but suggested we all meet for a drink after dinner. There were several requests to return to the Euro Seafood Garden Café as it had been such a success the first time some of us ate there. I got the shuttle into town and booked our tables. Next stop Nick the tailor to collect my clothes.

Soon after I got to Nick's I was joined by all the others who had ordered clothes and we had an impromptu fashion show. As I had masterminded the whole tailoring experience I was relieved when everyone declared themselves happy with their purchases and in particular Mark who looked amazing in his bespoke suit. Nick had done a good job. I was delighted with my new wardrobe and in particular my impulse purchase, a Thai silk jacket. When we got back to the hotel it was raining heavily and I splashed through the puddles back to my room to change before meeting the group in the bar.

After dinner we met up with Barnaby and Owen. A few days earlier Barnaby had claimed that he had found the display of escort girls in a local hotel and had been threatening to take us to see them. Now was as good a time as any. It was surprisingly tasteful. The girls were beautiful and they sat on banked rows of carpeted steps looking down demurely. It was a while before I realised they were watching a television at the bottom of the steps. At regular intervals someone would enter this area bearing a number and one of the girls would get up and leave. We moved on to another bar for a final drink before getting rickshaw bikes back to our hotel.

My breakfast was interrupted the following morning when Pansy arrived and insisted I went with her to speak to the manager regarding a bottle of brandy she claimed had disappeared from her room two days earlier. I had reported it at the time but the hotel clearly did not believe that anything could be taken from any of the rooms. Their theory was that Pansy had drunk it herself and then forgotten she had done it. I doubted that had happened although she could have taken it to another room as I knew they had been holding room parties. When we left that afternoon there was still no sign of the brandy and the deputy manager told her that she must fill in a form and they would deal with it and then write to her.

I had to turn my attention to the collection and checking of luggage ready to load onto our bus. I met Tata in reception when she had arrived with our bus to escort us back to Bangkok. It was lovely to see her again and she was already being super-efficient, and checking that all the cases were being collected. Eventually all the cases had been brought down, checked and loaded on to the bus and everyone was there ready to go. Three hours later we were at the airport checking in for our overnight flight. I had time to wander around the Duty Free where I had hoped to buy Pansy a bottle of brandy but it was much too expensive so I just gave her some money towards it. I would never know what had happened to that bottle of brandy.

* * * * * *

I did discover what happened to all the receipts the dissidents had collected from the hotel restaurant. Aimee called me a few days after I got home to inform me that they had been attached to a letter of complaint. The author was suggesting that my company swapped these receipts for a large refund. They had also received my receipts for the same number of meals but eaten locally, £60 in total. I suspected a £50 voucher for one of our holidays would be the best offer on the table.

As we chatted Aimee reminded me that after I had completed my first trip with them I had been offered a two week trip in Rhodes and I had accepted. I was surprised to be offered a trip so far in advance but was told it was a big group and would suit my organisational skills. I had repeated several times at my interview that I was used to dealing with groups of eighty-five people in a city centre hotel. But on that occasion we had been following a set programme. Holidaymakers, I had already discovered, did pretty much what they wanted. I could hardly believe that the nine months since I had agreed to lead this trip had already gone by and I was about to embark on my last trip as a holiday rep.

Chapter 12 - June

As I emerged from the luggage reclaim at Rhodes airport before I could collect my thoughts or my group I was enveloped in a bear hug and a voice boomed in my ear that she was pleased to see me. The company sign that the woman had been waving vigorously was relinquished to the young man beside her and then linking my arm she dragged me outside towards a bus. As we trotted along she introduced herself. She was Linda, our local agent. She had everything under control. I was commanded to get on board and wait with some other guests she had already found in Arrivals while she fielded the remaining guests who had been on my flight.

Linda was back again a few minutes later with some more guests. It was exhausting watching her scurrying to and fro. In between forays she had informed me that she would be meeting all the flights and dispatching the arrivals to our hotel. I was to be in reception to greet them and check them in. After the last few passengers had boarded Linda told me to meet her in reception the next morning so she could brief me regarding the optional excursions and then she was gone.

It was a short journey to the Hotel Cosmopolitan in the small resort of Ixia where we were staying. By the time we arrived everyone was desperate to fling their clothes off to catch some rays. One of them was Marjorie who raced back to reception to complain that her room did not have a balcony. I should have dealt with this through reception but Marjorie was hopping around impatiently and glancing outside as though she only had four hours to sunbathe and not fourteen days. To stem the hysteria I gave her the key to my room. She did not come back so I guessed it fitted the bill. I just had time to check my room before the next group was due to arrive. My generous gesture had backfired and I had allocated myself a cubbyhole next to reception and opposite the bar. I pleaded with reception to give me another room. At first they refused then I remembered that some of my group had not yet arrived. I suggested a swap. They were not happy but eventually decided they could offer me a room at the back of the hotel with views over a large building site and the countryside beyond. I accepted it gratefully.

The Welcome Drink was total chaos with forty-seven people milling around the trays of ouzo and fresh orange juice. I was still trying to check that everyone was there when the maître d' appeared. The tapping of his foot and constant glances at his watch soon made it clear he wanted us in the restaurant. We followed him to our four tables. Two of these tables, in the absence of an effective ban on smoking, were in the area where smoking was tolerated. There was a stampede for the table furthest away from the smoking zone. It was like a crazy form of musical chairs as guests barged each other out of the way. One man even moved a chair from one table to another and crammed it into a space that did not exist. When the maître d' pointed out it was a buffet everyone on the furthest table sat tight not daring to leave their seat empty. I had to negotiate a truce and quickly. I appealed to the smokers not to smoke until everyone had finished their meal. They agreed. The few people still lingering by the table hoping to grab a seat at a non-smoking table reluctantly took the remaining empty places.

Harmony was restored by the time I suggested that we all strolled down to the road below our hotel where there was a parade of bars and shops. Everyone decided to come. I could imagine the delight of the local bar owners when my crocodile of forty-eight people started walking along the parade. I had been down there earlier but had hastily retreated as I was constantly badgered by bar owners wanting me to take my group to their bar. I was not wearing my badge but they had an instinct for spotting Hostesses, even new ones like me. One in particular was very aggressive and shouted at me until I was out of sight. I was quite unnerved by this experience but was happy to run the gauntlet again with forty-seven companions. There were too many of us to fit into one of these small bars so we split up and some went to the History Bar while the others patronised the Nostalgia Bar. They were still propping up these bars when I went back to the hotel to meet my last two arrivals.

The excesses of the previous night were manifested in hangovers at breakfast the next morning and several absentees. Some of these did not attend the Information Meeting that followed. I did not have time to chase them up as Linda had insisted I was on parade thirty minutes before the meeting was due to start. She ran her groups with a military precision that was both admirable and irritating at the same time. When we finished putting out the chairs for our meeting we sat down to discuss our programme for the week. Linda invited me to call her Lindy but I struggled with this cute diminutive when applied to this stout, super-efficient character. Even before the meeting began she upset some of my group by barking at them to wait outside the room while we talked. She informed me that she must have a minimum of twenty to run a trip and immediate confirmation of numbers plus payment for the Lindos excursion the next day. As she went off to make some phone calls her parting shot was that I was responsible for the money and any short fall would come out of my pocket. I was quivering in my court shoes.

After she had gone people began drifting into the room – the first few requested permission to do so – we giggled together and speculated that Linda must have been a teacher in a former life. When she swept back into the room I suspected she might insist the group stood up and said 'good morning Miss'. She was very well organised and went through all the trips available that week and answered all the questions that were asked. She then left as grandly as she had entered and I started taking bookings and collecting money. I had no problem getting my minimum numbers but collecting the money was a nightmare of confusion as people shoved notes at me and then rushed off to start some serious sunbathing. I frantically scribbled down the trips that had been booked and the money that had been received. I would sort out the change later. I did notice one man inserting a note at the bottom of the pile and taking a note from the top saying that was the change due to him.

Later, when I counted the money I discovered I was €50 short. My secret payer had said he put in €100 and taken €50 in change but there were no €100 notes in the pile. There was one name that did not have an entry regarding the amount of money paid. That was Frederick. I hoped he had not done it deliberately and even if he had it would be difficult to prove. As I did not have the courage to approach my prime suspect directly I would have to make a general appeal and hope his better nature would come to the surface and he would own up. Since he had arrived Frederick had spent most of the time in the bar, his thin body hunched over a pint of beer as his short-sighted eyes gazed morosely at the contents.

Once all the money was stored in my safety deposit box I was free to explore the local vicinity. First I called into the supermarket close to the hotel entrance and met Mike the proprietor. He was charming and promised that if he did not stock any items my clients wanted he would order them for the next day. When I strolled along the promenade of shops and bars I was once again harassed by the pushy bar owner who had accosted me the previous day. His persistence was fuelled by the fact we had not patronised his bar the previous evening. He kept shouting that I was breaking the 'agreement'. I quickened my step to get past his frontage but he chased after me so I ran across the road and took refuge on the beach. I had given him the same response I had given all the other bar owners that I would let the group decide which bars and restaurants to patronize.

I strolled back along the beach until I had passed our hotel and then crossed back over the road where I found several other shops and some hotels. After all that exercise in the heat of the day it was time for a siesta. The noise from the building site below was quite soporific and I was able to catch up on some sleep. My first twenty-four hours had been really hectic and a rude awakening at five this morning when the bin men arrived had not helped. Fortunately I had set my alarm (I did this whenever I sat down in my room) and I had time for a swim before I had to ring 'Lindy' to confirm numbers for the next day. I confessed regarding the shortfall and received no sympathy just a reminder that it was my responsibility.

As soon as everyone in the group had assembled in the bar I asked them to be quiet so that I could speak to them. This was not easy, fifty excited clients all jabbering away about their first day in Rhodes. I had already decided I needed a notice board and wanted to draw their attention to its existence where the programme for each day would be displayed. When they were suitably quiet I asked if anyone remembered giving me the wrong note when they paid me for the trips as I was now €50 short. I did not expect a public confession so suggested if anyone had checked and found they had more money than they should have maybe they could tell me later. I had no doubt my prime suspect would check his money, discover he had too much and pay me back.

I socialised with everyone that evening running between the Nostalgia Bar and the History Bar. We filled both bars. Personally I preferred the former probably because the owners, Jan and Patrick, kept sending me half bottles of a very nice white wine made in a local monastery. It was the early hours of the next morning when we finally crept back into our hotel. But sleep evaded me. My prime suspect had not owned up so I was still missing some money. I remained optimistic that it would turn up eventually. I had searched my room and safety deposit box several times in the hope I may have mislaid it but I had not.

The following morning I joined the group on the Lindos trip which began with a tour of the island. I was concerned because I had not seen everyone at breakfast before I left. Late risers and large numbers meant I would have been hanging around until midday to see them all anyway. I left my mobile number with reception in case there were any problems.

We had several stops on the way to Lindos and the first was a leather factory attached to a huge showroom. We were encouraged to purchase souvenirs and presents at 'good' prices but some avid shoppers in the group had already explored the shops in Rhodes and assured us, in loud voices, that the same goods were cheaper there. Everyone took this hint and it was not long before we were on our way again. Our next stop was a monastery where we toured the underground church and visited the winery which was basically an exercise in selling wine and flavoured brandy.

After lunch and more shopping opportunities in Embona we finally arrived in Lindos. It was mid-afternoon and extremely hot especially for those of us who walked up to the Acropolis. Of course we could have hired donkeys but we felt it was unfair on the beasts. Our walk was punctuated with pleas from the many tablecloth sellers to view their wares spread out on the rocks beside the path. After the Acropolis we had some free time to explore. With one accord we set off for the beach bypassing the wooden walkways and running across the sand in our bare feet. We were soon hopping from one foot to another. The sand was red hot and the soles of our feet were on fire. We slumped on to some empty sun beds and were immediately asked to pay the full daily rate. Hastily pulling on our shoes we moved on and sought refuge under the shady awning of a beach bar. We stayed there until it was time to meet our coach.

We arrived back at the hotel just in time to meet up for pre-dinner drinks. I was surprised to find several people already in the bar when I arrived there thirty minutes before the appointed time. They all wanted to speak to me about their rooms. The people who had requested rooms with a sea view were troubled by the noise of the traffic on the road between the hotel and the beach. Those with a pool view claimed they were kept awake by the amorous croaking of the bull frogs in the ornamental ponds fringing the main pool. I made a list of requests and went to speak to the reception manager. The hotel was full and they only had one spare room on the ground floor of the small two-storey block by the pool. Harry, who found the traffic noise intolerable but relished the idea of being able to fall out of his bed into the pool bar, decided to accept this offer. One of the bull frog haters took his room on the road. I swapped my quiet room for a top floor pool view in the hope the ardour of the bull frogs would soon cool down. The others resigned themselves to waiting until more rooms became available or swapping amongst themselves. All the moves were scheduled for the next day which meant I had to find time to pack that night.

After dinner that evening we went to the usual two bars on the strip. I was sitting with the group in Nostalgia when the frequenters of History joined us, their faces so long they were nearly dragging along the floor. It seemed the unhappy patron had called the police to complain of the loud music in the bar five minutes past midnight (the watershed) and the police had arrived a few minutes later and shut the bar down. I knew the culprit would be hanging around outside to see the results of his efforts so I went outside to speak to him. The whole situation was getting out of hand and required one of us to be the grown up.

He was there and looking very smug. I pointed out that he was getting a lot of daytime trade as several people in my group favoured his establishment for a late, cooked breakfast rather than getting up early (by their standards) for the hotel's rather mundane buffet. But that could change if I spilled the beans about tonight's escapade. It was time for reason to prevail. His anger had stemmed from an agreement he claimed to have made with another rep whereby he had paid that person to take all our clients to his restaurant. I was not even sure that it was a rep from my company. I was doing my best to please everyone and when he agreed to withdraw his complaint about the music it seemed that I might be succeeding.

I took my own luggage to my new room after breakfast the next day and stuffed it all in the wardrobe so that the chambermaids could clean the room. I had arranged to walk into Rhodes with some of the group. It was my first opportunity to walk along the front into the town. We were side-tracked by the smell of fresh doughnuts in a small bakery by the roadside and stopped to sample some with a cup of coffee. Both were delicious. It did not take us long to reach the new town of Rhodes but we continued along the sea front until we reached one of the original gates through the city walls that took us into the old town. We split up to browse the shops that lined the pretty cobbled streets. After exploring the old town I walked through the new town where I was unable to resist the temptation of the pie shops.

I bought a fresh spinach pie or Spanakopita for my lunch. The filling, a mixture of spinach, herbs, onion and feta cheese was encased in paper thin sheets of phyllo pastry. These pies were originally made by shepherds in the mountainous region above Athens. I loved the salty tang of the feta cheese. I sat on a shady bench in the street to eat my pie. When I had finished I took a road out of town towards the Acropolis. I knew that this route would lead me back to our hotel. This acropolis was not a tourist attraction and no one was around so I sat up there for a while as it was very peaceful and cool.

I settled into my new room before meeting the group for pre-dinner drinks in the pool bar. Some of the group were spending most of their days there and had requested that this be our regular venue. I was happy to agree to the change and got there early as I could see from my new vantage point that people were already assembling there. It was a chance to catch up with those I had not seen very often that week as the group had soon split into two. I saw the early birds at breakfast every morning before they went off to pursue their chosen activities. Most of the night owls skipped breakfast and went straight to the pool bar for a midday snack. My concerns at having to deal with such a large group were, so far, proving to be unfounded as a regular pattern was developing. My announcements were all in black and white on our notice board in reception and I would also pass them on verbally when I met up with people during the day. Of course, this did mean I always had to be twenty-four hours ahead of myself but it was better than running around trying to find everyone every day.

The hotel entertainment that night was karaoke by the pool. I had a bird's eye view from my balcony and watched some of my group performing while I caught up with my paperwork. I would be able to discuss the merits of each performance at breakfast the next morning without admitting that I had not actually been present. When it finished I knew they would be in their usual haunts so I walked down to the History Bar and after a quick chat with the people there I said I was going to join the group in Nostalgia. I told this group I would be in the History Bar and then went back to my room to do my accounts. I also counted my money, yet again, in the hope the missing note may have miraculously appeared. It had not. It was too late now to confront my suspect.

The following day was the trip to Symi and Linda had given me permission to go as well. It was not a good start as our local guide missed the bus that took us to the harbour. As we waited to board the ferry for the three hour crossing to the island I prowled up and down the quay looking for him. A few minutes before the ferry was due to depart there was still no sign of him. I was concerned that I would have to lead the tour and regretted not having done more thorough research. The crew were casting off when a young man sprinted across the quay towards our boat. He scrambled aboard and when he got his breath back he introduced himself as Berkant, our missing guide. He had managed to hitch a ride to the harbour when the public bus did not turn up. Now I could relax and enjoy the day.

I could also ask questions instead of answering them. I had noticed a local woman had boarded the boat on her hands and knees. She was still on her hands and knees at the far end of the deck. Several people were standing with her but ignoring her. It was clearly not a temporary stance so I asked Berkant if the locals usually travelled in this position. The woman had transgressed and her punishment was to crawl to the monastery at Pandomitis, our first stop. One of her companions was her husband and the look on his face suggested he was suffering more than she was. We watched in amazement as she crawled off the boat and along the quay. Then we lost interest as our nostrils flared to the smell of baking. The local baker had just produced a fresh batch of the spinach pastries for which the area was famous and we joined the rapidly growing queue to sample them. There was just enough time before our boat set off again.

As soon as we arrived on Symi we gathered together for lunch in a small bar on the sea front. We were grateful for the sea breeze as the temperature was climbing into the forties. Immediately after lunch we went to the Symi Sponge Centre where the handsome Nikos gave us a very interesting and amusing talk about the history of the island and the sponge diving. It was not the big sell I had expected although, of course, after the lecture we were invited into the adjoining shop where we could purchase natural sponges. I suspect it was the charm of Nikos rather than the special properties of the sponges that enticed us to indulge. After paying for our purchases we strolled around the lovely little town of Symi before boarding our boat back to Rhodes.

I had to be a bit creative at dinner that evening. Several people had pointed out to me that in such a large group it was difficult to get to know everyone. They felt uncomfortable asking people their names so they would ask me. Just before we all went into dinner I suggested that everyone went in with someone they had not sat with at a meal. Most people rose to the challenge but the most ardent smokers would not join us and scuttled into the restaurant and took their usual places. They were adults and could do as they wished and smoking together was clearly a highlight of their holiday.

The following day Linda had organised an all-day boat trip for us with promises of beaches and a BBQ. However, the beaches were only seen in the distance, the lunch had never been near a BBQ and there was not even a bottle of barbecue sauce to season the meat. Nevertheless the twenty-nine of us who had been enticed aboard really enjoyed ourselves. This was probably due in large measure to the free bar which we just about drank dry. It was very relaxing spending the day at sea enjoying the slight breeze when the boat was in motion. We stopped four times to swim off the boat. The third stop was Kallithea where lots of water sports were available and boats came alongside to take people off to participate in different activities. No-one wanted to do anything more energetic than lazing on deck or floating in the sea around our boat. When we got back to Rhodes harbour neither Linda nor our coach was waiting for us as arranged. It was too hot to hang around for long so after waiting a short time some people got taxis back to the hotel and some went off for a drink. I sat on my own at the appointed meeting place, perched on a large black bollard in a patch of shade.

Eventually our bus arrived and I rounded up the drinkers and we went back to the hotel.

Frederick had decided to accept the challenge to integrate the group and organised a room party. I suspected he may be looking for a new companion as the woman he had travelled with had dumped him two days into the holiday. He was certainly struggling to make friends of either sex. We were all invited to join him after dinner. But everyone decided to go for a drink first and never came back. I felt sorry for Frederick and joined him for one drink but when I realised the party was not going to happen I walked back to my room. As I skirted the swimming pool the bull frogs began croaking. I stopped and looked in the water to see if I could see them. From the noise they made I expected they would be the size of a large toad but they were tiny and very difficult to spot. Their nightly warbling was taking their toll and I was so shattered I fell asleep over my report. I had not had my usual siesta that day and having once been of the opinion that sleeping during the day was for wimps now I was relying on it to keep me going.

The next day was the last full day for half the group but they would be replaced by another twenty-five people so there would be no respite for me. I would also have the added worry of integrating the new arrivals with the remaining guests. I was up early to finish my accounts and collect the tips from my departing guests. As I was having an early breakfast Marjorie appeared. She had been complaining of a sore throat but now it was closing up and she was worried. Reception advised that rather than getting a doctor to come to the hotel it would be quicker and cheaper to go to the hospital in Rhodes. They ordered a taxi for us and we set off. On the way I called Linda to postpone our meeting that morning. Her tone suggested that she thought that Marjorie could have picked a more convenient time to be ill.

On arrival at the hospital we were directed to the medical room. This room was empty and gave me hope that we would soon be on our way back to the hotel. After a cursory examination Marjorie was sent for an X-ray. First we had to pay for the X-ray and we joined the queue to do so. The length of the queue suggested that every patient was sent for an X-ray regardless of their ailment. Precious receipt obtained we went through to the waiting room. We had to listen very carefully for Marjorie's name as the Greek pronunciation of English names was often very strange and they got Christian names and surnames mixed up. Everything came to a standstill when an argument erupted because some patients were not in possession of the relevant piece of paper. Six people could have been X-rayed while this controversy raged. After the X-ray had been taken it was back to see the doctor and we had to queue again. Eventually a chest infection was diagnosed and we left with a prescription. We walked to a nearby hotel and I asked the receptionist to call a taxi for us. Back at the hotel Marjorie went off to relax by the pool and I walked to the local shops to get her prescription.

On my way back from the pharmacist I was hailed by Frederick who was drinking in a local bar not only because it was cheaper than the hotel but also because his erratic behaviour had resulted in him being ostracised by some of the group. He had a violent temper that had manifested itself a few times so most people were giving him a wide berth. I could not ignore him so I joined him for a quick drink and a senseless conversation. He had clearly been drinking all morning. I had seen this as an opportunity to discuss his erratic behaviour but there was no point so I finished my drink and walked back to the hotel. I got back to the hotel just in time to join some of the group for lunch. We had swapped dinner for lunch because we were going to a Greek Evening organised by Linda.

After lunch I sorted out the money and wrote out the accounts for Linda and then I delivered notes to those who were departing the following morning detailing the luggage collection and departure times. Next stop was reception for my delayed meeting with Linda. As we were going through the accounts I was given a fax that had just arrived from Aimee to say our Managing Director had booked one extra person for the following week but as there was no room at the hotel I would have to find alternative accommodation in a local bed and breakfast. Linda did not offer to help, just clucked impatiently while I read the fax, which I had said I must do immediately as it had urgent splashed all over it in big, black, capital letters.

I did not have time to start wandering around the locality looking for a bed and breakfast so I pleaded with the manger to find me a room in the hotel. He thought I might be able to stay where I was for another three nights but then I would have to move out. However, this could not be confirmed until the next day when the Rooms Manager arrived. I just had time to call Aimee to advise her of the situation before we set off for our Greek evening. When the coach arrived there were already a lot of people on board and it was clear that there was not enough room for everyone in my group. Jenny, the local guide, suggested that the rest of us go in taxis. She hastened to add that she would be paying the fares. While Jenny went into reception to organise the taxis I organised which of those in my group would travel on the bus and who would come in the taxis with me.

Reluctant though I had been to experience another 'unique' Greek evening I had been swayed by Linda's order to attend. It was much better than I had anticipated. Everybody entered into the spirit of it, no doubt aided by the mandatory raki that we had been offered on arrival. We started with a village tour, more like a village peep as it was over after a glimpse of two houses. The rest of the evening followed the 'usual' format. We ate in a large village hall where hundreds of people on small wooden chairs were crammed round trestle tables groaning under mountains of pre-cooked, reheated food washed down with wine that was just the right side of vinegar. We were entertained by a surprisingly tuneful duo. This prompted Marjorie, who had miraculously recovered her voice, to request a song for the people who were leaving the next day. I made the request for her but they said no. When I relayed this answer to Marjorie she stormed off to find Jenny, our local guide. Jenny made the same request with the same result. Soon after that Jenny shepherded us all back to the bus and organised the taxis for the overflow. When we said goodbye she apologised for being persuaded to try where I had failed. I just shrugged and said I wished she had succeeded and then Marjorie would have been happy. Maybe.

The following day was change-over day and I was very glad that Linda would be at the airport meeting, greeting and dispatching the arrivals while I stayed in the hotel packing up and sending off the departees. As we were waiting in the lobby surrounded by the luggage Frederick clapped his hands and asked everyone to be quiet. Frederick was staying for a second week so I wondered what he was going to say. He grandly announced that he had organised a collection to cover the money that I was missing in payment for the excursions that week. I was very touched by this kind gesture but could not help admire the cunning of this character in getting his companions to pay for his trips.

I had just waved the first group off when the Rooms Manager arrived and I would discover my fate. I had not had time to do any packing so it would be a disaster if I did have to change rooms. It was good news. I could keep my room for the next few days and then, for the two nights when the hotel was full, I could move into one of their courtesy rooms. These were basic but I think I would have slept on a couch in reception rather than have the hassle of moving out of the hotel for two nights and then moving back again. Once the first group had left I was free to join some of the group for lunch in a restaurant on the strip below the hotel. Since I had made my peace with the pushy patron he had continually invited me to eat in his restaurant and as my companions had been haunting the place I joined them there and enjoyed an excellent all day breakfast.

I had just waved goodbye to the second group when the first members of my new group arrived. There followed a flurry of checking in, pointing out the notice board and confirming the time for our Welcome Drink later. Some of the remaining guests were hanging around reception anxious to get a look at the new arrivals so I introduced them to each other. This was a good precursor to our meeting later and would help the integration of the new arrivals with the rest of the group. It soon became clear that the new arrivals included a social butterfly, Flossie. In the short time it took to check-into the hotel Flossie had introduced herself to everyone in reception including Frederick. He gallantly offered to carry her bags to her room for her. Off they went, the tall gangling Frederick bending down to catch every word uttered by the skinny Flossie draped like a Christmas tree in a stunning variety of patterns and styles.

When we met for our Information Meeting the following morning I suggested to Linda that she made it brief as half the group had heard it before and the other half had gleaned quite a lot of information from their companions the previous evening. She took this as an invitation to prolong the meeting with the result that everyone got bored and switched off. In the face of this lack of interest she gave up and left me to organise the trips for the following week. Not many of them wanted to commit to any trips just yet so they all went off to relax by the pool.

I joined some of the remaining group in the bar to hear the latest gossip. There had been a lot of intrigue amongst the group the previous week and I had kept my distance but I had discovered that Frederick was giving real cause for concern due to his flashes of temper. He had not only offended people in his own group but other guests in the hotel when he had shouted at their offspring for being noisy. It was clear I would have to address the issues that had been raised but first I needed more information. As we chatted I discovered that he was taking Melinda out to dinner that night. I was concerned as she appeared to be rather naïve. I could not interfere with their plans but to set my mind at rest I did listen at their respective doors and I was very relieved when I heard nothing but silence.

That was because they were not in their rooms. When I opened my door I heard a racket outside and stepped out onto my balcony to see what was going on. Some of my group were skinny dipping in the pool. I crept back downstairs and bumped into some of the women creeping back into the hotel still naked. They fled when they saw me their breasts flying free. I laughed out loud as their bare bottoms wobbled round the corner. It was exactly the reaction I had anticipated. When I got to the pool bar some of the group greeted me and suggested I joined them. I could see out of the corner of my eye that Frederick was still in the water with not a stitch on. He did not dare get out while I was there and I knew it. The others succeeded in their efforts to distract me and I never saw him emerge from the water.

Several people went on the Lindos trip the following morning but I did not join them as I had too much to do. Although it was strictly none of my business my conscience was pricking and I wanted to see Melinda to 'warn' her about Frederick. I saw the trippers off and then went into breakfast where I found Melinda and we had a chat. I told her that Frederick had a tendency to lose his temper and she said that although he had been okay with her she had felt uneasy in his company and would not be going out with him on her own again. My next task was to find somewhere for dinner that week as the group wanted to eat in town one evening. It was too hot to walk there so I caught the local bus and began my search in the old town. I was drawn to the Rustico by its promise of genuine home-cooked Greek cuisine. I decided to sample the food and sat at a table in the courtyard. I was joined by the owner, Konstantin, who chatted with me the whole time I was there. He was very happy to take my booking for the group and as I left he suggested that I stayed on Rhodes and went to work for him. No thanks. I had already met several downtrodden English women slaving for their Greek partners.

After a swim in the hotel pool to cool down I showered and settled down for a siesta but I was thwarted by a phone call from Flossie who wanted to go home because she was not coping with the heat and she was bored as well. Flossie was a real madam. She was very happy to let men pay for her meals and then she expressed surprise, usually in conversation during breakfast, when they wanted to kiss her. She had been taken out by three different men and now that she did not have a man she had taken to her room to bombard me with telephone calls requesting a flight home. I had to keep careful notes for my report and this was the sequence:

Flossie called to say she wanted to go home. I said she may have to pay but she said she had not got any money. The only possibility of getting a free transfer on to another flight would be if it was a medical emergency. Flossie said she suffered from a nervous complaint and the sun had caused it to flare up again.

I rang Aimee who said she would check to see if the ticket could be transferred but it was unlikely.

I rang Linda who said she could get her a flight home in the early hours of the following morning. It would cost €150 and she must have the money up front. Linda was adamant there was no chance on medical grounds.

I rang Flossie and gave her this information.

Flossie rang back and said she wanted to go home on medical grounds so I said she would have to see a doctor or go to the hospital. I warned her that she would have to pay for this service and then claim it back later on her insurance. She did not want to do this.

Flossie rang again to ask if I could find out if she could go home on medical grounds before she saw a doctor! I said I would try but I doubted it could be established without a medical opinion.

Aimee called back to say the flight was not transferable and Flossie would have to pay. If she could not pay herself someone would have to ring the office and pay by credit card. Repatriation on medical grounds was unlikely but it was up to the insurance company.

I rang Flossie and gave her the above options and she said no way and to try medical grounds.

Flossie rang back to say she would take the flight and pay for it.

I rang Linda and asked her to book the flight. Linda said Flossie had to pay me first.

I rang Flossie and said Linda would book the flight as soon as she had paid me. Flossie said she did not want the flight and that she was feeling ill and confused and did not know what to do.

I rang Linda and told her not to book the flight.

My whole afternoon had been spent on the telephone and I still had to copy out the menu for our dinner in town so that the group could see what the choices were for the set meal. I passed these around during pre-dinner drinks. When Flossie arrived I told her how sorry I was that she was not happy. She snapped back that the situation was making her ill again and that she did not want to end up in a Greek mental hospital. I retreated and concentrated on sorting out our dinner in town. Most people decided to join us at Rustico but some people also wanted to eat at Ta Kioupia having heard that it had a reputation as one of the best restaurants in the world. Ta Kioupia was expensive but I had called the manager and he had offered me a good deal for a set menu. Several people booked to eat there on our penultimate evening.

The next morning the weather was even hotter and we were officially experiencing a heat wave. It was too hot to be active and a day by the pool was the most popular option. I joined some of them there for coffee. Marjorie and her companions were very anxious to pass on the gossip most of which was completely inaccurate apart from the news that Flossie had been dumped by Frederick which would explain her request to go home early. I lay out in the sun very briefly before showering and lunching in the hotel as we were eating in town that evening. The heat was stifling and it was a relief to return to my room for a long siesta.

Even the invincible Linda seemed to be affected by the heat. When I called her with the numbers for the excursions that week she said she would have to call me back. Her timing was immaculate. She called when I was in reception trying to organise taxis to get thirty people into the old town of Rhodes simultaneously. I had just booked the relevant number of taxis and the receptionist was writing out slips of paper with our destination in Greek when eight other people arrived. Their destination was also the town as they were going to a concert. They had assured me they would organise their own taxis but had changed their minds and I was charged with that task as well. I hoped that the destinations would not get mixed up and everyone would arrive at the right venue. Some taxis had already departed by the time I finished talking to Linda. In the midst of this organised chaos the Rooms Manager appeared and told me that I would not have to move out of my room after all. That was really good news as I had forgotten to prepare for this possibility.

The only taxi that arrived at the wrong destination was my taxi. Our driver took us to a different gate but I did not realise the mistake at first. It soon dawned on me when there was no sign of the rest of the group who should have been waiting for us. We raced across the town to the restaurant. We arrived just as the others appeared round a corner coming from a different direction. I was so relieved to see them as I had not wanted to chase around the old town looking for them all. Everyone was soon seated at our tables and it seemed that I could relax and enjoy my meal. But then Marjorie announced that she had to get a taxi back to the hotel as she had broken a tooth.

As taxis could not drive into the old town and Marjorie could not remember the way back to the Marine Gate I walked there with her and put her in a taxi. By the time I had walked back to the restaurant I was exhausted and uncomfortably hot. I did not expect to see Marjorie again that evening so I was impressed when she managed to find her own way back to the restaurant. I had written down some landmarks for her to look for when walking through the old town. Our meal was really good although genuine Greek cooking is quite rustic and does not appeal to all palates. I had the kleftiko which is a lamb stew slow cooked in the intestine of a sheep. The name means in the style of the Klephts, marauding bandits, who did not have their own flocks of sheep so they would steal lambs or goats and cook the meat buried in a pit to contain the aroma of cooking and avoid the smoke being seen which would give them away. The meat was tender and tasty.

After the meal some people stayed in town to sample the nightlife there and the rest of us went back to the usual bars below our hotel. We had made a pact to stay up until midnight so we could sing Happy Birthday to Harry who was celebrating his birthday the next day. Finally I was free to return to the hotel and a short night's sleep. I was off to Symi again early the next morning as Linda had decreed it should be so. There were only eight people from my group booked on this trip so it had not been possible to include a local guide and I would be escorting them.

We set off the following morning in blistering heat. Thanks to the sea breeze it was tolerable on the boat but it was stifling at Panorimitis and Symi where it was registering 43°C in the shade. The day followed the usual pattern except that on the return journey we had to make a detour into Panorimitis to collect the wedding guests we had delivered there on the way to Symi. The boat was overcrowded and there was very little shade so most people draped their towels over their heads. I had never experienced heat like it. The newspapers were full of warnings about staying inside as much as possible. Milk was turning sour and butter was melting before shoppers could get it home from the supermarket.

We were back just in time to meet the rest of the group for dinner in the hotel. After dinner we were all going to squash into the Nostalgia bar as they had made a cake for Harry's birthday. Before I could join them I had to deal with another crisis. As we came back on the boat from Symi I had noticed that Frederick's shin had a nasty bright red rash. I asked him what had happened. He just muttered that he thought it was an allergy. I was not convinced but as he was not keen to seek medical advice I said I would check again later to see if it was any better. I did check when he arrived for dinner and the inflammation on his leg was getting worse. A nurse in our group thought we should go and see someone as soon as possible. But Frederick insisted on having dinner first. He clearly thought I was overreacting. As soon as we had finished eating we took a taxi to Rhodes hospital where he was examined, given an injection, prescribed antibiotics and told not to drink. We got a taxi back to Nostalgia where we arrived in time for some cake and champagne to celebrate with Harry. It was another two o'clock finish. Frederick was still happily ignoring the doctor's instructions not to drink alcohol when I left.

Several people went off on trips the following morning but I did not join any of them. My first task was to walk to the pharmacy to get Frederick's prescription. The weather was still boiling hot and the hotel was full to bursting so there was a lot of pressure on the sun beds around the pool. The fiercest competition related to the most comfortable of the three different types available. German guests were reserving the best beds with their towels at the crack of dawn and then going out for the day so the beds remained empty. I was asked to do something about this but the hotel manager refused to enforce the rule that sun beds could not be reserved before seven in the morning. As a joke I suggested that they store some of these beds overnight in Harry's bungalow when they came back from the bars.

I forgot this piece of advice as I worked my way through my list of things to do including confirmation of our booking at Ta Kioupia that evening. I was excited because some of the group had invited me to dine there with them as their guest. I really appreciated this lovely gesture. I had seen an article about the restaurant that had once been rated as one of the top ten restaurants in the world. I felt I needed to find something dressy for the occasion so I went into Rhodes where I found a nice two piece in a boutique in the old town. I went back to the hotel for a much needed siesta before writing out the details for our departure two days hence and delivering them to the rooms.

Ta Kioupia was excellent. It was in the village of Tris not far from our hotel. We sat outside in the courtyard of some converted farm buildings. On arrival we had walked through the kitchens where all the staff resplendent in long black aprons, were busy chopping up fresh produce. The meal was amazing, one huge Greek *mezze* of about forty different dishes but all very small portions so we managed to taste everything. We started eating at eight thirty and finished just after midnight. After we finished eating we were served raki which arrived in a basket of ice with the bottle nestling in the middle and the glasses arranged around the edge. The whole evening was a fabulous experience.

During breakfast the following morning I heard people shouting outside. When I looked through the window there was pandemonium around the pool. The battle of the sun beds was in full swing. A tug of war was going on between Frederick and a German guest each one clinging to either end of one of the most comfortable sun beds. All the other sun beds of this variety had vanished. Then I saw Harry sneaking out of his bungalow with a sun bed under his arm. It dawned on me that the group had taken to heart my jest about storing some sun beds in Harry's bungalow. I crept outside in case I needed to take action. By that time the manager had been summoned and the tirade was directed at him but he had no idea what they were angry about. I slid past them and went back into breakfast hoping my air of innocence was convincing.

I had just resumed my meal when Christabel arrived looking very glum. She had slipped on her bedroom floor and fallen onto the end of her bed the previous evening. Now she had decided that the pain was so bad she needed to have an X-ray. She also wanted to change to an earlier flight home so that she could travel with George who could help her with her luggage. I had a meeting arranged with Linda that morning and she would already be on her way so I asked Christabel if she could wait until after my meeting to go to the hospital. She agreed and then George volunteered to take her to the hospital and off they went.

They called me while I was still with Linda to say Christabel had been X-rayed as soon as they got there and the results had revealed a suspected cracked rib. Linda had already called the airline to try to change Christabel's flight but without success as the earlier flight was full. I waited for Christabel to get back and told her that I would help her with her luggage the next day as we were both on the same flight. When I went outside a second offensive in the sun bed war had just erupted. I arrived at the poolside just in time to see an angry German woman spitting at Marjorie who was prone on the sun bed the women considered to be hers. Several people in my group leapt to their feet to protect her. Fortunately the husband intervened and dragged her away before there was open warfare. My group were very shocked at this violent reaction but once everyone had calmed down we saw the funny side – it had been a brilliant coup. Sadly I could not boast that it had been my idea.

As it was the last evening for everyone I had decided to do something special for our pre-dinner drinks and the hotel manager had given me permission to organise drinks on the flat roof above Harry's bungalow. It was a brilliant venue with great panoramic views and we were all chatting and having fun when a head popped up over the parapet. It was our German adversary in the sun bed war earlier that day. She was furious and demanded that we leave immediately. I referred her to the hotel manager and she stomped off. We did a bit of stamping around ourselves before taking some group photographs and then going into dinner. We finished the evening at our usual bars. I left them there and returned to the hotel to pack. During the evening I had received several presents from members of the group – mostly bottles of booze – and somehow these had to be crammed into my suitcase.

The next day we were on three different flights and departing at different times. I left with the last group on the afternoon flight. When we arrived at the airport we discovered that our flight was delayed for three hours. It took forty-five minutes to check us in and then we were escorted to a taverna across the road where we joined three hundred other stranded travellers. We were packed into a large, hot airless room and served an apology of a meal that consisted of dried bread and wafer thin slices of salami. Despite the instructions to remain where we were some of my group decided to walk to the village of Paradiso just five minutes away. A few of them took a taxi back to our hotel to laze by the pool. All the other tourists were kept in order by the representatives patrolling the taverna. I could feel them glaring at me and my nearly empty table. My fingers were tightly crossed. If they suddenly found a plane and started boarding us I would never get them all back in time.

Despite the threat of 'extra capacity' arriving imminently we were still in the taverna when my flock reassembled around our table. An hour after the predicted time we were herded back across the tarmac as our transport home taxied down the runway. The arrivals were whisked off the plane and we were soon on board. But despite the pilot's best efforts we arrived at Gatwick after the last train had left. I had no option but to curl up on a bench in Arrivals and wait until the first train departed the next morning.

Despite my exhaustion a creaking escalator and regular announcements, in several languages, not to leave luggage unattended made it impossible to sleep. Images of the past twelve months rolled through my mind. I dozed off and in my dreams I revisited the mountains I had climbed, the beaches I had swum off and the cities I had explored. I was woken by the sound of shutters being lifted and the smell of coffee percolating as the airport came to life. People milled around me all of them at the start of their journey. Wistfully I watched them scurrying around bumping into each other and trying to cram trolleys into lifts already full of people and pushchairs. My travels were over. Or were they?